praise for
Racial Paranoia

"Brutally honest and brilliantly original, *Racial Paranoia* diagnoses an urgent problem: the suspicion and the reality of racism on the down-low. John Jackson takes us on a stunning whirlwind tour through a landscape peopled by everyone from Frederick Douglass to Dave Chappelle. The picture that emerges is of a new reality where race is everywhere and nowhere, seen and unseen, felt and ignored. Jackson's insight into what he calls the *de cardio* racism inscribed on American hearts is destined to make this book a classic."
—NOAH FELDMAN, Professor of Law,
Harvard University, author of *Fall
and Rise of the Islamic State*

"Provocative and insightful. . . . Highly recommended."
—*Choice*

"*Racial Paranoia*—an unusually entertaining volume whose take on contemporary racial divisions and conspiracy theories proved prescient when coverage of Barack Obama's presidential campaign was hijacked last spring by the sensation that was the Rev. Jeremiah Wright."
—*The Penn Gazette*

"Illuminating and penetrating . . . one of the finest examinations of hip-hop in American culture . . . Mr. Jackson is brilliant when analyzing hip-hop or the

comic styling of Dave Chappelle. . . . For those who want to better understand the feel of contemporary racial issues, *Racial Paranoia* should be placed alongside Cornel West's magisterial *Race Matters*."
—EDWARD J. BLUM,
National Catholic Reporter

"Provocative and groundbreaking . . . worthwhile reading for any serious student of race relations."
—*Virginian-Pilot*

"John L. Jackson, Jr., once again puts conventional wisdom on its head with a smart, imaginative and humorous conversation about race in contemporary America."
—MARK ANTHONY NEAL,
author of *New Black Man*

"A rigorous and fresh examination of the new axis of race relations in America."
—RANDALL ROBINSON, author of
An Unbroken Agony: Haiti, from Revolution to the Kidnapping of a President

"Thought-provoking. . . . Jackson's well-reasoned analysis is right on target."
—*Booklist*

RACIAL
PARANOIA

ALSO BY JOHN L. JACKSON, JR.

Real Black: Adventures in Racial Sincerity

Harlemworld: Doing Race and Class in Contemporary Black America

RACIAL PARANOIA

The Unintended Consequences
of Political Correctness

The New Reality of Race in America

JOHN L. JACKSON, JR.

CIVITAS
BOOKS

A Member of the Perseus Books Group
New York

Books published by Basic Civitas books are available at
special discounts for bulk purchases in the United States by
corporations, institutions, and other organizations. For more
information, please contact the Special Markets Department at
the Perseus Books Group, 2300 Chestnut Street, Suite 200,
Philadelphia, PA 19103, or call (800) 810-4145, ext. 5000,
or e-mail special.markets@perseusbooks.com.

Designed by Trish Wilkinson
Set in 11.5-point Sabon

The Library of Congress has cataloged the hardcover as follows:

Jackson, John L., Jr.
   Racial paranoia : the unintended consequences of political
correctness : the new reality of race in America / John L. Jackson, Jr.
      p.   cm.
   Includes bibliographical references and index.
   ISBN 978-0-465-00216-0 (alk. paper)
   1. Political correctness—United States. 2. United States—Race
relations—Political aspects. I. Title.
JK1726.J33 2008
305.800973—dc22   2007042052

Paperback ISBN: 978-0-465-01813-0

10 9 8 7 6 5 4 3 2 1

Contents

Preface

African American comedian Dave Chappelle shocked his fans in 2005 when he walked away from the third season of his hit Comedy Central television program, *Chappelle's Show*, and away from the $50 million he was supposed to earn making it. Chappelle simply left the set one day, headed to a New York City airport, and took off on an impromptu flight for South Africa, departing on a whim and without even telling his wife and children ahead of time. What drove Chappelle to Africa, what compelled him to forfeit such an enormous payday, was one evocative version of the inescapable contemporary experience of race and racism in America.

The comic who headed for Africa that day had only recently morphed from a moderately successful nightclub act into a bona fide Hollywood superstar, his idiosyncratic wit just starting to attract a truly national audience. As graduate students in New York City during the mid-1990s, a few classmates and I spent what little disposable income we could spare catching stand-up comedians perform all around the city. We saw Chappelle's routines at least five or six times. In those days, Chappelle was hardly a household name, but he could already boast several fairly high-profile appearances on cable TV specials and in feature films, including Eddie Murphy's *The Nutty Professor* in 1996. The skinny, mild-mannered comedian from the nation's capital was just beginning to build something of a cult following among audiences entertained by his brand of humor, a brand that definitely isn't for everybody.

Chappelle's comedy is notorious for its crassness and vulgarity, for pairing endless drug references with pointed social satire. He offers skits laced with words like "bitch" and "nigger" to poke fun at the hazards of contemporary dating and the crazy antics of hip-hop's more eccentric performers, mixing a self-conscious toilet-bowl aesthetic with irreverent send-ups of conventional racial stereotypes. But even though Chappelle's jokes incessantly (even obsessively) reference racial differences, there aren't many fans who would mistake him for more obvious comedic "race-men" of the Dick Gregory or Paul Mooney variety, entertainers who explicitly tell racial jokes to make unapologetically political statements about continuing white racism.[1]

It wouldn't be a stretch to imagine Gregory or Mooney jumping on a plane and popping up in Africa somewhere. Even a traditionally race-neutral figure such as Bill Cosby, once dubbed "America's favorite dad," might show up on the African continent with some kind of political project to launch, especially since he has been putting his money (million-dollar donations to important African American institutions) and his mouth (controversial criticisms of poorer African Americans' cultural pathologies) smack-dab into the middle of public debates about contemporary black life.[2] Cosby, Mooney, or Gregory might make such a transatlantic homage to connect their exploits in America to larger global issues, bringing media attention to the problems of debt relief and government-fostered genocide, blood diamonds, and the AIDS crisis. To many of his biggest fans, however, Chappelle's surfacing in Africa, after walking out on his hit comedy show, seemed a little more out of character. If anything, he was usually the performer lampooning such racial gestures, caricaturing them as either absurd or disingenuous. There are no sacred cows for Chappelle, and African Americans' commitments to "Mother Africa" merit just as much ribbing as, say, nonsensical hip-hop emcees (his spoof on the multiplatinum recording artist Lil John) or classic children's television shows unrealistically set on the dangerous curbsides of urban America (his spin on Sesame Street as a drug-infested slum), two recurring targets of his acerbic wit.

So, when the press found out that Chappelle was spending time sauntering around Durban, South Africa, instead of working on his show, they were pretty shocked, and their sensational stories about the matter demonstrated just that. Chappelle had gone crazy, they said. Meanwhile, others reported that the funnyman had checked into a psychiatric treatment clinic over there. Or was it a detox center? In one account, Chappelle had been brainwashed into renouncing earthly possessions and joining some obscure tribal cult out in the jungle.

These Chappelle stories made the rounds in major magazines and newspapers, on Viacom's cable music triumvirate (MTV, BET, and VH1), and all over the Web. Further digging only netted more gossip, weirder and wilder reports, even mock stories about black celebrities, everyone from Oprah Winfrey to Al Sharpton, conspiring to get the show cancelled because it made black people look bad. When Chappelle finally made his way back from Africa and granted interviews to major media outlets, he spent the bulk of his time dispelling these rumors and clarifying his reasons for leaving the show, the country, and all that money. Chappelle's tale about his final day on the set is fascinating for its combination of both heavy-handedness and restraint, of straightforward race talk and subtle attempts at reading between racial lines. It also showcases some of what makes the contemporary experience of race in America so different from just about anything this country has had to negotiate before.

While taping one particular skit on that fateful day, Chappelle played a character donning blackface makeup, a not-so-subtle nod to the minstrel tradition that demanded nineteenth- and early twentieth-century actors darken their faces while parodying blacks on stage and screen.[3] The actors, black and white, would use burnt cork or greasepaint to cover their skin. They'd contrast that with exaggerated red or white lips and then top the entire image off with a wig that satirized the kinkiness of blacks' hair. Al Jolson's 1927 film *The Jazz Singer,* the first feature-length "talkie" to come out of Hollywood, enshrined the theatrical practice of minstrelsy in its famous closing sequence, in which a would-be cantor puts on blackface and sings "My Mammy" to his mother. Even though a few actors tried to nuance and humanize their portrayals, blackface was the height of racist ridicule and derision in American theater.

In Chappelle's skit during that final day of taping, he was playing a pint-sized, blackfaced "pixie" who appeared out of thin air whenever racial groups saw their own worst stereotypes explicitly or inadvertently invoked. Playing a well-heeled passenger on a commercial airline flight, Chappelle has to decide whether or not to have chicken as his in-flight meal once the stewardess informs him that they are out of fish. Black people are supposed to love chicken, Chappelle thinks to himself, and so he doesn't want to reinforce that stereotype by eating chicken—fried chicken, at that—in mixed racial company. The pixie, a specter from that passenger's racial subconscious, whose blackface, the comedian explains, is supposed to represent "the visual personification of the 'N' word," magically appears out of nowhere to coax Chappelle into ordering chicken, singing and tap-dancing his appeal: "You can't beat fate, nigga. Get the chicken. . . . Make way for the bird."

Chappelle is famous for these kinds of racially provocative gestures. To his fans, this controversial humor defuses the power of popular stereotypes and allows people to laugh at the absurdities and irrationalities of American racism. To critics who read him less generously, Chappelle simply reinforces all of our worst racial assumptions and gives young kids, especially his white viewers, license to laugh away their own racisms.

This pixie skit is quintessential Chappelle, a controversial and complicated message that takes racism on directly, fearlessly, with bare knuckles instead of kid gloves. Did it critique and unmask traditional blackface performances or merely reenergize them for a new generation? Obviously, people have very different opinions about how to answer that question, even if many of them believe that playing with blackface is always a dangerous game. Think of the trouble that Ted Danson and Whoopi Goldberg got themselves into when he tried to roast her in blackface at the Friars Club in 1993. Clearly, he knew the implications; he might even have thought it was a clever critique of Hollywood's racist history. When it made the news, however, most people just considered it to be in extremely bad taste.

More recently, there was that fascinating story of a group of white female students on a college softball team in central Florida. The women borrowed jerseys from the black guys on the school's basketball team and (with the basketball players' explicit blessing) attended a campus party in blackface—as those very basketball players. Members of both teams were flummoxed by the school administration's disapproving response. The softballers certainly didn't mean it in a racist way, and the basketball players had signed off. So, what was all the fuss about? It isn't absurd to think that Chappelle's racy humor helps to promote these kinds of public gestures. If Chappelle can do it, the students might ask, why can't we?

Furthermore, it isn't far-fetched to assume that Chappelle had a critical, even antiracist, agenda behind that pixie skit, but even he started to second-guess his ability to make such an agenda clear and unequivocal, especially as he looked around at the cast and crew watching his blackface performance. Chappelle says that he glanced over at one of his crewmembers and felt disturbed by the way this person, a white man, was laughing at his racial caricature. Relaying the story to Oprah Winfrey, Chappelle claims that he had a sinking suspicion that the person was laughing *at* him, laughing *at* black people, and relishing these racial stereotypes in a destructive way.

But how did he know? Chappelle admits that the guy hadn't said anything explicit that bothered him. There was nothing he could point to and clearly put his finger on. He just had an inkling, a feeling. There was something intangible and unnerving about how this guy laughed at the pixie's antics, something that didn't sit well with Chappelle. "There was a good-spirited intention behind [doing the skit]," Chappelle explained. "So then when I'm on the set, and we're finally taping the sketch, [he] laughed in such a way—I know the difference between people laughing with me and people laughing at me—and it was the first time I had ever gotten a laugh that I was uncomfortable with. Not just uncomfortable, but like, should I fire this person?"[4]

Race relations have irrevocably changed in the last, restless half century of our country's history, and this popcultural tidbit highlights some of the radical differences between the contemporary reality of race relations and earlier forms of American racism. For one thing, Chappelle is in charge in this scenario. It is his show. The alleged racist culprit works for him, not vice versa. He has the authority to hire and fire, so he isn't simply afraid that a powerful white boss will drum him out of the business unless he degrades himself in blackface. It is Chappelle's decision. Bert

Williams, the famous Antiguan-born actor from the late nineteenth and early twentieth centuries, performed in blackface throughout his career, but that was because many of the most powerful producers of the time wouldn't have it any other way.[5] For Williams, it was work in blackface or risk not working at all. Chappelle chose blackface himself, probably because squeamish television executives today would wish that he not. He is pushing other people's buttons, not having his strings pulled.

The most marked difference between Chappelle's contemporary experience of racial enmity and earlier narratives is that Chappelle's telling of the story lacks any transparent and in-your-face racism. There is only a hard-to-pin-down suspicion that Chappelle feels while deciphering a lackey's wordless laugh. The crewmember didn't call Chappelle a "nigger" or remark that he thought all blacks were really just like that blackfaced pixie. In fact, he didn't say or do anything except what the skit called for: he laughed. If Chappelle tries to explain what was so different, what was so racist, about that laugh, words mostly fail him.

He can only tell you that he felt it, really felt it, and that he trusts his knack for determining the difference between a goodhearted laugh and a racist one.[6] This ambiguous and nonfalsifiable sense of racial distrust is at the heart of the new reality of race in America. Chappelle didn't just go crazy that day he left the country, and he wasn't simply being hypersensitive. He was feeling the subtle sting of racial paranoia, a decidedly new spin on an old American problem.

Introduction
The Paranoid
Paradoxes of Race

Were those levees in New Orleans blown up on purpose during Hurricane Katrina? It might sound absurd, maybe too crazy to even dignify with an earnest dismissal, but that's exactly what the Nation of Islam's controversial leader, Minister Louis Farrakhan, speculated about as soon as the storm's winds subsided. The germ-infested waters had only just stopped rising. Journalists had barely begun to dig themselves in for twenty-four-hour news coverage. Rotting corpses were still floating along the murky waterways that were once city sidewalks, and Minister Farrakhan was already asking his followers—and anyone else within earshot—to think the unthinkable.

"I heard from a very reliable source who saw a twenty-five-foot-deep crater under the levee breach," he offered, preaching to a congregation in Charlotte, North Carolina. "It may have been blown up to destroy the black part of town and keep the white part dry."

Even if many African Americans find Farrakhan's contention downright ridiculous, describing him as a fanatic and insisting that nobody purposefully blew up anything, many of those same dissenters would still give serious consideration to the claim that the Federal Emergency Management Agency (FEMA) dragged its institutional feet in sending aid and assistance to those citizens trapped in a flooded New Orleans almost exclusively because of race, because the bodies dangling from open windows and perched on soggy rooftops were mostly black instead of white.[1]

The Grammy-winning hip-hop superstar Kanye West put a finer point (and name) on the race-based Katrina accusations during a national telethon for the relief effort when he exclaimed, "George Bush doesn't care about black people." The subsequently released evidence of former FEMA head Michael Brown warning President Bush ahead of time about the horrific magnitude of what was likely to happen in New Orleans in the wake of Katrina might only further indict the president's seemingly lackluster response. For some, the question of intention remains: was the government just inept or more deliberately (and racially) neglectful? And Farrakhan, even with all of his ideological extremism, is still somewhat representative of where a lot of African Americans come down on that particular question.[2]

These alarmist and conspiratorial attitudes and assumptions always seem to emerge during national events and catastrophes, whenever race is one of the prominent variables animating the latest media firestorm du jour. Farrakhan and West epitomize "hard" and "soft" versions of what I'm calling racial paranoia: distrustful conjecture about purposeful race-based maliciousness and the "benign neglect" of racial indifference.[3]

Racism often serves as a crucial explanation for unnecessary social suffering and governmental disregard. To many African Americans, it may just be one social factor among many, but it is still decisive. And even African Americans prone to dismissing Farrakhan's claims out of hand might ponder past racial injustices (a forty-year study in Alabama in which government scientists allowed black men to die of syphilis, merely pretending to treat them; the "1877 Compromise" between North and South that disenfranchised newly freed slaves just after the Civil War liberated them; the throwing of Japanese Americans into internment camps by President Franklin D. Roosevelt during World War II) and wonder to themselves, however fleetingly, if it's not a bit naive to dismiss such accusations out of hand.

Most racial misgivings and misunderstandings are predicated on fears that fan the flames of America's worst racial conflagrations. This fear explains African Americans' angry reactions to former education secretary William Bennett's hypothetical comments about racial genocide in 2005. Aborting all African American fetuses would lessen crime, he stated matter-of-factly, but it would still be morally reprehensible. There are surely unspoken racial fears hidden beneath Bennett's inclination to suggest such a callous illustration, and the fear at the kernel of African Americans' hostile responses to Bennett came out of wary discomfort with the fact that he could even imagine such a scenario—and then use it to equate all black babies with criminality. These same white fears of violent blacks explain why Duke University administrators in that same year chose to advise their students (in a long and carefully drafted mass e-mail) against congregating on the sidewalk in front of the house where white lacrosse players were accused of raping a black exotic dancer—on a "tip" that black gang members from the local community were planning a retaliatory drive-by against Duke students in honor of the alleged victim, a black college student at North Carolina Central, as though Crips and Bloods operate like some kind of urban al Qaeda cell, sending out hostile terrorist chatter before striking their targets.[4]

Racism is characterized by hatred and power: the hate people express for other racial groups and the relative power they possess to turn that hatred into palpable discrimination or material advantage.[5] The concept of racial paranoia, however, stresses the fears I've been talking about, fears people harbor about other groups potentially hating or mistreating them, gaining a leg up at their expense. Racial paranoia is racism's flipside, even if those two analytically discrete sides can sometimes effortlessly meet.

All Americans share the fears that underpin racial paranoia; it's the specifics that differ, translating into mutually exclusive (and sometimes antagonistic) interpretations of everyday life. We find major race-based differences of opinion on everything from party politics and social policy-making to mundane choices people make about what television shows they watch: *Seinfeld* versus *Martin*; HBO's *Sex and the City* versus UPN's *Girlfriends*.

In such an atmosphere of stark racial differences of opinion, what looks like paranoia to one group can seem quite logical to another. Things that blacks sometimes take for granted whites easily dismiss as unreasonable, insane, pure nonsense—and vice versa. For example, most white Americans would probably consider the racial nationalism of someone like Marcus Garvey (with his early-twentieth-century emigration scheme of relocating black Americans to Africa) a fairly bizarre form of racial extremism, but nowadays we have prominent black political figures, including bestselling author Randall Robinson, making their own individual Garvey-esque voyages to foreign lands—and explaining to everyone else why they are finally "Quitting America" for good.[6] There is a long history of prominent African Americans leaving the United States for new homes in faraway places: James Baldwin's years in Turkey, novelist Richard Wright's second life in Paris, dancer Josephine Baker's stints throughout Europe, and on and on. For many African Americans, these relocations have often seemed like quite reasonable, even necessary, responses to their fears about continued racism and discrimination in America.

Of course, every fear isn't racial paranoia, and Americans have to *learn* how to be paranoid about race. It isn't fundamentally hardwired into us. We have to teach ourselves— and our children. One way we learn is through the mass media; journalists can frame issues in ways that challenge or reinforce our own worst racial clichés and stereotypes: complicated college rape investigations are reduced to simplistic racial melodramas; news wire services caption Katrina photographs so that white victims merely "find" food while black ones explicitly "loot" for it. The media are usually condemned as racist for such complicities and biases, for its oversights and cover-ups. I know several African Americans who only half-jokingly declare that CNN must secretly stand for *Conning Niggers Nowadays*.

As a particularly flamboyant representative of the television news media, conservative pundit Tucker Carlson voices many of the denials and protestations that only serve to reinforce blacks' suspicions. Carlson exemplifies how exasperated other Americans can get whenever African Americans start talking about racism as a smoking gun for every form of social discrimination, even and especially without specific proof. He grows particularly annoyed when wealthy African Americans (people he believes should certainly know better) do anything short of totally dismissing other blacks' race-based conspiracy theories out of hand. He has reprimanded pop-cultural icons like hip-hop artist Chuck D and filmmaker Spike Lee for just such "irresponsibility" with respect to Farrakhan's aforementioned levee allegations. According to Carlson, any claim that people purposefully blew up levees in New Orleans or that the government willfully withheld federal aid to the flooded areas (to kill as many black people as possible) is a crackpot, fringe belief that should hardly be dignified with serious consideration.

"You're a smart guy," Carlson compliments Chuck D during an episode of Carlson's TV program. "You know that white people didn't blow up the levees to kill Black people. You've got to know that didn't happen."[7] Where's the evidence for any actual bombing, he argues, or proof that the Feds sat around cabalistically rubbing their hands together with nefarious intent? Chuck D's response to Carlson's queries was carefully equivocal: "I can't say unless I know for sure what's the actual facts and what's actually false." And Chuck D may never know enough, not definitively, to denounce Farrakhan's racial accusation.

Carlson is a perfect example of America's too-quick willingness to dismiss the significance of racial paranoia. Of course, such dismissal allows everyone to sleep better at night, believing that a few racial cranks say nothing meaningful about more general racial suspicions in American society, but we can't begin to understand race today (or the volatile racial fault lines of contemporary national politics) without taking such beliefs (as wild as they may seem) quite seriously—not as points of fact but as organizing principles for how people make sense of their everyday lives and the forces potentially allied against them.

What I am calling racial paranoia delineates something essential about how all Americans confront social differences in their lives, a racial paranoia constituted by extremist thinking, general social distrust, the nonfalsifiable embrace of intuition, and an unflinching commitment to contradictory thinking. All of these features contribute to the paranoid reasoning that characterizes American understandings of race and difference today. And this doesn't only include the fringe theories of an irrational few.[8] *Racial Paranoia: The Unintended Consequences of Political Correctness* is a story about the historical and contemporary manifestations of racial distrust in American society, about how that story has shifted with structural changes in the power relations between blacks and whites, between minorities and the machinery of the nation-state. The fact is, racial paranoia won't just go away, and every future social disaster (or CNN-covered news story) provides more fodder for its growth and development—even as it unfolds in potentially unpredictable ways.

In the 1950s and 1960s, "consensus historians" such as Richard Hofstadter argued that large swaths of the American public displayed a "paranoid style" of political analysis that made them incapable of productively participating in truly rational and reasonable debate. This "sick" style promoted a preoccupation with "the way in which ideas are believed and advocated rather than with the truth or falsity of their content."[9] Hofstadter argued that the rise of "mass society" (defined by the dominance of radio, television, and film) made twentieth-century American paranoia different from anything that had come before it. I would argue that an emphasis on *race* and *racism* productively distinguishes twenty-first-century discussions of paranoia from older media-spawned versions stressed by Hofstadter.

Since the civil rights movement helped to formally outlaw racial discrimination, social science research has shown that subtler forms of racism, forms more difficult to define or even see, have actually made it tougher to operationalize the phenomenon today. Of course, there are still a plethora of audit studies proving that, statistically speaking, blacks (even with identical credentials) have a harder time than whites getting everything from new cars to new homes, landing job interviews, or bringing home an equal wage for the same work. According to sociologist David Wellman, these differences aren't just about white prejudice. Racism isn't just prejudice at all; it is based on "culturally sanctioned, rational responses to struggles over scarce resources . . . regardless of [individual] intentions" or public bans on racially insensitive speech.[10]

When racism was explicit, obvious, and legal, there was little need to be paranoid about it. For the most part, what blacks saw was what they got. However, after the social changes of the 1960s, African Americans have become more secure in their legal citizenship but concomitantly less sure about other things, such as when they're being victimized by silent and undeclared racisms.[11] This uncertainty can make people all the more paranoid about the smallest slights, the subtlest glances, the tiniest inconveniences. Any of those can be telltale signs of "two-faced racism," of hidden racial animus dressed up to look politically correct, racial conspiracies cloaked in public niceties and social graces.[12]

Racial Paranoia is about the post–civil rights lives of "affirmative action babies" brought up experiencing legal segregation as little more than black-and-white images from one PBS special or another, or as family stories passed down through the generations.[13] This book tries to explain why race, especially in the form of racial paranoia, is so hard for all segments of America to shake. It is about the suspicions black people beat back whenever, say, an idle white salesperson at their local drugstore or supermarket sees them beckoning with a question but ignores them anyway—or when that same salesperson takes a few seconds longer than needed to furrow his brows and sigh himself into an unenthusiastic response. Insignificant, I know, petty even—offensively so. It may sound like so much more hollow bourgeois angst. But it is exactly within the crevices of such real, imagined, or hallucinated trivialities that the seeds of larger racial paranoia grow. When talking about race and racism, we shouldn't underestimate the potential significance of seemingly inconsequential acts. *Racial Paranoia* takes a broad look at African Americans in the twenty-first century as they attempt to see something that can't always be seen, to touch something that may not be there, and to make sense of a small voice inside their heads that whispers and whispers and whispers.

In some ways, race was easier to understand and discuss when it was that obvious impetus for public water hosings and police dog attacks, when it was emblematized by socially meaningful lines separating the fronts from the backs of buses. Fortunately, that version of racial reality is dead. However, many people are still using pre–civil rights sensibilities and understandings of race to talk about it today. We have achieved a modicum of racial equality in the law, but we are far less skilled at figuring out what this recent change in race (from blatant to subtle, from explicit to inferential, from biological to cultural) means for how we relate to one another after the courts adjourn and the unabashed bigots have been publicly lambasted.

Racial Paranoia shows that understanding race means disregarding almost everything we accepted about it prior to the 1960s. This is part of the reason why something like hip-hop, which I discuss at length in chapter 5, is potentially important to the story. It's a specifically post–civil rights phenomenon with a radically contemporary sensibility that mirrors racial paranoia's internal dynamic.

The point isn't that race is less important now than it was before.[14] It's just more schizophrenic, more paradoxical. We continue to commit to its social significance on many levels, but we seem to disavow that commitment at one and the same time. Race is real, but it isn't. It has value, but it doesn't. It explains social difference, but it couldn't possibly. This kind of racial doublethink drives us all crazy, makes us so suspicious of one another, and fans the flames of racial paranoia. Nothing is innocent, and one bumps into conspirators everywhere.

Case in point: My wife and I pass a fancy hotel in our adopted hometown of Philadelphia, a bitter wind howling and whipping up trash all around us. We have been playing tourists for the weekend, exploring the many famous sites of Benjamin Franklin's historic city. As she heads across the street, continuing our hunt for a casual lunch spot, I lag a bit behind, lingering at that hotel entrance to eavesdrop on an animated conversation between the hotel's doorman and valet parking attendant. The latter rubs his hands against a haggard copy of a book I've seen many times before, *The Unseen Hand,* by A. Ralph Epperson, a conspiracy theorist who claims that just about every major event in the history of the world was purposefully orchestrated by a secretive group of international elites determined to control the planet. I had already written about another one of Epperson's books, *New World Order,* which espouses similar claims, so I was interested to hear how these two men would talk about the author's conspiratorial arguments.[15]

As I stood in the lobby, stealing not-so-furtive glances their way, the doorman was listening attentively as his coworker explained the book's premise.

"They are talking about the Illuminati," he stated calmly, matter-of-factly, "trying to take over the world, doing it, taking over the world and controlling Bush and them so that they can keep themselves secret."

The two twenty-something black workers were soon approached by a thirtyish blonde, a guest at the hotel, who had arrived to retrieve her valet-parked car. The men continued discussing Epperson, seemingly oblivious to her presence, until the woman actually chimed in to ask for more details about the book. A little nonplussed, the valet handed the woman her keys and stashed the book under his shoulder. Genuinely interested, she asked a few more questions, jotting down the title and author, and then headed for her Range Rover. The SUV hadn't even turned the corner before the men got back to their conversation about the Illuminati's scheme, linking it to current events in Iraq and implicating several major American politicians in the plot.

This brief exchange highlights part of what is so important about race and paranoia in contemporary American society: the deeply entrenched everydayness of it, a doorman and a valet comparing notes on global conspiracy, racial suspicions metastasizing into conspiratorial worldviews right in the middle of a busy hotel lobby. If these two guys are anything like the many other African Americans I have talked with about Epperson's theories of global conspiracy, they also bring a distinctively racial reading to it, a reading its white author would probably not endorse: that the Illuminati (or Trilateral Commission or any other such nefariously secretive organization) is actually just a stand-in for whiteness, for White America. *The Da Vinci Code* meets Alex Haley's *Roots*. In this version, Robert Langdon is in serious danger because he knows that the Catholic Church has covered up the fact that Jesus wasn't just married, he was also black. In this racial retelling, the Illuminati wants to take over the entire world, but particularly relishes the idea of destroying black people along the way.

This racial slant to Epperson's book helps explain the men's uneasiness about that white hotel guest's inquisitiveness and their lukewarm response to her interest. Even though Epperson never mentions it at all in his book, many of his black readers see race as the ultimate cause of African American hardships, and they tend to combine that belief with otherwise nonracial conspiracies of contemporary and historic events. *Racial Paranoia* links such extreme racial conspiracies to the everyday forms of racial paranoia and distrust that periodically manifest themselves in screaming charges of racism, charges that sometimes seem to come out of the blue and over very little—maybe with the accused not even knowing what she did wrong.

As an anthropologist, I'm trained to examine racial paranoia ethnographically: as a behavioral and ideological repertoire that creates (and is created by) complex cultural forces. To get at some of that, I ask basic questions about racial paranoia: Where does it come from? What are compelling past examples of it in American society? Has race always functioned in such ways? How do these paranoid views manifest themselves in everyday life? And is there anything we can do about it?

Again, this racial paranoia isn't just "a black thing." Whites also exhibit race-based paranoia—in big and small ways: clutching purses in slow-moving elevators, continually reanimating age-old arguments about the biological bases of intellectual differences, dismissing any invocation of racism as mere victimology and insincerity. We've become so good at anticipating the other's next move that there is little need even to listen out for the trains rumbling across the racial tracks dividing us from an assortment of thems.

Dismissing racial paranoia as extremist implies that race is being used to justify something so far from the mainstream that its invocation is absurd, outlandish. Of course, this is always a context-specific judgment, especially since our notion of the mainstream changes over time. For example, many Americans once believed that God created Africans simply to serve as chattel slaves for their white masters, so fanciful stories about God's cursing Ham with dark skin (a story I'll unpack a bit in chapter 2) were hardly considered extremist. If such biblical interpretations are relegated to the ideological provinces of neo-Nazis and Ku Klux Klan members today, they were bandied about quite matter-of-factly throughout the nineteenth century— and by congressmen and presidents, no less. Some of these same statesmen helped found the American Colonization Society at the beginning of that same century. This was a group expressly committed to sending free blacks back to Africa, a proposition considered quite reasonable in its time, even if few whites would publicly admit to endorsing such a position today.

To miss this point about context would mean thinking far too anachronistically about social life and racial ideologies. Labeling anything as extreme can be complicated by highlighting differences in time and place. Overly confident dismissals of racial paranoia underestimate this fact—and miscalculate its significance. Even still, there is an assumption about racial thinking that imagines we can identify our collective mainstream (whatever it is at the time) and define some ideas as marginal to it, even if those centers and margins change massively with each passing era.

This extremism is usually coupled with a lack of social trust that can be writ large or small. Farrakhan's levee discussion is a clear case of distrust at a wider societal level. The proverbial clutched bag on the elevator (when an unknown black man enters) is a more intimate form, one that many people explain away with recourse to statistical links between race and crime, the founding premise for William Bennett's aforementioned race-based hypothetical. These instances of distrust are important because racial paranoia translates fear into social action. We decide, for instance, to cross the street, just to be careful, when we see a "suspicious" African American walking toward us. A cautious cab driver passes Cornel West's lightbrown outstretched hand and justifies it as a form of protection and self-preservation.[16] Even if FEMA was just inept and not truly malicious, distrust greases the wheel for the latter appraisal, anyway. If individuals can be counted on to convert fear into practice, is it really that huge a jump to imbue organizations (run by these same individuals)—FEMA, the Illuminati, CNN, or anything else—with that exact same capacity?

Distrust is one of the most important features of racial paranoia. Without it, racism and racial discrimination would have little social traction. And this distrust feeds our doubts. Employers fear that black workers will be lazy and confrontational, which is part of the reason why they may pass them over for jobs or promotions. White law school applicants fear that less-qualified minorities will get accepted to schools that deny them entry, which propels some to file lawsuits claiming reverse discrimination. And we can complicate this picture even further by admitting that individuals sometimes internalize the fears and distrust others attribute to their own ostensible racial group. For example, African Americans can also readily cross the street when they see other African Americans approaching. What do we make of claims that black cab drivers are not that much more likely to stop for black would-be passengers than their white counterparts? This fear can characterize relations across racial lines or within racial camps. Either way, we have a lack of trust that racial paranoia feasts on.

And this distrust is not just cognitive. It is also intuited, felt, sensed, which is an incredibly important part of racial paranoia's power. Malcolm Gladwell's critically acclaimed bestseller *Blink: The Power of Thinking without Thinking* argues that snap judgments often work as effectively as careful and long-term contemplation when it comes to making important decisions. Gladwell argues that these snap decisions are only valuable when they have been shorn of biases based on irrationalities like racism, even citing the infamous Amadou Diallo shooting as an example of the havoc racism wreaks on intuitive thinking.[17] But searching for this pristine intuition, unsullied by racist thinking, might be a little bit like digging around for one of those proverbial needles in a haystack, little more than an unrealistic and utopian goal, especially since racism itself is defined not just by careful, long-term reflection, but also by quick, snap judgments that predetermine our actions even before we have time to think them through.

Racial paranoia thrives within the very blinklike moment that Gladwell champions. It is precisely what gets *intuited* and *assumed* as much as reasonably *concluded*. Racism doesn't just do damage to an otherwise discerning intuition; it actually constitutes that intuition through and through. This intuitive aspect of racial paranoia is key because it is exactly what makes, say, Farrakhan's aforementioned levee claim impossible to debate away. It feels like a kind of truth to him—instinctively and immediately, even before he ever heard someone else describe the supposed crater left in a levee that he's probably never seen. Many of his African American listeners share a similarly instinctive presentiment, and no amount of argumentation can easily debunk such an intangible and slippery sixth-sense kind of feeling.

Racial paranoia inhabits the gut, not the mind. It is a hunch as much as a proven fact. It is a rapid-fire assessment that can hardly be dispelled with recourse to claims about contrary evidence or logical analysis. This makes racial paranoia impervious to scientific appeals, and this is part of what explains its entrenched nature and long-term staying power. (Gladwell does a good job of chronicling research studies that seem to show just how ingrained racial biases can be. He simply posits a gut-level space before those biases take root, a supposition that might be a little too neat and easy.)

Racial paranoia can also thrive when its arguments seem, prima facie, self-contradictory. There is always a fundamental contradiction at racial paranoia's core: cries of reverse discrimination and unfairness when a black person gets promoted over her white peers at work but little anger about the paltry number of blacks in the firm to begin with. How can one justify the first concern and ignore the second? One answer is bald self-interest. It helps us to make sense of things that might potentially disadvantage us, not things that work in our favor. Many African Americans rail against continued racial discrimination, but they may not focus the same degree of attention on the substantial rights won since the 1960s. In some ways, these kinds of selective analyses make pragmatic sense. Focusing too much on racial victories might allow disingenuous others to justify placing less emphasis on contemporary racial discrimination in favor of competing social issues. To talk about the lack of minority members in the law firm really could create an environment that might put a white worker's job prospects in jeopardy: to level that playing field could actually require letting some whites go (not just hiring more blacks). In each of these cases, racial paranoia helps people to live with contradictions of all stripes, particularly when they privilege self-serving claims on social resources and remedies.[18]

When I was listening to that conversation about Epperson's Illuminati conspiracy in a downtown Philadelphia hotel, I was eavesdropping on the everydayness of contemporary exchanges about pernicious global plots and unthinkable worldwide deceptions. And the young African American men who exchanged tales about the implications of such schemes showcase the uncanny ability of many contemporary Americans, those susceptible to the seductions of racial paranoia, to live and work and play squarely in the middle of mainstream America, even when and if they seem to fear, in mixed company (i.e., if a young white hotel guest beckons for her car keys), that other people might find their ideas bizarre or threatening.

Racial Paranoia examines how Americans can be both mainstream and extreme at the same time, especially when it comes to race and racism. In fact, racial thinking demands this kind of paradox. It necessitates logical contradictions and creates not only a world where levees are possibly blown away by evil bureaucrats, but one that can't be imagined to exist any other way.

We are all inhabitants of just such a topsy-turvy world; the difference is that some of us want to pretend that we can reason ourselves out of it, instead of listening to people talk about where these seemingly cockamamie ideas come from and why they feel so plausible. Using a mixture of historical analysis and contemporary ethnography, of archival research and media criticism, *Racial Paranoia* considers some of the reasons why we are all so paranoid about race—and how that paranoia makes itself known. I examine historical texts and listen to present-day Americans in an attempt to explain how racial paranoia shapes our everyday lives. I argue that "racial paranoia" (1) is much more common than many people would imagine, (2) has become even more entrenched and powerful than earlier American versions, and (3) represents a useful way to define some of what is most important about contemporary racial antagonisms in American society.

We can hardly employ racism as explicitly or wholeheartedly as we did in the past, not without recourse to the absoluteness of supremacist ideologies or conspiracies about blown-up levees and secret societies committed to racial oppression. However, we can't totally extricate ourselves from race either. Thinking seriously about race and racism in the twenty-first century means starting with this paradoxical realization: we don't want race to rule our lives, yet we can't seem to live together without obeying its calls. Successfully dealing with racism means creating social policy and embracing personal politics that recognize the paranoid power of this knotty impasse confounding us all.

Contemporary racism is subtler than anything America could have boasted in the past. That subtlety leaves room for plausible deniability. Nobody goes on CNN or FOX to admit that they simply hate blacks or Jews or Arabs, at least not if they want more than fifteen minutes in the mainstream spotlight—and the lucrative lifestyle that comes with it. That kind of talk is simply beyond the pale of public discourse, rightly shunned from the core of legitimate social debate. Political correctness has cleaned up our conversations, but there's a catch. This cleansing means that lip service to racial equality isn't taken at face value. And racial paranoia has become one of the primary ways of divining hidden race-based animosity in someone who would never willingly show it. This can be a quite frustrating and anxiety-producing way of ferreting out racists. It is also just about impossible to prove, especially for the victims who claim to experience subtle racism in a fleeting laugh or a stolen glance.

Racial Paranoia attempts to make an argument for the importance of racial paranoia as a distinct analytical lens for understanding contemporary America, a country that now carries its potential racisms in truly unprecedented ways. America's racial logic has changed dramatically in the last two hundred years, and mostly for the better. But our analysis of it lags far behind, especially in terms of the issues we emphasize, the questions we ask. This book tries to rewrite some of those old questions into new ones, far more than it can hope to fully answer: How do Americans experience this contemporary version of racism, a kind that can't safely speak its own name, a kind that must deny the accusation (even if it's secretly true)? What tools do people use to uncork traditional racism's bottled-up swagger? And why do we even need to disentangle racism from racial paranoia if we want to chart a productive future? These are the issues *Racial Paranoia* attempts to explore. The chapters move swiftly, attempting to lay out the conceptual groundwork for an important moment of self-recognition and recalibration in the history of American race relations. Racial paranoia isn't about seeing racism where it doesn't exist. It is a rudimentary and imperfect recognition that spotting racism at all these days demands new ways of seeing altogether.

CHAPTER 1

What Dave Chappelle Can Teach Us about American History

B efore the last applause sign went dark on the set of *Chappelle's Show,* one skit from the comedy program's first season, "The Player Hater's Ball," depicted a group of wanna-be pimps who constantly played the dozens, exchanging witty putdowns in an ongoing game of verbal one-upsmanship. They swapped "yo' mama" jokes and poked fun at each other's clothes and physical features: "Why don't you click your heels together three times and go back to Africa?" "You are so dark, when you touch yourself, it's like black-on-black crime." "What can I say about that suit that hasn't already been said about Afghanistan? It looks bombed-out and depleted." The skit opens with player haters from all over the world convening for the ninth annual Player Hater's Ball, a gala affair staged to crown the new Player Hater of the Year: the cruelest, most spiteful and misanthropic "verbal abuser on the planet." Such a title isn't just about dispensing funny quips, though. You also need to show a general mean-spiritedness and disdain for just about everybody else on earth. Dave Chappelle's character, Silky Johnson, ends up winning that year's competition for "calling in a bomb threat to the Special Olympics."

A second installment of the Player Haters segment has these same would-be pimps taking their show on the road—to the antebellum South. In the process, they provide contemporary viewers with a short history lesson in American race relations. Of course, it probably makes more sense to learn facts about the past from trained historians, not comedians, but the Player Haters sketch distills a pivotal piece of this nation's racial history in ways that can help to frame a productive discussion about race and paranoia in contemporary society. The skit highlights what is so new and different about race-based distrust today, what makes its present incarnation distinct from anything that might have characterized Americans' earlier racial interactions.

In that second Player Haters skit, these modern-day pimps create a time machine and travel back through the ages simply and exclusively "to hate on people," other people, with their trademark insults. They first drop in on Adolf Hitler, abusing him verbally and physically. Their next stop is a slave plantation in the Deep South. Wearing colorful fedoras, shiny suits, slick hairdos (one player hater, Beautiful, sports a Jheri curl), gators on their feet, and even a cape (donned by Silky Johnson himself), the three black player haters (along with the Korean player hater, Mr. Roboto, who actually invented the machine) find themselves back in the 1840s, watching black slaves forced to work the land under a scorching sun.

When the slaves' master spots these odd-looking outsiders, he hurriedly approaches, whip at the ready, intent
on keeping these potential troublemakers away from his
seemingly docile and hardworking slaves. The master advances, but the player haters seem little more than amused.
Unfazed and intrepid, they begin to taunt him with their
"snaps": "We traveled all the way back through time to
call you a cracker"; "You better watch your mouth, white
boy, before I put these gators up your ass and give your
insides some style."

Incidentally, Buc Nasty, the player hater wearing those
aforementioned gators, glimpses one of his own ancestors
dutifully working right alongside the other slaves, but if his
nineteenth-century forefather has any of the quick-witted
bravado of his wisecracking and pimped-out progeny, he
doesn't show it. He just quietly toils away with everyone
else, only stopping long enough to make eye contact with
Buc Nasty and to recognize the striking resemblance between them (both characters are played by the same actor).
Nasty's doppelganger ancestor could have been feeling all
kinds of anger and ill will toward his white master, but he
could not so glibly play with the idea of expressing it. And
he definitely would have to think twice before voicing a
colorful retort about lodging shoes up his master's rear end.
However, the twenty-first-century player haters share none
of this reticence.

After calling the master a "honky," Silky Johnson offers
the confused slaves a quick primer on the term's history,
linking its usage to *The Jeffersons,* which he tells them will
become a popular sitcom in another hundred years or so.

Silky presents this little TV factoid in a purposefully sober and almost schoolmarmish way, with a measured and fairly serious tone. He even offers them a description of George Jefferson's life, quoting lyrics from the show's opening jingle to provide the details. His point, he says, is simply to let the slaves know that in the future, "blacks will be free." After the slaves wonder aloud about when they themselves will taste freedom, Silky aims his gun at the slave master's chest and fires. "How about nowish," Silky declares, the master's limp whip clearly no match for the hard steel Silky Johnson is carrying.[1]

When the sketch aired, as part of a special show dedicated to bits that "went too far," it ended with a series of looped jump cuts showing the same shot of that slave master getting gunned down over and over and over again. Chappelle could hardly control his laughter as he watched the skit replayed along with his studio audience. "Apparently, shooting a slave master isn't funny to anyone except me and Neal [Brennan, the show's white cocreator]," he chuckled. "If I could, I'd do it every episode."

Chappelle's Time Haters segment plays on a simple, but important, anachronism: the contemporary stereotype of that smart-mouthed, back-talking, no-nonsense black person teleported to a slavocratic past. Besides the obvious joke of wisecracking pimps wormholing through time and space, there is another punch line at play, one based on the categorically uneven relationship between blacks and whites during slavery: today's haughty and "cool-posing" black men would have had a more in-your-face (George Jeffersonian) response to yesterday's white slave masters.[2] They'd call things like they saw them. They'd walk around fearlessly, like the badasses they are supposed to be. That is, they'd do exactly what real slaves in the eighteenth and nineteenth century couldn't do—at least not without fear of brutal reprisals. Eddie Murphy played with the same idea in one of his classic concert performances, telling a joke about a contemporary black man who boasts to his friends that if he had been a slave in the Old South, he would have told his master to bale the hay himself. Today's black man wasn't going to be baling anything for anybody—not now, not then.

These jokes say something quite serious about race relations during and after slavery. First of all, they're premised on a clear and purposeful recognition of the harsh racial treatment meted out to African slaves in the early decades of the American republic. Of course, any consideration of chattel slavery should be careful not to paint too monochromatic a portrait. "In mainline North America," historian Ira Berlin reminds us, "slaves (like their owners) were simply not the same people in 1819 that they had been in 1719 or 1619, although the origins and color of the slave population had not changed."[3] Slaves had different experiences in different times and places. You might work alongside a small farmer who could only afford a few slaves or be part of a vast plantation with hundreds. The daily lives of Southern slaves also varied by region. The cotton South was distinct from, say, the tobacco South. In the 1700s, before cotton really became king, slaves in the low country of South Carolina generally faced a harsher life than those working in the Chesapeake area.[4] Indeed, freedom itself meant different things to different slaves, depending on what part of the country their masters called home.[5] Even still, we've been left with many moving slave narratives documenting the systematically brutal tactics of slave masters, traders, breakers, and overseers throughout the slavery period and in many different parts of the country, both before and after America became a sovereign nation.

Frederick Douglass, America's most famous nineteenth-century black abolitionist, writes about being starved, whipped, and shipped off to a notoriously violent "slave breaker" when he resisted his master's demands. Similarly, Sojourner Truth relates disturbing tales of having her hands tied and back whipped until the blood gushed down her spine. Even though recently uncovered evidence seems to suggest that he might have fabricated the story of his birth on the continent of Africa, no one questions eighteenth-century slave-turned-abolitionist Olaudah Equiano's claims about seeing slaves grotesquely tortured with thumbscrews and other horrific contraptions.[6] Before escaping across the Atlantic, Moses Roper spent many of his days walking around literally chained to other slaves, a futile attempt to stop him from pulling off future escapes. Roper even saw masters weigh down their recently recaptured slaves with large bell-covered metal harnesses, the weight of the harness and the ringing from those bells conspiring to make any subsequent escape attempts that much more difficult.

No slave was safe. Historian Jacqueline Jones emphasizes the fact that sometimes slave masters and overseers would take out their pent-up aggression on the weaker relatives of more menacing and intimidating slaves, which meant that your own good behavior couldn't keep you out of harm's way.[7] Nobody was spared the master's wrath. Jones even describes pregnant slaves being forced to stretch out on the ground with their bellies in ditches dug out from the dirt specifically to protect their unborn babies, the master's future workers, while their mothers endured brutal floggings. Slavery even had its inadvertent hazards. Harriet Tubman describes how she was almost killed in her teens when an overseer accidentally hit her in the head with a blunt object meant for another slave, an injury that caused her painful seizures for the rest of her life.

There are many other school-taught tales of slave masters willing to suffer very little in the way of backtalk or defiance. The confrontational attitude of the pimps in that Player Haters skit would have gotten them whipped, branded, or killed. Slaves understood their vulnerable position, even if they didn't always keep up with official court rulings on the matter, such as the Supreme Court's infamous 1857 Dred Scott decision. The majority opinion in that case, as penned by Chief Justice Roger Taney, declared that "Negroes"—slave or free—"had no rights which the white man was bound to respect." And with that explicit backdrop (along with laws banning slaves from reading, testifying against whites, and wandering around town without permission), what could slaves do? Racism was thoroughly codified and sanctioned by the laws of the land. This was the pinnacle of de jure racism in antebellum America, a legalized racial discrimination that wouldn't be dealt its most massive deathblow for another hundred years.

It wasn't that people hadn't tried to fight de jure racism earlier than that. They certainly did. Four years after it became a national law, Wisconsin's supreme court justice, Abraham Smith, tried to declare the 1850 Fugitive Slave Act (requiring that free states return runaways to their slave masters) unconstitutional. In Illinois, a judge named William Denning did the exact same thing.[8] The U.S. Supreme Court summarily overturned their decisions, but people didn't give up in the face of such defeat. In Wisconsin, for instance, the state legislature then tried to pass a law making it illegal to enforce the 1850 act in that state, resting its claims on the very same "states' rights" cries that would embolden the South to secede from the Union little over a decade later.

Even if Northerners were hesitant to return runaways, there was still the threat of slaves (or free blacks) being kidnapped and smuggled to the South anyway. Rachel Parker was but one "free colored girl" kidnapped from West Nottingham, Pennsylvania, and taken to Baltimore in 1851. Many more "free" blacks met a similar fate.

Abolitionists would sometimes find ways to free kidnapped blacks. They'd engineer daring escapes, hazarding "rescue trials" convened against them once caught, or they could try to buy back the freedom of recaptured escapees. Even still, the threat of slave kidnappers was very real, and many blacks died trying to fend them off. Pockets of judicial protest, such as the acts of defiance exemplified by Wisconsin and Illinois in the 1850s, provided little protective cover for America's blacks—and few real options for dealing with interracial grievances, especially those of slaves against their masters. This all meant that slaves had to be circumspect about what they said and did. Any missteps were usually met with sanctioned retribution.[9]

Now, if the dynamics of race in antebellum America gave slaves every reason to remain potentially secretive toward their masters about their true feelings and budding runaway plans, there was little equivalent need for whites to mask their racist thoughts about blacks. Although some slave masters might have chosen to be generous and paternalistic with their slaves (and some bounty hunters would pose as abolitionists to catch runaways), there wasn't the same compulsion for all whites to bottle up their racial beliefs, to overly parse words or muffle phrases before uttering them. Even those who euphemized an exploitative system by calling slaves "servants" did it more to convince themselves of their own benevolence than to hide any of their contempt for Negroes from Negroes. The white planter class was generally unabashed about its low regard for the abilities of the "inferior" races (and classes) beneath them, and there was little need to hide it.

Masters also oscillated somewhere between implicitly trusting slaves and dreading their potential for rebellion or revolt, especially once the unthinkable had happened in Haiti and the island's slaves threw off their colonial shackles. During the Civil War, some slave owners were disappointed by the disloyalty of their seemingly contented charges. Many white southerners had come to believe their own rhetoric about slavery's generous gifts to the enslaved, and they were shocked and alarmed upon learning that things were not all as they had pretended. "This war has taught us the perfect impossibility of placing the least confidence in the Negro," a slave master wrote in 1862. "In too numerous instances those we esteemed the most have been the first to desert us."[10] It might seem hard to imagine now, but there is probably some real sincerity here, true paternalistic disappointment at ungrateful slaves fleeing plantations for their freedom. A slave justifiably running from bondage was almost unthinkable to slave masters. This was a time when some nineteenth-century physicians considered a slave's very urge to run away a kind of mental disorder, "drapetomania," which could be treated, of course, with severe beatings. Given such a diagnosis of pathology, it stands to reason that some slave masters wouldn't think twice about killing disobedient slaves, justifying that inhumanity by imagining their more submissive slaves as better suited for life than those mentally disturbed runaways.[11]

Many masters wanted to believe that if they treated their slaves well, with a modicum of respect and decency, then the slaves would appreciate it and relish their connection to such benevolent owners. And some slaves did. But planters and plantation owners couldn't really know when seemingly "lovable ol' darkies" weren't really plotting imminent escape or bloody revenge.[12] The motif of the happy slave, warmly incorporated into the white family, stood side by side with the possibility that those smiles and nods and honorific terms ("auntie," "uncle," etc.) might have hidden secrets much more sinister.

Slave owners worried about this all the time. They feared being burned alive in their beds or poisoned by their cooks.

According to historian Betty Wood, eighteenth-century slave masters "were so paranoid about the possibility of being poisoned by their slaves, be it by herbs or by arsenic and the like, that what might well have been natural deaths from ailments such as gastroenteritis were blamed on slaves, who could find themselves on trial for their lives" in front of a jury "consisting of local slave owners."[13] So, even as some planters expressed unshakable trust in their slaves, many more couldn't bring themselves to do so—not entirely. They even feared allowing slaves to bury their dead at night or to play their drums during the day, just in case these practices were mere ruses for planning insurrection. Of course, slaves did find ways to hide their illicit actions in plain sight, cloaking preparations for rebellion in the singing of spirituals and forging manumission documents (or passing for Indian, as the "mulatto" Moses Roper did) once on the road to freedom. And it was obvious enough to most slave masters that their slaves' smiles and ritualistic practices could be convenient masks for connivance.

African American abolitionist Harriet Tubman had a price on her head all her life for the role she played in shuttling slaves to freedom via the secretive network of safe houses that made up the Underground Railroad, a project that only worked because slaves didn't let on about when they were leaving and because the owners of safe houses along their route kept their practices hidden from anti-abolitionists and their racist legal codes. Tubman is always pictured as serious, menacing, someone who looked whites squarely in their faces, rarely mincing words. However, to be as good as she was at sneaking slaves out of slave states, she probably had to be equally adept at various masking techniques (the wide smile, the averted eyes, the bowed head) if she wanted to draw the least amount of attention to her efforts. What slave masters saw in the smiling resignation of their slaves was not necessarily what the slaves were thinking and feeling. If the slaves were smart, their masters would only see what was most pragmatic and safe for the slaves to show them. If you dreamed every night of stealing away, you had better be careful about broadcasting those fantasies in the light of day.

Trust was an issue both inside the master's house and out in the slaves' quarters. Slaves couldn't necessarily have confidence in one another either. Masters would sometimes use certain slaves to flog and "drive" others, a privileged position that some slaves embraced with dastardly relish. If rumor of potential rebellion passed the ears of a slave who considered it more prudent to expose the plot than to risk worse consequences (for everyone) if the scheme was actually carried out, it would not be too long before the slave master knew the intimate workings of the conspiracy. Tipping whites off about a forthcoming revolt could even win slaves their very freedom, the ultimate incentive for promoting betrayal. A slave named Gabriel was planning a rebellion in Richmond, Virginia, in 1800, but two slaves informed his master, and he was hanged with his coconspirators before they could begin their insurrection. South Carolinian slave Denmark Vesey planned his uprising for Bastille Day in 1822, after which he intended to head off to Haiti and take advantage of President Jean-Pierre Boyer's open-door policy toward Africans in the Americas. Some slaves opposed to Vesey's plan leaked as much as they could to the authorities, and Vesey was executed with more than thirty of his alleged accomplices well short of Sans Souci, the once majestic palace in northern Haiti built by a former slave who became "King of Haiti" in the early nineteenth century, Henri Christophe.[14] Most famously, when Nat Turner tried to organize a slave rebellion in Virginia in 1831, he was careful to keep his plans hidden from everyone except his most trusted coconspirators. Turner's revolt was also quashed, but the plans were fertilized and hatched under the cover of complacency and contentment, Turner and his band strategically needing to hide the fact that anything like an uprising was brewing.

The demand for secrecy and silent acquiescence to white authority wasn't just an issue for blacks below the Mason-Dixon Line. Slavery was supposed to be the South's "peculiar institution," but cities in the North benefited from its fruits as well, all the way up to the Civil War. And even in those Northern cities, blacks had to be very careful about how they represented their true feelings in public. For example, those fugitive slaves fortunate enough to escape to the North would arrive in, say, New York City only to discover that they needed to avoid other fugitive slaves and free blacks once they got there. Posing as friends and allies, these racemates might be spies for Southern interests committed to repatriating fugitives to their Southern masters. Runaway Frederick Bailey fled Maryland for New York in 1838. "Soon after arriving," according to historian Fergus Bordewich, "he encountered another fugitive slave whom he had once known in Maryland, who warned him forcefully that no one in New York could be trusted. The city, he said, was full of Southerners and hired men on the lookout for fugitives, and even blacks would betray him for a few dollars. The man was even frightened of Bailey, for fear that he too might be a spy."[15] Runaway slave Basil White was led away from Philadelphia and right into the hands of his Southern kidnappers "by a colored man named John Dorsey."[16] Some former slaves even trafficked in slavery themselves once they gained their own freedom. America's version of race-based slavery meant that blacks had to be careful around everyone—even other blacks and even in the North.

Born a slave in North Carolina but working as an abolitionist freeman in Boston, David Walker wrote *Walker's Appeal, in Four Articles; Together with a Preamble, to the Coloured Citizens of the World, but in Particular, and Very Expressly, to Those of the United States of America,* a courageous plea for the emancipation of America's slaves. He even sanctioned armed rebellion as a form of justified self-defense against the inhumanities of slavery. That was in 1829. In 1830, he was found dead in the street. The official cause was tuberculosis, but with various bounties on his head from white plantation owners, many black Bostonians believed that he had been poisoned—the cost, they knew, even in the North, for explicit racial candor and openness. That was the ultimate reason why most blacks, slave or free, watched their every word.

Until the mid-twentieth century, during the golden era of de jure racism, of legalized race-based discrimination and second-class citizenship for black Americans, there was still little reason for whites to temper their position on "the race question," no matter how potentially hateful or small-minded that position might have been. Not only were whites allowed to make their vilest racial feelings known, but they weren't generally subject to criminal prosecution if those same feelings turned into murderous actions. As early as the beginning of the eighteenth century, Virginia passed a law declaring that any master who accidentally killed a recalcitrant slave would "be free of all punishment . . . as if such accident never happened." North Carolina passed a similar law in 1830, deeming it logically impossible for a master to be found guilty of destroying his own property. Even if a white man was actually convicted for killing a slave, he would usually be pardoned by a governor—or, like the South Carolinian white man uncharacteristically sentenced to die in 1839 for killing a black person, he would "escape" before the sentence could be enforced.

After slaves were emancipated in the 1860s, the threat of white vigilantism increased throughout the South, especially with the Ku Klux Klan's emergence in 1866, the brainchild of disaffected Confederates. While still a professor at Princeton University, America's future president Woodrow Wilson was hardly an outlier when he virtually crowed in print about the inferiority of Southern Negroes and the emergence of "the great Ku Klux Klan . . . to protect the Southern Country."[17] This is what many Americans believed and the assumption upon which they based their everyday lives. There was no reason to pretend otherwise.

Finally, with the Northern victory in the Civil War, America would begin to see the unraveling of slavery's legal stitches, progress made slowly, one tiny thread at a time. After the 1877 compromise, when the North left the recently freed and enfranchised slaves to fend for themselves in the soon-to-be "Redeemed" South, the sweet promises of emancipation soured as white Southerners slowly relegislated (and terrorized) away the racial gains that had been won during the early years of Reconstruction. The "slave codes" became the "black codes" as America's legal system remained an explicit handmaiden to continued racial discrimination, and all the more so once slavery no longer provided blanket protection against blacks' claims to belonging and citizenship.

So, after emancipation, there was still little need for whites to paper over their true feelings about blacks, even as blacks continued to nurture reasonable fears about the consequences of anything but dissimulation in their own cross-racial exchanges. The law was aligned against "free" African American "citizens" to the point where whites could still commit the most heinous atrocities with little fear of being brought to justice. In June 2007, the Federal Bureau of Investigation released damning evidence that linked the 1940s lynchings of two black couples in Monroe, Georgia, to then governor Eugene Talmadge. In some ways, this revelation isn't necessarily surprising. Even well after slavery ended, whites were used to assaulting blacks with relative impunity. Think of those infamous photographs, sometimes made into postcards, that depict white townspeople standing in front of the charred bodies of recently hanged blacks throughout the late nineteenth and early twentieth centuries. Moms and dads, sons and daughters, all posing with smiles on their faces as rotting and castrated corpses dangled from nearby trees. There was no need to feel ashamed, to shield children's eyes from the gruesome sight. There was no pang of contrition, no compunction, no compulsion to hide the deed, and certainly no sense of self-immolating "white guilt."[18]

Of course, there have always been whites valiantly fighting for the rights of African Americans, even in the eighteenth and nineteenth centuries (Susan B. Anthony, Sherman Booth, Charles Sumner, Thaddeus Stevens, Harriet Beecher Stowe, William Lloyd Garrison, etc.), but John Brown is probably the most infamous and violent of them all. Brown was executed after leading several like-minded whites (along with a few blacks) in an 1859 plot to take over a federal arsenal in Harpers Ferry, Virginia. He had hoped that his actions would start a larger slave revolution across the South, and the other men he led into battle that year were clearly willing to give their lives for the same cause.[19]

Americans not necessarily as single-minded (or suicidal) in their commitments to racial justice did put a great deal of time and energy into the abolitionist movement. They published antislavery newspapers. They bought individual slaves their freedom. They drafted writs of habeas corpus to bring kidnappers to trial. They allowed their homes to serve as stops on the Underground Railroad and smuggled escapees farther north to Canada. Nevertheless, these activists were probably more the exceptions than the rule. And American history is littered with white-led race riots and mob violence against blacks that seemed to galvanize much more momentum (much more quickly) than the slow burn of these antiracist activities. There were vicious draft riots in Manhattan during the Civil War that turned white ethnics against darker-skinned New Yorkers. Twenty-two blacks were killed by white supremacists in North Carolina during the Wilmington Race Riot of 1898. At the beginning of the twentieth century, America experienced some of its most infamous acts of antiblack rioting. Greenwood, Oklahoma, a black town outside of Tulsa, was decimated by whites in 1921 when a female elevator operator accused a black shoe-shine boy of attacking her. There was Rosewood, a black town in Florida burned to the ground in 1923 after a white woman claimed that she had been raped by a black assailant. With such quick and deadly consequences, blacks were taught to know their place and to avoid any form of public confrontation with whites, especially white women. If, at one end of the spectrum, black female slaves had been considered nothing more than the sexual property of their masters, white women were always placed on a pedestal at the other end of that continuum, a pedestal that was supposed to elevate them safely beyond the reach of black men's desires.

The lessons learned in places like Rosewood and Greenwood helped to reinforce an almost mythical concern for the powerful "black buck," the long-standing white fear about strong and dangerous black slaves who were not as obsequious as they should be and who used their massive physical presence to intimidate genteel white men and women without saying a word. The specter of this animalistic black beast would often incite race-based mob violence in the early twentieth century, especially when the sanctity of white femininity was at stake (as the examples above highlight).[20] The black buck had to be stringently policed—killed, if necessary. His fate made an example for other blacks to internalize.

This image of the black buck reverberated around the black community and demanded a careful response. Parents tried to teach their children how to safely negotiate the larger white world. No matter how individually powerful a black man was, he was fighting some long odds when going up against the structural forces of America's entrenched racial order. With that knowledge in mind, kids were instructed to perform a version of themselves that was least threatening to whites. If they didn't, the consequences could be dire.

Emmett Till's open casket in 1955 is one of the most famous mid-century examples of "white justice" in the face of black haughtiness, of a racist society that demanded quiet resignation—or else. Till, a Chicago-born fourteen-year-old, had been warned that he had to "mind his manners" around Southern whites, which was code for the kinds of obsequious behaviors that slaves had mastered many generations before. But Till allegedly didn't heed the advice, either groping for or whistling at (depending on who tells the story) a local white woman just a couple of days into his summer vacation. Less than seventy-two hours later, the woman's enraged husband and his brother had killed the teenager. And only one more month passed before an all-white jury acquitted them both for the crime. This was American justice, and the lesson for blacks was clear: strong and silent were safer than proud, loud, and self-assured.

Political philosopher Danielle Allen characterizes the 1950s (and all of the postbellum to pre–civil rights era) as a time when blacks and whites exhibited "a different etiquette of citizenship: dominance on the one hand and acquiescence on the other."[21] With the coming of the civil rights movement and "black power," Emmett Till's martyrdom and the graphic media images of white incivility toward blacks, especially against young black children integrating public schools, would help to animate a new version of black identity, a brand of black masculinity that refused public obsequiousness and emphatically removed "the mask that grins and lies."[22] The erstwhile black buck would be reincarnated as Shaft.

Tragic incidents such as the murder of Emmett Till proved that the end of slavery didn't mean the end of codified forms of racial discrimination, which is why *Brown v. Board of Education of Topeka* in 1954 and the Civil Rights and Voting Rights acts of the mid-1960s were such groundbreaking achievements. Those new mid-century laws and reinterpretations of old laws meant that discrimination would no longer have explicit legislative or judicial cover. For most scholars of race in the United States, this is also the moment when racism and discrimination became more difficult to fight. An unabashedly racist law might be overturned, but what can you do about a functionally racist and discriminatory social order without overt legal backing? Historians often describe this as the moment when America went from de jure to de facto racism, from a racism steeped in the law to a racism that perpetuated itself without the same degree of explicit recourse to our legal justice system. For example, the backlash against that 1954 *Brown* decision (and the subsequent rulings that started to pick away at its gains almost immediately) carefully argued on other than exclusively racial or racist grounds.[23] And even without laws to keep blacks out of certain occupations, neighborhoods, or restaurants, blacks still only crossed hard and fast social lines at their own risk—and backroom deals (such as buildings with "restricted covenants" forbidding residency to certain groups) operated just one shade below officially stated policy. As Alexis de Tocqueville noted in 1848, "Inequality cuts deep into mores as it is effaced from laws."[24] Whites had to be more careful about how they represented any potentially discriminatory practices, but social division continued its hardwired connection to racial difference, even without the nineteenth century's brand of rubber-stamping by the Supreme Court.

In part, this means that America experienced the beginnings of a racial role reversal after the 1960s. Instead of a defenseless Emmett Till terrorized by the fearless white vigilante protected from legal prosecution, instead of the undaunted white slave master and the silent black sycophant, extreme types in slave-era racial relations, we have the confrontational African American (distrustful of whites and newly emboldened to take any grievances to the courts) and unabashedly racist whites increasingly marginalized in the public sphere (and not nearly as unapologetically backed by the laws of the land).[25] And blacks could now get away with confronting whites (especially in Northern cities where their numbers had grown during the "great migration") without worrying that white citizens would return to lynch them at will.[26]

As America has attempted to deal with the psychic and physical scars left in the wake of our country's troubled racial past, the imagery and terminology of slavery and Jim Crowism continually reemerge in public conversations and debates. Today, much of that talk is organized around the question of reparations for *all* blacks, but in the 1960s, Malcolm X famously drew a stark distinction between "house" and "field" slaves, a distinction implying that some slaves might actually deserve more recompense than others. The field slaves, he said, prayed long and hard for their masters' demise, fantasizing every day about the end of their enslaved plight, while the house slaves so identified with their masters, so relished their relatively cushy position in the big house, that they were essentially invested in their masters' well-being.[27] When the master became ill, Malcolm X satirized, the field slave prayed it was terminal; the house slave overidentified with the master and longed to bear the illness in his stead.

While Malcolm X's distinction worked extremely well, rhetorically speaking, as a not-so-subtle criticism of middle-class blacks and political accommodationism in the 1960s, his version of antebellum history is far too cut-and-dried. If anything, with so much more interracial face time, the house slaves probably had to disguise their real feelings even more consistently than field hands did, especially because the tiniest whiff of insubordination might mean sure-fire punishment. Plus, even if the field hands wished their masters a speedy death, it wasn't like they could just run into the sick men's bedrooms, curse them out to high heaven, and make their feelings known, much less brandish a blade and finish their masters off—not without confronting the certainty of lynch-mob retaliation. All slaves, even and especially house slaves, had to hide their feelings, and it is folly to assume that they enjoyed a categorically cozier relationship to slave masters and mistresses, especially since many slave families cut across the house-field divide altogether.

If we look at those three most infamous architects of potential slave rebellions—Gabriel, Turner, and Vesey—we have, if not quite house slaves, three "members of the slave elite" plotting bloody uprisings.[28] House slaves and other more skilled blacks were the ones with the most intimate knowledge of how the master's family lived—and how to use those details against them. Even with full knowledge of the obvious dangers, "the number of reports of owners and their families being poisoned by their house slaves, by those whom they had previously considered entirely trustworthy, runs completely counter to the notion that these women and men were uncritically devoted to those who held them in captivity."[29]

Recognizing that slave masters possessed substantial (almost absolute) social and legal power over their slaves, acknowledging "the full weight and meaning of the slave-holder's dominion," doesn't mean that the slaves were simply helpless. The master and slave had what historian Ira Berlin has called a "negotiated relationship," where the master held all the power but still needed to make small concessions to slaves in order for the system to work.[30] Even before slaves started to assert themselves during the Civil War, striking and walking off farms, they had other ways to defend their inter-ests: "Female slaves sassed, they loafed, they engaged in vari-ous sorts of sabotage."[31] They possessed some small agency. Many did talk back (or even fight back) and lived to tell about it. But the brave or reckless few seem to have been far outnumbered by those bondmen and women who simply tried to get themselves and their families through the day safe and sound.[32]

For historians struck by how few slaves in the United States organized formal rebellions (as compared to the higher frequencies of such attempts in the Caribbean and South America), there were disputes about the supposedly unusual harshness of North American slavery, a harshness that scholars such as Stanley Elkins claimed had extin-guished slaves' very desire for liberty—or their ability to take full advantage of it once it came.[33] Social scientists have used the specifics of American slavery to explain much of contemporary black culture today. Dispropor-tionately low black marriage rates and strained relations between the sexes, a growing preponderance of female-headed black households, and the "dysfunctional" aspects of contemporary "ghetto" culture have all been linked to slavery's horrific legacy.[34]

TransAfrica founder Randall Robinson argues that most ordinary Americans don't think about slavery nearly enough. He believes that we've done a masterful job of hiding its remnants from public view, ignoring its foundational connections to some of our most hallowed history, as though not seeing it will make it go away. Well, it does, and it doesn't. Robinson makes his case for slavery reparations by placing those hidden and unacknowledged slaves front and center, a move, he maintains, that can get young black people talking productively and constructively about their contemporary lives by placing those discussions into a more substantial historical context.[35]

Contrary to some common reactionary assumptions about a supposedly self-pitying embrace of victimhood within the black community, the ultimate trump card for such a position, chattel slavery, is hardly something, as Robinson notes, that black Americans dwell on—or even bring up.[36] Far from using it as a crutch, they barely discuss it most of the time. Blacks may talk about racism, past and present, but not necessarily about slavery. Perhaps by avoiding that discussion, we hope to fend off any twinges of humiliation or emasculation. Are these the shameful feelings for which we overcompensate by calling one another "nigger," reclaiming that word as a way of defusing racism's antebellum power? Whatever the reason, slavery isn't a major theme of contemporary black culture and conversation. Outside of a few hip-hop artists, contemporary black music doesn't emphasize it: KRS-One traces a line from overseers to officers, Nas talks metaphorically about ruling the world and freeing his sons, and other "conscious rappers" make brief and passing references, but most comprehensive books about hip-hop can comfortably tell its entire story without a single reference to slavery.[37]

Likewise, there isn't a slew of black movie directors churning out filmic meditations on the antebellum South, which is why Haile Gerima's 1993 *Sankofa* was such an important moment in independent black cinema. On the political front, black leaders found themselves publicly criticized throughout the 1990s for not taking vocal enough moral stands against contemporary slavery in Africa and against the rulers who benefit most from it. And the black press didn't talk about that slavery as substantively as many activists would have liked either. It seems that few members of the black community want to linger on slavery much anymore at all.[38]

This relative silence about slavery in contemporary black America (whether due to shame, as some scholars argue, or something else) is crucial to any discussion about race and racism today. That's because slavery's de-emphasis is at least partially a function of its seeming self-evidence. The uncertainties and ambiguities that define contemporary interactions between individual whites and individual blacks are radically different from the imagined absoluteness of the master-slave relationship.

Despite the neglectful stance taken by many toward the contemporary significance of chattel slavery, there was a stretch in the 1970s when slavery did become a kind of household obsession in America, thanks, in no small part, to television. Journalist and genealogist Alex Haley's embellished work of family history, *Roots,* became a significant TV hit at that time. It highlighted the life of one of Haley's ancestors, a proud and feisty slave named Kunta Kinte, a Mandinka from the Gambia who was captured, enslaved, and brought to the United States in the late 1700s.[39] Of course, there were many such feisty figures in American history, slaves who either made their way back to Africa in the late eighteenth century or died boldly trying.

Roots was so popular among African Americans, at least partially, because it was the tale of a defiant slave who would not easily consent to his own captivity. Kunta Kinte's story of black recalcitrance had more than a little bit of 1970s flavor to it. His willingness to stand up for his manhood in the face of overwhelming odds struck a chord with African Americans, especially during the height of Black Power. Even if Kunta Kinte was eventually "broken," black viewers could still see—and admire—his early defiance, his unwillingness to acquiesce. It is a post–civil rights desire for brave resistance written back into America's antebellum past, Dave Chappelle's player haters without so many witty one-liners.

In important ways, the racial tables had turned noticeably by the time *Roots* aired; the Black Power awakening (somewhat ironically reinforced by the more substantive incorporation of blacks into American society after the legal advances of the 1950s and 1960s) was a major pivot point for the change. That's part of the reason why Chappelle's mention of George Jefferson in the aforementioned Player Haters sketch is so appropriate. George Jefferson is a short black man with a chip on his shoulder. He doesn't bite his tongue, and he isn't afraid to "call a cracker, a cracker." And that's not just because he's a middle-class property owner with his own penthouse and a dry-cleaning business to boot. Even his maid, Florence, has an acerbic tongue. She will tell anyone off in a second, including her Napoleonic boss. George keeps her gainfully employed, of course, because he appreciates her sincerity, her nerve, and her fearlessness. And the show wouldn't have been a success if there weren't something hilarious about the lengths to which George and Florence both go in telling folks off, giving people a piece of their minds.

What makes George particularly laughable, even if still sympathetic, is that we're supposed to consider the man's obsessive willingness to make his antiwhite feelings known mildly inappropriate and odd. The joke seems to be that he takes things too far, especially since the whites in his building are hardly the racist ogres that his former neighbor, Archie Bunker, personifies. To be sure, the Georges and Florences of the world need their Archies, their overt and obvious racists, for the entire system to work. But even Archie saw the writing on the wall. He couldn't talk about race, sexuality, and other forms of difference with nearly the impunity he once enjoyed—or that his father and his father's father could exploit.

The subtler racism gets, however, the more paranoid people become about hidden racial motivations and intentions. For the slave masters who had to discern the cloaked sarcasms and possible insincerities of their self-protective slaves, it could feel like violent rebellion was always just around the corner—if not from their own slaves, then from slaves on another plantation. And even though blacks faced a very different kind of threat, a ubiquitous threat, from whites during the antebellum period, they also learned to fear the capricious absoluteness of societal aggression. Such "congealed boundaries of distrust" formed over decades (even centuries) are hard to dissolve.[40]

Even without the explicit codification of racism in America's legal code, most blacks today can still see racism. They see it in the small things, the seemingly innocuous gestures, not just global conspiracies and vast racial differences in social outcomes. Racism might actually feel more powerful and scary when it seems to play possum, preparing to pounce on any naive person who takes words (or even deeds) as the unequivocal reflection of inner feelings. Vulnerable slaves and their masters both understood this implicitly. If they could somehow travel through time like Chappelle's raucous player haters, antebellum slaves and their masters might best be able convince us all that seeing is never simply believing when squinting across America's fraught color lines.

CHAPTER 2

The Birth of Political Correctness and the White Man's Newest Burden

While it was economics that drew Europeans to Africa in search of inexpensive overseas labor power for their expanding global empire, labor they used in their colonies to produce cheaper raw materials for the consumer products demanded by their growing populations back home, slavery also rested on religious foundations. When America's founding fathers threw off the shackles of colonial "slavery" (and its "taxation without representation"), declaring themselves free and sovereign (liberated from "foreign" tyranny by way of a new constitution), they still possessed a powerful rationale justifying their continued enslavement of Africans, justification as much for themselves as for anyone else. This prevailing theological explanation would keep racial slavery alive in the United States for many more years than the British Commonwealth would tolerate it. Religion would be one of the many validations for slavery in the United States after the American Revolution, but it also provided traction for subsequent antiracist activism. Not all whites were morally conflicted about slavery, but those who were found justifications in religious orthodoxy, even if that doctrinal validation didn't last forever.[1]

Bringing God's Holy Word to the world's unenlightened savages helped Europeans to defend their pith-helmeted excursions into the Dark Continent and provided them with a more positive psychological upside to the brutal realities of chattel slavery. Civilizing heathens was considered the "white man's burden," a phrase popularized by a Rudyard Kipling poem and that seems to imply only the most grudging acceptance of Europe's imperial mandate. According to one dominant characterization of conversion during the colonial period (and there were many religious figures, including Catholic popes, publicly denouncing this position as early as the fifteenth century), Christian slaves were supposed to humbly accept their enslavement and be thankful for the eternal salvation that came with it. Slavery on earth was a small price to pay for the rewards of eternal life after death.

And this was hardly just the feeble excuse of slave masters. Many African American slaves and former slaves talked about slavery—and their own horrible experiences with it—in just these vindicating terms. Some of them claimed to appreciate the higher spiritual good they had found by way of slavery's rugged and lowly path. Eighteenth-century slave Phillis Wheatley probably put it most poetically. "'Twas mercy brought me from my Pagan land," she wrote. "Taught my benighted soul to understand." Without slavery's introduction of God's mercy and grace, Africans would have never learned the teachings of Jesus Christ—or been compelled to love him. Whether or not some slaves were engaging in a bit of antebellum real-politik (Wheatley herself uses the rest of that same poem to gently remind hypocritical Christians that "Negroes may be refined and join the angelic train"), many were quite sincere in their assessment of slavery's salvific upside, and even more so after visits with their "heathen" brethren back in Africa. Former slave and longtime abolitionist Henry McNeal Turner even suggested that African Americans emigrate to Africa and enslave the Africans still there (but only for seven years) in an attempt to civilize and Christianize them for the backward and ungodly Africans' own good—the "white man's burden" in blackface.[2]

Clearly, many former slaves, especially those sent off as missionaries, did feel fortunate to enjoy the fruits that came with living in a prosperous new nation like America, even if they only received those fruits once propertied white men had first discarded them. In the North, free blacks also maintained their faith when the congregations that had converted them only offered a lukewarm embrace once they were in the fold. Denominations such as the African Methodist Episcopal church were founded because predominantly white churches in the nineteenth century often treated their black worshippers like second-class Christians. Instead of throwing out the religious baby with the racist bathwater, blacks struck out on their own to create spiritual institutions that treated them as full inheritors of God's glorious bounty.

Many white Christians considered slavery to be the divine will of God, an ordained mechanism for spreading the news of His promise to the damned and forgotten.[3] God had even explained why Africans were supposed to be slaves, how they had earned that miserable status. Time and time again in the eighteenth and nineteenth centuries, scholars, politicians, slave masters, and even slaves themselves invoked the "curse of Ham" to account for racial differences and for slavery's existence in one fell swoop: Noah had placed a curse on his son Ham's son, Canaan, in the book of Genesis. After the flood, when Noah and his family were replenishing the earth, Noah got drunk, disrobed, and was inadvertently seen in all his nakedness by his youngest son, Ham. Ham immediately relayed the event to his two brothers, and they went back to cover the old man's body, careful not to catch a glimpse of him in the process. But it was already too late for Ham. The damage had been done. Mortified and dishonored, Noah proclaimed, "Cursed be Canaan; a servant of servants shall he be unto his brethren."[4] Servant was easily translated as slave ("servant" being the most common euphemism for "slave" in the paternalistic South), and Africans' degraded standing was deemed duly fated by God. To mark Canaan's offspring, God's curse also made their skin dark, which explained the difference in pigmentation between Europeans and Africans. And there it was. The curse of Ham gave race-based slavery the imprimatur of destiny, of providential inevitability.[5]

America's early commitments to such biblical interpretations cut both ways. They simultaneously excluded and included blacks.[6] For Africans to be preordained slaves by an antediluvian messiah figure, religious scholars had to demand that those Africans at least be considered human, descendants of Adam, not dehumanized and imagined as part of some separate origin story. The curse of Ham was a kind of backhanded form of recognition. At least it meant that Africans were a part of the species—and this at a time when it wasn't a foregone conclusion that Africans were people at all. Even as recently as the early twentieth century, Ota Benga, an African from the Congo, was brought to the United States by missionaries and purposefully exhibited alongside animals in the Bronx Zoo. The jury was still out on how to classify such "primitive" Africans, where they fit along that Great Chain of Being. Many serious thinkers posited at least two Adams—maybe more. Africans could have been pre-Adamic or post-Adamic. During the Renaissance, the polygenists (imagining different Adams for different racial groups, if they believed in the Adam story at all) locked horns with monogenists (mostly theologians and church officials), who demanded one founding story for all humankind. In the United States, even in the South, the monogenist argument won out, and Ham's curse provided a useful way to justify slavery without having to think about slaves as something other than human beings.[7] These beasts were humans, just a cursed form, relegated to slavery by the most sacred of texts.

Religion served as a linchpin for many early Americans' relationships to the nation and to one another. And it certainly validated all kinds of political positions. Historical sociologist Orlando Patterson reminds us that the Ku Klux

Klan wasn't just a disorganized band of racist vigilantes up to no good.[8] It was more of a religious cult, one committed to a Christian America and fighting for the Hamitic divisions they considered sanctioned by the Old Testament. Of course, that's part of the reason why their calling card was a burning cross. It was a resolutely religious symbol. It represented the Cross on Calvary, a cross burning with indignation at the abominations of miscegenation and racial equality. It was the Klan's commitment to the Bible, a literal reading with racial inflections, that provided moral weight for their holy crusade against racial amalgamation and blacks' short-lived political gains during Reconstruction.

The nineteenth-century Reconstruction project was beaten back by the forces of retrenchment and "Redemption"; newly elected African American officials in states like Alabama and South Carolina for instance, were unfairly removed from office by murder or mischief throughout the 1870s.[9] Some scholars have labeled the civil rights movement America's "Second Reconstruction," an homage to that thwarted first go-round less than one hundred years earlier.[10] For the 1960s Reconstructionists, victory meant palpable and lasting social transformations in electoral politics and beyond. It meant appealing to morality and religion (not just the law) in an attempt to reconfigure America's racial order. And they won many significant battles with that strategy, all predicated on their victory in the fight over racism's moral worth.

Unlike the Radical Republicans (who valiantly but unsuccessfully pushed hard against the grain of moderate Lincoln

Republicanism and Confederate obstinacy, fighting for the full legal rights of newly freed slaves), the mid-twentieth-century activists in America's Second Reconstruction didn't immediately lose all the measurable gains they had acquired. In fact, despite whatever criticism might be aimed at the men and women who marched nonviolently, braved those freedom rides, staged sit-ins, and organized community boycotts in the 1950s and 1960s, they waged a systematic and powerful counterattack against the most pernicious features of legalized racial discrimination

Those mid-twentieth-century battles over the future of America's racial democracy weren't just about the law. And they weren't only fought through litigation. While Charles Houston, George Hayes, Spottswood Robinson, Robert Carter, James Nabrit, and Thurgood Marshall toiled away in America's courtrooms, arguing for the full and universal application of the Constitution's Fifth (due process) and Fourteenth (equal protection) amendments, Fred Shuttlesworth, Ralph Abernathy, Martin Luther King, Jr., and others worked their magic from the pulpit.[11] They wanted to make American racism a specifically religious issue, but a different kind of religious issue than it had been in the past. They intended to take Christianity back from the likes of the Klan, using its moral authority as a way of grounding African American claims to citizenship and humanity.

There is a long and growing body of literature on "liberation theology" as a philosophical and practical foundation for various kinds of political activity.[12] In an American context, liberation theology might even be made to mark the very mentality that meshed religious commitments with calls for social revolution dating all the way back to the earliest settlements in the New World, to spiritual communities built by people of faith longing to escape religious intolerance and discrimination in their native lands. Of course, traditions of spirituality fomenting political and social action go back far before the founding of America and stretch well beyond its borders. Every major civilization on this planet has dealt (in one way or another) with potential conflicts between faith and freedom, religion and revolution, piety and politics. It is one of those quintessential human dilemmas.

Serious political activism tends to demand the kind of existential footing that religious faith can provide. Writing about contemporary Nicaragua, anthropologist Roger Lancaster argues that the history of revolutionary social movements there or anywhere else is just about incomprehensible without making links to the moral authority and galvanizing power that Christianity helped establish.[13] Marxism and religion are usually assumed to operate at cross-purposes, especially since social theorist Karl Marx famously dismissed religious beliefs as delusions, ideological tricks that purposefully keep people focused on heaven instead of their earthbound troubles. But Christian socialisms clearly predated (and even informed) Marx's very own theory of revolutionary change, Christian socialisms that had long grounded demands for equality in a language of spiritual brotherhood and righteous anger.[14]

And this isn't just a Christian thing. The histories of resistance to exploitation and material inequities all around the world are steeped in complicated religious justifications for societal changes that have always used sacred texts, religious stories, and deific laws to authorize political demands, especially demands by the exploited and disenfranchised for social autonomy and equality. Religion doesn't simply distract people from politics; it can also radicalize them, offering an idiom to express their concerns and an unshakable faith that higher powers are on their side. America's long history of religiously validating political claims foreshadows the Religious Right's recent scale tipping in electoral politics—or even our current fears of "fundamentalist Islam" as a threat to national security.[15]

As late as the 1940s, most scholars of African American culture and history couldn't predict the political relevance of African American religious practices, describing black communities as "overchurched" and otherworldly (at the expense of real engagement with social issues), something analogous to Marx's analysis of religion as a weapon of the powerful that the powerless get fooled into wielding on themselves. With the Southern Christian Leadership Conference's institutional role in the civil rights struggle, much of that discussion of black religion and politics has been radically reworked in the last forty or fifty years. Black churches have become central to any discussion of political activism in the black community, serving as bunkers in the 1960s for vulnerable activists, ground zero for the dangers of heartless antiblack backlash (think of the four little girls killed in that Birmingham church). And just like before, when black abolitionists and rebels such as David Walker and Nat Turner used religion to justify their unswerving attacks on slavery, Martin Luther King, Jr., and others used Christianity to challenge American racism in the twentieth century.

Since one of the traditional pillars of white racial superiority was steeped in biblical considerations, the civil rights struggle's redeployment of Christianity (mixed with nonviolent public action) was prescient. It could appeal to (and revise) those biblical stories, pivoting on America's age-old investment in its own moral and religious integrity. In fact, King argued that racism was an alternative religion for Americans, a form of apostasy that flouted Christian ideals. Racism was a false God. "Racism is evil," he said, "and we must see it for what it is: racism is a faith, a form of idolatry . . . [with] the ultimate arrogance of saying God made a creative mistake." For King and those working with him, racism shouldn't just be considered an attack on black people. It should be reframed as an attack on Christianity, an attack on God, and an attack on the very religious foundations that made America "one nation under God." The implications were clear: how could any country last if its basic moral framework was compromised, if it was disobeying (and misconstruing) the will of God, the command to love thy neighbor as thyself?

The civil rights movement perfected this religious critique of nationalist hypocrisy. Its supporters argued that white Americans couldn't really love God (or this country) if they didn't treat Negroes the way they themselves would want to be treated. Offering an early version of that 1990s Christian slogan WWJD (What Would Jesus Do?), they asked Christians to imagine how Jesus might deal with

American racism. And they provided their own answer. He would rail against it, fight it. He certainly wouldn't discriminate against others, curse and spit at children for trying to go to school. Black Powerites eventually criticized King for his integrationist message, but he was arguing for inclusion on truly (even radically) biblical terms, inclusion into the "Beloved Community."

The civil rights movement's success wasn't just about redefining Christianity—and wasn't simply won by better sermonizing. It was also clearly spurred on (and assisted) by the newly invented television's powerful nightly telecasts. King tested America's religious conscience, but none of that would have worked nearly as well without the creation of broadcast television as a ready-made national stage for the representation of righteous, nonviolent resistance and discontent. As a new communication medium, television came of age in the 1950s, just in time to chronicle and disseminate news of those civil rights battles.[16]

It was one thing to read about water hoses and vicious dogs being unleashed against women and children peacefully marching for their equality. It was entirely another to see those graphic images beamed into your living room. Inevitably, the aggressors (police or violent white reactionaries) came off as the bad guys in these nightly narratives, with the stoic black protestors playing the role of innocent victims. Even when right-wing pundits tried to recast civil rights rallies as little more than glorified sex orgies, there was little denying the visual facts of these uneven and inhumane confrontations captured by television cameras.[17]

Of course, there are some powerful still photographs from this era as well, photos depicting white-hot rage at, say, black students attempting to desegregate schools or sitting down at all-white lunch counters. These photos also did the work of casting white anger as unjust and unfair, wicked and sinful. But it was the television set that unfurled this drama as a live-action event for all Americans to see, searing those moving images into people's hearts and minds. The television became a window into America's soul, and the view wasn't pretty. For blacks, these images of outrage were frightening and enraging. For whites, they were depictions of a whiteness that most would just as soon distance themselves, at least their "better selves," from, especially in mixed racial company.

And these television images weren't just for American consumption. Angry white racism didn't play well overseas either. During the 1930s and 1940s, many blacks explicitly invoked the irony of being asked to fight fascism and Nazism abroad when American racism was still alive and well at home. Indeed, once the Nazis started to use both religion and science to justify their own racist practices in Europe, those tactics became even less acceptable in an American nation trying to define itself (and its global aspirations) in contradistinction to the machinations and maneuverings of Adolf Hitler. For example, America's early love affair with eugenics, the project of genetically engineering future generations by way of selective breeding and sterilization, a field systematized and championed by Francis Galton in the late nineteenth century, quickly ended, at least explicitly, once the Nuremberg Trials revealed the atrocities carried out by the Nazis under its scientific auspices.

Even after the Allies won the war and marginalized Germany in the 1940s, American racism was still a very serious issue for the nation's international image. During the cold war, the Communist threat posed by the Soviet Union was heightened by the fact that black Americans portrayed their native land as a racially oppressive and undemocratic place. In the 1960s, when Jim Crow denied African dignitaries access to empty rooms in vacant Southern hotels, such slights further damaged America's reputation abroad and opened up space for the Soviet Union to get that much cozier with leaders from these newly decolonized countries.[18] It was very important for America to walk the walk it had talked all along, even if just to keep the Soviets from forming more dangerous allegiances with the Third World. The United States's push to reimagine itself as a global superpower required making the case that its own house was in order, but America's conspicuous hypocrisies around issues of race made that a very hard sell.

Up until this point in the nation's history, racism was unremarkably mainstream. From the "curse of Ham" to presidential declarations of the Ku Klux Klan's redemptive ethos, racism wasn't something most people thought about hiding or downplaying. There was no need. It simply defined how life was lived. Even politicians, ever coy and careful with their public pronouncements, didn't feel required to be particularly cautious about supporting racial inequality. They made no bones about the fact that they believed blacks were inherently inferior to whites; even many of those political figures who fought against slavery and for equal rights feared that Africans might truly be hereditarily inferior.

George Wallace has become canonized as the poster child for segregationist politics in the mid-twentieth century, most especially because of his heartfelt mantra of "segregation now, segregation tomorrow, segregation forever," delivered in public and at a podium, not in a backroom somewhere safely away from prying eyes and ears. This emotionally charged snippet from one of his inaugural speeches, his throwing down of "the gauntlet" on behalf of "the greatest people that have ever trod this earth," is replayed every February, during Black History Month, as part of the ceremonial retelling of our collective drama about how blacks won their equal rights. Each year, Wallace's 1963 figure gets more and more grotesque, more and more unreal. His time-frozen image plays a two-part role. One is straightforward. He's the black-hatted racist of old, the villain unapologetically hunkered down against an inevitable legal equality that we now know was just over the horizon. He's also a useful (even cathartic) symbol of what contemporary America is not—brash, bold, and brutal about its racialism: he represents the last gasp of unembarrassed public racism. Part of the ritualistic significance of those rebroadcasts stems from the fact that they allow us all to be frightened (by our own racial ghosts) and rewarded (for our continued racial progress) every single

February. (Selma's Eugene "Bull" Connor often gets cast to play the very same role Wallace did along with former Arkansas governor Orval Faubus.)

Wallace had his heyday during an era that privileged America's last group of unabashed public racists, and even Wallace recanted his segregationist position later in life— at about the time that he became a born-again Christian. Most of the major figures putting up their fight against those seemingly anarchistic and radical dreams of racial egalitarianism during that Second Reconstruction changed their explicit tunes soon after the 1960s. Jerry Falwell, who has always deftly split the difference between politics and religion, used the story of Ham's curse to explain black inferiority and justify racial segregation well into the late 1950s. By 1988, he had publicly reversed his stance on segregation and recanted his earlier interpretations of Genesis as misguided and just plain "wrong." He even later claimed that he knew in his heart that segregation was a sin against God's will even while he was openly espousing it in the 1950s, but he just didn't have the courage to challenge what he had been taught in Bible school.[19] The 1950s, it seems, restricted Falwell from speaking his true heart vis-à-vis the travesty of segregation and racism, but it wasn't racists who had to cloak their beliefs. Falwell had to hide (and fight) his antiracist impulses for fear of backlash from the other end of the ideological spectrum.

What you saw before the 1960s was a decidedly brash and brazen American racism. Racists were out in the open, embodying the exactness of posted placards, a confidence

born of explicit police support and long-standing black
acquiescence to governmental indifference. They had vocal
advocates like George Wallace guarding the schoolhouse
steps. Men like South Carolina governor and senator Strom
Thurmond won election after election on conspicuously
racialist platforms. But a funny thing happened on the way
to the twenty-first century. The American mainstream
changed direction. For all the reasons already discussed, it
became less prudent for Americans, especially public figures, to espouse racist beliefs in public. Racialist responses
were deemed offensive, hostile, and insensitive and immediately connected the speakers to those water hoses and
police dogs of yore that were set on young, defenseless,
peaceful, and decidedly Christian black marchers. Racism
was redefined as a social and moral evil of catechistic proportions. The white man's new burden was guilt and shame
for moral failings around race. What used to be common
sense was now a cancer, a deadly sin. Something everyone
once took for granted (on religious grounds) was now de-
nounced just as adamantly (and by way of a similarly religious inflection).

Scientists had to deal with the same reversal. Where
they once voiced their opinions about black inferiority
without compunction, they had to start worrying that
people would accuse them of racism based on the social
implications of their research. When scholars such as
Arthur Jensen, J. Phillipe Rushton, and William Shockley
(the scholarly trifecta for such discussions) updated age-
old theories steeped in genetic explanations for black intel-

lectual underachievement in the 1970s and 1980s, they felt pummeled by their colleagues and responded by denouncing those critics for their supposed use of ideological and political commitments as justification for suppressing legitimate scientific inquiry about racial differences. And this works even if the racial valences are reversed. When Leonard Jeffries talked about whites as "ice people" with a genetic predisposition for genocidal violence, he was pilloried in the press and dismissed by other scholars as a charlatan.

Learning a key lesson from these early public relations nightmares and public floggings, the most recent racialist readings of group differences have had to couch their work very carefully, explicitly anticipating and trying to head off accusations of racism. This has gotten to the point where "race" is barely mentioned at all (sixteen pages or so out of some eight hundred) in a book such as *The Bell Curve,* an early 1990s attempt to repackage arguments about why the cognitive differences between successful and unsuccessful people have more to do with natural endowments than with social inequalities or unfair forms of discrimination. Even without positioning "race" as a major concern of the book (or even a minor one), critics still read between the lines of that controversial offering and accused its authors of scientific racism in disguise.[20]

Of course, the need to read between the lines is already a far cry from George Wallace–like candidness. And such readings are simply met with hasty denials and defensiveness (as well as accompanying cries of reverse racism). The public debate about race in America has become little more than accusation and counteraccusation, claim and counter-claim. Unless the offending party gets caught with a hand in the cookie jar (for instance, Michael Richards being videotaped spewing "nigger" at black audience members in a Los Angeles nightclub), most public discourse about race leaves space for plausible deniability around questions of racist intentions. Even when things are seemingly unam-biguous (Howard Cosell calling black football players monkeys, Mel Gibson attributing all the world's problems to conspiring Jews, or Richards's ode-to-lynching tirade in response to those hecklers), individuals apologize, deny racist motivations, and try to move on. They don't dig in their heels and champion the cause of racial difference. They don't defend their racialist ideals at the schoolhouse door. They chalk things up to alcohol, fatigue, a bad joke, whatever, and then rush to put the entire episode behind them. Sometimes it works, and sometimes it doesn't.

As early as 1976, Agriculture Secretary Earl Butz prema-turely left his cabinet post under Gerald Ford after the news-papers reported an off-color comment he had made about African Americans on an airplane ride back from that year's Republican National Convention. Butz responded to a question about why more blacks didn't vote with "the party of Lincoln" by claiming that "the only things the coloreds are looking for in life are tight pussy, loose shoes and a warm place to shit." He made the remark in late September, and he was gone four days into October. Such clearly offen-sive race talk was no longer acceptable, especially not for public officials, even when speaking in private.

When psychiatrist Frederick Goodwin compared inner-city youths to monkeys in the wild (suggesting that the notion of an urban "jungle" might be more than just a simple metaphor) during a speech to the National Advisory Mental Health Council in February 1992, he was head of the Alcohol, Drug Abuse, and Mental Health Administration and one of the government's most powerful medical researchers. Within a week, the Congressional Black Caucus was asking for his head, and he was apologizing profusely for his unintended offense. By the next month, he'd resigned. In Goodwin's case, he left one lucrative job for another, an even more prestigious post as head of the National Institute of Mental Health. (Most mea culpas around such issues usually result in quite a bit more time out in the wilderness before the perpetrators have been rehabilitated and integrated back into society, which they usually are.) Even still, these changes in public punishments around racially inappropriate speech weren't accepted in all quarters. Editorials in the *Wall Street Journal* that year, for instance, roundly criticized the "Speech Police" for going after Goodwin over nothing.

If you weren't at Goodwin's address to the National Advisory Mental Health Council, you had to consult the transcripts for details about what he had said, but when former Virginia senator George Allen called a young nonwhite member of his audience "macaca, or whatever his name is" and asked an almost all-white Appalachian crowd to "welcome macaca . . . [to] America and the real world of Virginia," it became a national news story that helped seal Allen's losing bid for the Senate in 2006. That's because "macaca" (which is supposedly slang for "monkey") had a video camera with him and was able to capture the entire thing on tape for those of us not in attendance.

Anything "macaca"-like on videotape is the kiss of death, and actual footage certainly adds a little something extra to the buzz around these kinds of controversial moments. It is part of what made the mug shot remnant of Mel Gibson's off-camera rant play differently than the TMZ video of Richards's meltdown, with the latter all over the Web and nightly news programs for several days.[21] We had unflattering photos of Gibson but not the infraction itself. With Richards, we were almost at the comedy club with him, watching the entire thing, rewinding the muffled parts, counting the number of "niggers" for ourselves. That is exactly what sunk Howard Dean's bid for the presidency. It wasn't what he said or even how he said it; it was that the news channels could heighten the story by playing the offending clip incessantly. This partially explains why Jessie Jackson's "Hymie Town" reference didn't get the kind of media traction (although it did get some) that radio DJ Don Imus received for calling the Rutgers women's basketball team "some nappy-headed hos." Jackson voiced his slur, he thought, off the record and to a reporter who didn't sell a tape of the comment to a tabloid TV show. Imus and his producer's "nappy-headed hos" comment could be played ad infinitum. And it was. In the age of "technological reproducibility," that makes a major difference.[22] Without the tape, it can be denied and dismissed. Howard Cosell and Jerry Falwell both denied what they were accused of saying until the tapes were produced, and they couldn't refute the recordings themselves. That helps distinguish Lewinskygate from the rumors circling John F. Kennedy and Marilyn Monroe. Monica Lewinsky had the technological goods: audiotapes, scientifically testable bodily fluids, and CNN replays of previous (seemingly innocent) kisses between the two. Media scholars have said it before and in many ways: the media constitute a productive force. They don't just passively represent the world; they also craft it.

Even invoking past racisms, especially in public and on camera, can get you into trouble, with people calling for your head. During a December 2002 party for Strom Thurmond, former Senate majority leader Trent Lott waxed approvingly of having voted for Thurmond in 1948, when the South Carolinian made a bid for the White House. "When Strom Thurmond ran for president, we voted for him," Lott declared. "We're proud of it. And if the rest of the country had followed our lead, we wouldn't have had all these problems over the years, either." Of course, he was talking about the same Thurmond who championed segregation in 1948, which means that before the end of that very month, Lott was replaced as majority leader by Bill Frist. Again, in 1948 Thurmond could be what most American politicians had always been: explicit and no-nonsense about his segregationist commitments, an unreconstructed racist. By 2002, the mere hint of support for that position, even if not stated explicitly, was a major political blunder—and cost its perpetrator dearly. For the first time in our

country's history, would-be racist whites would have to dis-
simulate and misrepresent many of the negative feelings
they held about blacks, especially out in the public sphere,
or risk a form of "social death" by public censure.[23] They
would have to steal a page from the book of America's antebellum slaves.

Of course, this isn't the end of the conversation. Invariably, these accusations of racism are usually met with organized defenses—from those aforementioned editorials in
the *Wall Street Journal* in defense of Goodwin to an army
of news-scouring libertarian and neoconservative bloggers
online. The rejoinders usually start with the assumption
that racism is gone, banished, and so these obsessions with
"mere discourse" are attempts to create racial issues where
they no longer exist.

By the late 1970s, even black social scientists were arguing for "the declining significance of race"[24] as an explanation for perpetual and disproportionate black poverty.
Since racism was losing its impact on the social world, this
obsession with potentially racist language was considered
just another attempt to let black people off the hook
for their own shortcomings, blaming white America for
blacks' pathologies.[25] Sociologist William Julius Wilson's
argument for the declining significance of race, however,
wasn't about absolving white America of social responsi-
bility vis-à-vis their darker neighbors. It was more like the
theory of "institutionalized racism" in that it tried to show
how racially disproportionate outcomes could persist without the work of active racists. Of course, the declining

significance of race wasn't really about institutional racism. Instead, it offered a description of the newfangled class-based vulnerabilities of poor urban blacks, something that explained their intergenerational failures in comparison to the relative successes of a suburbanizing black middle class. Even still, Wilson's catchy phrase was music to the ears of many people who wanted to forget about the country's history of racial oppression, who wanted to deny that race or racism mattered in the meritocratic America born in the years following the legal gains of the civil rights movement.

There were controversial school-busing initiatives and the media-covered enforcement of other antidiscriminatory measures to bolster the claims made by those who wanted to believe that America had solved its racism problem. Some of these programs or laws were new; others had long been on the books but were only ever weakly enforced. Winning the war against de jure racism and de facto complacencies entailed gaining federal commitments to racial equality in access to public services and employment, or a thumb on the scale (i.e., affirmative action) as a way to address current symptoms of historical racial injustices. It eventually meant the return of black elected officials to statewide office in the South. The civil rights era also translated into legislation that made crimes based on racism and group-based discrimination "hate crimes," their own particularly shunned and harshly penalized category of unlawfulness. Of course, killing someone is always terrible, but killing someone (or well short of that)

solely because of the victim's identity—especially if that
victim is a member of a traditionally marginalized social
group and attempting, say, to cast his or her vote in a local
or national election—has been deemed a distinctively heinous and punishable offense.

These were all significant accomplishments that fundamentally reconfigured American society. Laws changed,
and some of America's cultural assumptions changed with
them. That recalibration helped trigger drastic alterations
to the public culture of race and racism—not a trivial thing
at all. The 1960s witnessed the beginnings of the end of
blatant and unabashed forms of racism in mainstream
America. At least, it meant the end of barefaced expressions of racial hatred that could be openly displayed
without wider public condemnation. Archie Bunker might
be able to get away with saying whatever he wanted to say
in the privacy of his own home, or maybe during informal
events with friends and neighbors in his working-class
Queens community, but he needed to be careful about voicing his ethnocentric beliefs too loudly in public settings,
especially if anybody was there with a video camera.[26]

That is an amazing transformation, and its significance
shouldn't be underestimated. The 1960s redefined how
Americans talk and think about race. The civil rights
movement—in conjunction with other political and social
movements of the time that were working for the equal
rights of Native Americans, Chicanos, women, and members of the lesbian, gay, bisexual and transgendered community—heralded a new degree of sensitivity in public

speech about social differences. Banning vicious racisms and lecherous sexisms, it ushered in the beginning of what is disparagingly branded as "political correctness."

Most people who actually call something "politically correct" (PC) are dismissing it as silly and pointless, a form of social censorship that makes Americans, especially white Americans, overly precious with their language while simultaneously promoting thin-skinnedness among minorities, a mixture that many argue suppresses honest and open civic debate. Others believe that all the things detractors dismiss as PC are the necessary rules of common decency and mutual respect that actually facilitate productive conversations across entrenched lines of social difference. No matter where one stands on this issue, however, the debate is usually only framed as a discussion about navigating the political minefield of political correctness, the capricious (say some) or crucial (others respond) policing and euphemizing of public language that the label PC pejoratively signifies.[27]

Most commentators don't emphasize, however, that the stakes of political correctness are located in a slightly different place than our conversations on the matter imply. The culture of political correctness actually generates one of the essential foundations of contemporary racial distrust. Since most Americans aren't as transparent as Archie Bunker (even when he's trying to hide his ethnocentrism), PC policies actually lose their ability to cultivate the kinds of good-faith dialogues they are meant to foster. Instead, blacks are stuck in the structural position (vis-à-vis white interlocutors) of their ancestors' slave masters: they see smiles on white faces and hear kind words spilling from white mouths without the least bit of certainty about whether those gestures are representative of the speakers' hearts. "The American Negro problem," wrote Swedish economist Gunnar Myrdal in the 1940s, "is a problem in the heart of the American. It is there that the interracial tension has its focus. It is there that the decisive struggle goes on."[28] And it is there that the search for racial honesty and truth continues today. But not in the same ways that Myrdal emphasized.

When individuals' words and some of their actions can no longer be trusted, we look for other seemingly invisible and interior clues about people's racial positions. We long to look past calculated performances and into the very hearts of men and women. Social analysts should take the features of this need, this search for *de cardio* racism, seriously—this racism attributed to the hearts of other-than-explicitly racist actors. *De cardio* racism is imagined to be a kind of hidden or cloaked racism, a racism of euphemism and innuendo, not heels-dug-in pronouncements of innate black inferiority.[29]

We're living in a moment when what I'm calling *de cardio* racism has elbowed out room for itself at the head of America's political table, right alongside still operative de jure and de facto forms (think of sentencing disparities for possession of crack versus powder cocaine as a contemporary version of the former and our seemingly effortless, self-perpetuating reproductions of residential and educational segregation along racial lines as a twenty-first-century instance of the latter).[30]

Given this newfangled reckoning of American racism's potentially cloaked animosities, the white man's newest burden is hardly lightened by political correctness—just as black people's deepest racial suspicions are only bolstered by America's current penchant for dressing up every ideological position (no matter how reactionary or elitist, partisan or self-interested) as simply another better version of egalitarianism.

CHAPTER 3

De Cardio Racism

· *Hunting for Racial
Wolves in Sheep's Clothing*

In the winter of 1984, NBC's *Saturday Night Live* first aired "White Like Me," a film short that humorously exaggerates the real essence of racial distrust and paranoia in contemporary America. In the skit, comedian Eddie Murphy talks directly to the camera, directly to the television audience, and informs them that he has decided to pass for a white person so that he can determine how whites really act when they think blacks aren't around. In light of the civil rights movement's moral recalibrations and the ascendance of political correctness as the normative standard for public conversations, Murphy thinks "talk is cheap," especially when the talk is about race and racism. He knows that he can't necessarily trust everything whites profess about race in mixed company, so the only way for him to determine if racial discrimination is still a defining feature of American life is "to go underground and experience America as a white man."

After the makeup and wig are applied, once Murphy has practiced his Hallmark-card-inspired renditions of white speech and body language, he strikes out into the world as a white person, "Mr. White." The joke, if you haven't seen the skit, is that he discovers something shocking. White people treat each other very differently than they treat blacks. They aren't spitting out racist epithets or conspiring to keep black people locked up in prison or anything like that. They actually aren't treating individual blacks all that badly. They're just treating one another much better.

Mr. White meets white store owners who refuse to accept money from white patrons, plying them with free merchandise instead. He finds that white passengers on public buses have parties (complete with music and scantily clad cocktail waitresses) whenever they have those buses all to themselves, the celebrations starting as soon as the last black rider exits. A whitefaced Murphy also learns that white bankers pass out huge wads of cash to white customers without demanding collateral or conducting background checks—or even requesting to see identification. Whites speak to blacks politely, kindly, but Murphy exposes this politeness as simply a ruse for more traditional forms of racial favoritism.

"White Like Me" parodies the sneaking suspicion that really animates American versions of racial distrust today: fear that discriminating and racist hearts might hide behind even the most benevolent smiles. Although Mr. White lives in a world that has turned its back on the brash, outspoken racisms of a curmudgeonly Archie Bunker and a defiant George Wallace, it is clearly not a place completely devoid of racial discriminations. And Murphy's make-believe undercover experiences are meant to dramatize what such hidden discriminations might feel like to the people usually blocked from seeing them.

Murphy and the rest of the cast in that *Saturday Night Live* segment implicitly challenge and reinforce the bourgeois perspective on race relations at the same time, a bourgeois perspective that might have us all blushingly ignore the harsher realities of intractable racism in contemporary society, a racism that still stands as one of America's most serious domestic issues. Of course, white store owners would find it tough to stay in business if they secretly gave all their goods away to white patrons, and the historical red-lining practices of American banks fell far short of tellers simply handing currency over to any white person who strolled into a local branch, no questions asked. So, the skit could be seen as a simple critique of the irrational excesses that allow blacks to consider racism the singular driving force in American life, a bogeyman that does most of its haunting under the cover of darkness, when its victims can't see.

But "White Like Me" might also be understood as another way that people "laugh to keep from crying," as the old adage goes, to find a humorous way to defuse the explosive anxieties and tensions that might otherwise eat you alive. The skit's embellishments raise the stakes to caricatured proportions, but they don't fundamentally debunk

the frightening idea that whites might just act a little differently, even feel a bit differently, when other groups, especially blacks, aren't around. If psychologists Jennifer
Richeson and Sophie Trawalter can show that whites find
"interracial contact" mentally "depleting," particularly in
a politically correct context where "individuals who harbor
relatively high levels of racial bias" have to hide that bias
from public view, it stands to reason that those very same
people might also feel like exhaling a bit whenever they can
let their racial guards down.[1] The psychological and cognitive toll of keeping such racial biases, or what could be
(mis)construed as racial bias, under wraps might explain,
say, why whites prefer not to live around a lot of black
neighbors. It would take up too much psychic energy.[2]

Anyone who feels like the legal advances of the last several decades have wiped the racial slate clean, cleansed the
soul of the American people, would probably prefer a version of multiculturalism that celebrates the colorfulness of
other traditions and the spiciness of people's ethnic cuisines
without unnecessarily wallowing in bygone moments of
our painful, shameful racial past, moments that still inform
how we view one another today through the obstructive
looking glass of race.[3] Whites may not be secretly partying
on "out-of-service" all-white buses these days, but some
did far worse than that just to keep parts of America decidedly all white in the past, a project that was made illegal,
but not unthinkable, after the 1950s and 1960s.

As a society we should never pretend that we have successfully reasoned or legislated our way out of race's suffo-

cating grasp. Our historical investment in it is too dynamic and affective for that, too irrational and deep-seated. We are being naive if we think that we can sit down and intellectualize ourselves out of its sticky clutches, if we imagine that ending explicit commitments to blatant types of racial discrimination must mean that we are done with racism's awful legacy for good. It is a trap that scholars fall into as well, assuming that all they have to do is objectively "deconstruct" race, prove it isn't real in the biological ways that we once thought, and then imagine that by doing so they have somehow inoculated us all against its most hazardous features, dulled its sharpest talons.[4] That isn't nearly true.

We want to believe something very similar about racism and accusations of racism. If we can prove that a particular allegation of racism is unfounded or untrue, we can all breathe a collective sigh of relief and try to move on. That is part of racism's power. It tricks us into thinking that we can wish it away with a string of logical premises and conclusions, with a singular decree of guilt or innocence. We fantasize about isolating this thing and determining its measurable impact once and for all, especially now that blatant forms of racism have been so thoroughly demonized in mainstream society.

With the destruction of obvious government-backed de jure and de facto racisms, the old racial arguments just don't work anymore. And our old racial glasses, the ones we used to make out traditional forms of racism, the ones that got us this far, really can't help us see with clarity like they used to. We need new ways of thinking about these issues, new ways of talking about race's subtler dynamic, and new ways of spying racial conflict in the twenty-first century.

In the decades following the civil rights movement, a new paradigm of race relations has arisen from the smoldering ashes of de jure and de facto racisms. Not only have legislative and economic discrimination—segregation and physical coercion or violence—predicated on race been explicitly outlawed, but statements betraying any personally held racial biases are altogether unacceptable in most of the public sphere. As a result, explicit racism has gone underground, at least partially, relegated to people's hearts and inner thoughts. To define oneself publicly as a racist, to claim that identity and commitment to older forms of blatant racism, is to embrace one's place on the fringes of society. Of course, some people relish such marginality; most fear it like the plague.

One precondition for the cultural evolution of American racism was the dream that we had attained a truly color-blind society with the end of legalized racism and state-sanctioned segregation. But those obvious victories only mean that potentially racist hearts become that much more important sites of debate and contestation, hearts that serve as one of the few remaining places where racism can stretch itself out unfettered. The era of *de cardio* racism, of a racism banned from the public sphere and reimagined as snug within the inaccessible hearts of other people, requires new methods of analytical engagement, methods far from anything we've ever used to make sense of the racial ties that bind us together.

Unlike America's previous mode of racial experience (blatant white racism accompanied by potentially disingenuous black obsequiousness), contemporary *de cardio* racism emphasizes something close to the opposite: black defiance and anger in the face of potentially disingenuous white acquiescence to political correctness. It highlights the difference between what people do and what they say, what people do and why they do it. This is not about whether or not we've achieved equality under the law—or as mandated social custom. *De cardio* racism is about what the law can't touch, what won't be easily proved or disproved, what can't be simply criminalized and deemed unconstitutional. It is racism that is most terrifying because it is hidden, secret, papered over with public niceties and politically correct jargon. It is a very powerful way that many Americans think about race today, as a subtle by-product of the ineluctably human fact that people feel things they'll never admit (sometimes, not even to themselves), particularly when the topic of discussion is race.

This trend toward a racial distrust and suspicion that is decidedly distinct from blatant racist practices of the past forces us to read against the grain of public speech more than ever before. *De cardio* racism assumes that if we hope to ascertain another person's private beliefs or motivations vis-à-vis race, we have to find tools that allow us to see past what they say, or even do, into their very hearts. We can't just take their smiles and egalitarian rhetoric at face value. And just because they "do the right thing" when we're around doesn't mean they aren't still secretly trying to do us in. It might not even be a conscious thing. Although nobody went on CNN or Fox after the Hurricane Katrina disaster to proclaim that they would like to donate money to white victims instead of black ones, a *Washington Post*/Stanford University study found that white Americans were willing to provide more financial assistance to white victims than black ones, to the tune of about $1,000 extra a year. And the darker the victim, the less money she would have received, with lighter-skinned blacks benefiting from about $100 more per month than those who couldn't pass the brown-paper-bag test (i.e., those not lighter than a brown shopping bag). Americans may hardly admit it in public, but they are clearly willing to put their money where their color biases are.

This contemporary lack of transparency regarding issues of race means that the progress we've made since the move from de jure and de facto to *de cardio* racism is circumscribed by the very impossibility of legislating private sentiment and personal morality. Rather than just confronting tangible foes (a federal government that segregates its armed forces or a discriminating landlord that makes no bones about restrictions against black tenants), today's would-be champions of racial equality often find themselves opposed by all the right rhetoric about racial equality—if not just by palpable silence.

As an anthropologist studying how black people talk about race, I've heard this silence described many times and in many ways, but one young security guard in Brooklyn, New York, captured the thrust of the *de cardio* racism critique most succinctly: "They were sending dogs to maul black kids in the street forty years ago, and all of a sudden there are no racists in America *at all*." *De cardio* racism asks, where did all of yesterday's racial wolves go, and why do all these sheep seem to be standing around licking their chops?

As strange as it might sound, the progressive elements in our culture (and, for very different reasons, the less progressive ones as well) might actually long for the racial clarity of "Whites Only" placards on store entrances. That's why a comedian's "nigger"-laced ode-to-lynching (Michael Richards), a would-be Senator's "macaca" gaffe (George Allen), and an alcoholic actor's conspiracy-fueled anti-Semitism (Mel Gibson) can be almost cathartic moments for us as a nation. At times like those, we can turn to our increasingly antiquated methods for dealing with overt racists, everything from public shaming to legal prosecution, and shake our collective index finger at their impudence. Our cultural and legislative engines for social justice are less effective, however, when dealing with people who may never feel comfortable exposing their racial thoughts to public scrutiny, people who recognize the dangers of making potentially racist motivations explicit and clear.

The eighteenth-century French philosopher Voltaire once claimed that human beings really only speak to conceal what they truly feel, as much to miscommunicate as anything else. Humans are complicated and dissimulating

creatures with the uncanny ability to misrepresent themselves and their deepest inner thoughts, to be purposefully
economical with the truth. It could be as harmless as a
"little white lie" about how good your child was in the
school play or as catastrophic as a governmental cover-up
of Watergate-like proportions. And there are few areas of
public life where people put these gifts to work as often as
they do in the context of discussions about race.

When dealing with such thorny topics today, we are
forced to confront the impenetrability of other people's most
secret views. Ultimately, we can only speculate about their
inner feelings, even those of the folks we think we know
best. *De cardio* racism uses that inescapable fact as the suspicious backdrop for any and all interracial communication
in our politically charged and politically corrected present.

In the era of *de cardio* racism, naive versions of political
correctness can make a bad racial situation even worse.
Self-conscious mandates about respectful speech are intended as a social salve, something to soften harsh and
offensive language so that everyone feels welcome to join
the national conversation, but it has also exacerbated the
scary disconnect between the specifics of what gets said
and the hazy possibilities of what kinds of things are truly
meant. People say things not simply because they believe
them but also because they know that saying something
else might get them into a whole lot of trouble, might be
met with public sanction and disdain, might get them labeled a racist.

From a psychological or sociological perspective, it is
incredibly important to acknowledge the relative newness

of this American dilemma: a racial context so conspicuously different from historical versions of American race
relations. One major driving force behind contemporary
public rhetoric around racial issues, especially for white
Americans, is a palpable anxiety about whether or not a
particular gesture will be construed as racist and used to
demonize the gesturer. We can't overemphasize the significance of this fact, that Americans now feel the need to
conceal potentially racist (and other xenophobic) beliefs
in ways that they never did before.

The demonization of public racism is clearly a social and
moral victory, but it has come at a cost. Political correctness has proven tragically effective at hiding racism, not
just healing it. In sacrificing noisy and potentially combat-
ive racial discussions for the politeness of political correctness, we face an even more pernicious racism, a racism
that's almost never explicitly declared, except among the
closest of confidants. But as the "White Like Me" skit's
lampoon shows, people recognize the fact that racism
might be even more effectual under the cover of color
blindness and rhetorical silence. That anxious possibility is
only compounded by the fact that race has become such a
sensitive issue. And language is the first place that sensitivity gets played out.

After all, what does it really mean to call someone "Native American" instead of "Indian," "Asian" instead of
"Oriental?" It is probably supposed to translate into something like, I respect your history and your desire to name
yourself. So, I'll discontinue the name I'm used to calling
you and call you something that you'd prefer. It could

mean that. However, it might also just mean, I don't really want the headache that comes with calling you what you don't want to be called, even though I couldn't really care less about your damned history.

In spite of lip service to the well-meaning ideologies behind such politically correct speech, many old ideas about race persist and continue to make their presence felt in public life. The most striking difference is that today's racial cues and references are largely submerged and sublimated. They are often coded and cloaked, subtly appealing to older stereotypes that can no longer be explicitly invoked. Instead of declarations about blacks being, say, "natural" criminals, we have images of violent crime that just happen to use a black example—most famously in George W. Bush's 1998 Willie Horton campaign ads. Instead of public affirmations of people's commitments to "segregation now, segregation tomorrow, and segregation forever," we have mere nods to and winks at the unspoken threat of racial miscegenation: for instance, another campaign ad, this time from 2006, in which a white woman claims that she met Tennessee's black senatorial candidate, Harold Ford, at a party in the Playboy Mansion and flirtatiously asks him to call her, drudging up a long—and previously more explicit—history of fears about black men cavorting with white women. In Harold Ford's case, according to the campaign ad, this potentially romantic link between Ford and a blonde woman is seemingly part of the reason why he's "just not right" for Tennessee. Even if that was the intended meaning (and maybe it wasn't), the ad couldn't dare say such a thing explicitly. Nobody could face the camera and just explain to Ford that his kind of race mixing still isn't welcome in the Volunteer State. If intended, racial stereotypes have to be implied, and each of us has to look past the de jure and de facto rhetoric of egalitarianism on the surface of things and into the hidden *de cardio* racisms that may still animate the darkest insides of campaigners playing to people's basest racial fears.

The suspicion of (and search for) such dark insides cuts both ways: it can protect a cautious person from potentially discriminatory practices or, at its worst, encourage hypersensitivity and a propensity for spotting racism even where it's probably not. Several psychological researchers from the University of Tulsa, the University of North Carolina at Chapel Hill (UNC), and Fayetteville State University published a study in 2006 linking "perceived racism" to forms of social paranoia. They hypothesize a direct correlation between "perceived racism" and "nonclinical paranoia" among African Americans.[5] Using 128 African American undergraduates from private, state-funded, and historically black schools as subjects, the researchers argue that black college students who perceive more instances of racism in their daily environment exhibit greater "cultural mistrust" of others and higher levels of nonclinical paranoia. Social psychologist Sherman James has already shown that African Americans' dealings with everyday racism lead to negative physical effects like hypertension, so it stands to reason that negotiating perceived racism day in and day out might have a deleterious psychological impact too.[6]

One thing to remember, however, is that perceived racism is not simply a transparent index of actual racism. It tables the entire question of racism (in fact) for a qualitatively different one of racism as something personally and subjectively assessed. The very idea of perceived racism implies uncertainty and ambiguity in the matter. Perceived racism is not *necessarily* racism. Can you imagine a study on African Americans' perceived racism in, say, Montgomery, Alabama, in the 1940s? How about the 1890s? It might not even make sense for social scientists to talk about perceived racism in such contexts, times of overt and obvious societal commitments to racial discrimination.

In that 2006 study on perceived racism, those researchers from Tulsa, UNC, and Fayetteville State aren't talking about the string-someone-up-on-a-tree kinds of racism. It is much subtler than that, less brutal and boosterish. Perceived racism leads to higher levels of paranoia among African Americans specifically because such perceptions of hidden or subtle racism are more difficult to confirm unequivocally than they were in the past—and that's precisely because we aren't usually talking about universally recognized examples of traditional racism. These are efforts to peer past formal racial egalitarianism, to look beyond surface civilities in search of possible *de cardio* malice.

In this MySpace generation, even things that would have signaled indisputable racism in the past seem more muddled and confusing now. Remember that private university in central Florida, the one where members of an all-white women's softball team borrowed jerseys from their black friends on the men's basketball squad, put on blackface, and went to a campus party as those black basketball players. The women didn't think they had done anything wrong; their black friends from the basketball team knew exactly what they were up to and even helped them apply the makeup, hence their surprise at being publicly scolded over what was meant as harmless fun. If psychologists have shown that people don't even necessarily know what makes them happy, they may not be able to identify exactly what makes them potentially hateful or discriminatory either. If we can "stumble on happiness," we might be able to stumble right into prejudice as well.[7]

The more blatantly racist a society has been in the past, the steeper its climb out of explicit racial discrimination and the harder it is for contemporary citizens to shake fears of *de cardio* racism. The farther we advance from overt racist doctrines and laws, the more material traces those past sins leave behind, which means all the more surfaces to which contemporary racially charged paranoia might stick.

The country's history of racial oppression has created a "culture of racial paranoia" at the heart of contemporary American life.[8] It's difficult for descendants of past victims (and perpetrators) to believe that they are truly safe from racial hatred and discrimination today, even and especially when they can't see it.[9] Race-based paranoia becomes a simplistic "racism detector" that attempts to see past superficial racial egalitarianism and into the hidden heart of *de cardio* racisms that may never see the light of day.

Racial paranoia is a way of thinking about race and fearing racism that is immune to outward signs of racial acceptance and benevolence. Racial paranoia is preoccupied with insincerity, with our intrinsic ability to misrepresent inner beliefs, to misrepresent ourselves. Using the logic of racial paranoia, public tolerance doesn't necessarily mean the absence of racism (especially in a self-consciously "politically correct" moment), and liberalism could just as likely be a cover for continued racial malice, racism with a poker face instead of a Klansman's mask.

To make sense of this racial paranoia, a racial paranoia that is less pathological than simply overprotective, it is crucial to understand that most common ways we invoke race are always linked to suspicious, hostile, and paranoid perspectives on social difference. At some level, race talk is always paranoid talk—whenever you hear it, whoever is doing the speaking.

Still, racial paranoia is distinct from racism, and racial paranoia actually increases as explicit expressions of racism decrease. The two things are not only analytically distinct; they are inversely proportional. Without taking this into account, we can lose sight of the fact that naive forms of political correctness reduce instances of explicitly racist discourse only to have racial paranoia blossom that much bigger in its place.

Ultimately, racial paranoia provides a valuable way to comprehend the lingering impact of America's history. Continued racism isn't enough to explain racial paranoia. To be paranoid about race, you need something more like the situation we have in the early decades of the twenty-first century: a precipitous climb out of a past steeped in explicit racial discrimination, Jim Crowism, and legalized second-class citizenship. Part of the fear is that we can always backslide, which makes it hard to accept the appearance of racial equality as anything other than just that, an appearance, maybe a mirage. It all happened so fast, in just a generation or so, the end of unapologetic public racism. Racial paranoia has a theory about where some of those 1960s wolves went: to buy some fresh wool for their new sheep costumes.

After twelve years of public service to her country, Congresswoman Cynthia McKinney may be best known for accusing one ostensible sheep of being a wolf. McKinney found herself at the center of controversy in March 2006 after allegedly hitting a Capitol Hill police officer for grabbing her in a congressional office building. The congresswoman maintained that the guard had singled her out because of her race, but she was soundly thrashed by both right-wing critics and her usual Democratic allies. They all publicly reprimanded her for crying racism in vain.

McKinney was criticized for playing the proverbial "race card," for unjustifiably claiming that that security guard had misrecognized and accosted her because he was a semi-closeted racist. It wasn't the first time she was stopped on her way to work, but on that particular day in March of 2006, she had had enough. After first calling herself a victim of "racial profiling," she eventually apologized for the entire incident, barely avoiding a lawsuit rumored to have been brewing among the attorneys representing the white officer who stopped her, Paul McKenna. McKenna maintained that he needed her to show identification because she wasn't wearing the requisite congressional pin that would have made it clear to him that she belonged in the building. He insisted that it had nothing to do with her race.

Interesting and telling about their altercation is the fact that much of the "story" pivoted exclusively on the accusation itself, an accusation that was met with everything from disgust to angry defensiveness but little of the "white guilt" theorist Shelby Steele uses to explain the "code of decency that defines [explicitly racist] views as shameful," a white guilt, he says, that is "quite literally the same thing as black power."[10] Instead of white guilt fueling public reactions to McKinney's claims, a different kind of righteous indignation was at play, a different guilt-trip. Conservative bloggers had a field day with McKinney when the incident made the news. She was scolded for invoking race at all, for trivializing real racism. Critics dismissed her for playing dirty, for being disingenuous and insincere. Part of what was going on during those days right after the incident was a clear demonstration of how the moral high ground around issues of racism has again been reclaimed. Where Martin Luther King, Jr., could make the spitting, rage-filled white suburbanite America's unequivocal racist villain, now the person who accuses others of racism—a "racism" far less obvious and transparent than placard-holding Klansmen—has become the new racial sinner, hypocritical and hypersensitive for throwing stones over nothing. To detractors, such people should be stoned themselves—for bearing false racial witness and embodying a new kind of moral failure.

Most fascinating about the McKinney-McKenna affair, however, is that McKinney never once claimed that McKenna had said anything inappropriate or racist to her. He hadn't systematically targeted her for ridicule. He never subjected her to racial slurs. He simply didn't recognize her as she bypassed the building's metal detectors and then hurriedly called out after her, giving chase and finally stopping her when she didn't initially respond to his calls. If this is racism, this is a "kinder and gentler" form of racism than most of what African Americans have had to negotiate in the past. This isn't about McKinney being categorically and explicitly barred entrance to the building. Instead of being victimized by legalized racial discrimination, McKinney was more the casualty of racial invisibility, of racism's invisibility. The problem wasn't that she was being prohibited from the building *tout court* but that she still felt somewhat unseen (and unaccepted) once she was already there.

In the improbable hunt for signs of *de cardio* racism, stopping a black congresswoman who has spent over a decade in the House of Representatives (going into and out of the same buildings) might be construed as the newest and sneakiest way of saying "nigger" without having to utter a word. But is it? This uncertain paranoia divorces racist attitudes (what people feel in their hearts) from racist actions (clear practices of discrimination).

Regardless of its origins, such a dynamic is currently taken for granted (and even somewhat accounted for by pollsters) in public commentaries about American politics. During the 2006 senatorial elections, for example, CNN political commentator Candy Crowley matter-of-factly offered the commonsense supposition that pollsters do not trust white voters in exit polls whenever black candidates are involved. White voters can feel pressure to say one thing in public (that they voted for a black candidate), even if they pulled the lever for someone else (decidedly *not* the black candidate) while behind the anonymous curtain of the voting booth.

Cynthia McKinney's blowup is representative of how race operates in such a two-faced moment, a time when most racism cowers away from explicit public expression. To critics, McKinney seems to have jumped off the racial deep end, overreacting to racially innocent gestures, making mountains out of molehills. But in a slightly different light, those same molehills might look like the tips of mountaintops buried beneath mounds of artificial and trucked-in dirt. Uncertainty about what could potentially lie below the surface of every smile and social nicety fuels racial distrust, and molehills are probably the topographic feature of choice for most racial paranoiacs surveying America's current social landscape. In fact, racial paranoia's most powerful playing field is usually insignificance, ostensible triviality. The minor details of everyday life prove central. You might almost say that the more petty and subtle the situation, the more paranoia it produces.

De cardio racism pivots on the subtle slight as telltale indication of hidden ill will. Seemingly minor affronts and everyday misunderstandings often result in illuminating case studies on racial paranoia, and award-winning novelist Gloria Naylor provides one idiosyncratic example of how a relatively minor offense can grease the wheel for more serious commitments to racial distrust and paranoia.

Naylor is the critically acclaimed author of several novels, most famously *The Women of Brewster Place*, which won a National Book Award in 1983 and was later turned into a made-for-TV miniseries, produced by (and starring) Oprah Winfrey. Since then, Naylor has continued to write fiction, but her 2005 offering, a "fictionalized memoir" called *1996*, has had some people talking about her with real concern, questioning her very sanity.[11]

1996 chronicles that summer in the life of its main character, Gloria Naylor, presenting a first-person account of how she was systematically monitored and harassed by government operatives while attempting to write a novel on a quiet island off the coast of South Carolina. As Naylor's self-named character relays the story, she was simply trying to mind her own business and get some writing done (the remainder of her time consumed with tending a small garden on the property) when a curmudgeonly old woman, an especially unfriendly neighbor, set off a chain reaction of surreptitious events that culminated in the National Security Agency's (NSA) scrutinizing Naylor's most trivial movements, covertly following her on daily errands, even stealing and returning her laptop computer on a whim (just to prove to themselves that they could do it). As Naylor recounts things, the government eventually began inspecting her inner thoughts (with some kind of top-secret spy machine) and even deployed a more advanced bit of technology to actually place ideas inside her head, self-destructive and suicidal thoughts that they specifically wanted her to act upon.

Naylor labels *1996* a "fictionalized memoir" not because she believes that any of the aforementioned details are made up or fanciful. She stands by the veracity and factuality of the devices she depicts, even going so far as to include an appendix with materials documenting other people's research on government-sponsored mind-reading techniques. Naylor only characterizes her memoir as "fictionalized" because it takes creative license with the inner lives of her tormentors, purporting to know their deepest thoughts and most hidden motivations.[12]

Naylor imbues Eunice, her mean-spirited neighbor, with an unquenchable and irrational hostility. Eunice blames the writer for spitefully killing one of her cats and then goes on a crusade to brand Naylor an anti-Semite as a consequence. Naylor paints Eunice's brother, a high-ranking NSA agent, as someone with a cold distrust of his reclusive sister and her claims about a black female writer he's never heard of, only allowing himself to be dragged deeper and deeper into the surveillance operation as a result of his own insatiable ego.

Naylor doesn't really know these people, and she couldn't possibly know most of these details about them.

Instead, she's connecting the dots, making up particulars, trying to find a way to explain the inexplicable events she experienced during that difficult summer (strange noises outside her home, cars tailing her during local drives, poison placed in her tomato garden). For all its invented psychological dot filling, Naylor's point is simple: the government is capable of doing some very dastardly and seemingly impossible things under the cover of darkness, and it often does—for no good reason.[13]

Naylor's story contains all the classic elements of racial paranoia: the spark provided by a relatively petty dispute (over cats in a garden patch), government complicity, insensitive mockery (by her purported harassers), and hidden motivations. A key feature of the story, of course, is Naylor's race. The fact that she's African American gets mentioned again and again in her retelling of the tale. It is represented as a major obsession of those unscrupulous attackers who decry her interminable stubbornness while assessing their clandestine operation's daily progress.

As far as Naylor can tell, it must have been her sympathetic remarks about the Louis Farrakhan–sponsored Million Man March in 1995 that sealed her fate as a victim of this massive government surveillance operation. She became guilty of anti-Semitism by association. And this is yet another important element of the entire scenario. Most of the people behind the plot she depicts are Jewish and motivated by their own fears and paranoia about anti-Semitism. Of course, a paranoid response to other people's ostensible paranoia is the psychological equivalent of fighting fire with fire, a pact of mutual self-destruction. So, by emphasizing her belief that Jews were the conspiratorial ringleaders of the illegal surveillance operation, Naylor just reinforces those same anti-Semitic accusations that she tries her best to dismiss throughout the book (by, for example, downplaying her actual connection to Farrakhan). But her own racial paranoia makes the ethnic and religious accusation necessary, even though it is based on some arguably flimsy evidence: her supposed ability to discern the Jewish facial features of government agents as they quickly speed by her country home, vanishing around the bend almost as soon as they appear. Though she feels certain of their ethnicity, many skeptics would simply place her xenophobic suspicions right alongside age-old accusations of Jewish conspiracies that date all the way back to the infamous publication of *The Protocols of the Elders of Zion*, an anti-Semitic hoax penned in the late nineteenth century, and much earlier as well.[14]

Although most of her tale also fits within the genre of "racial conspiracy," there is at least one thing that makes Naylor's story specifically representative of racial paranoia, even though that same detail is uncommon in most race-based conspiracy theories. The reason for this heavy-handed governmental effort to go after her first stems from something pretty inconsequential: she upset a grumpy old neighbor by poisoning one of the woman's cats. The cats would periodically enter Naylor's garden and muck around in her vegetables, even after she complained to her neighbor about it, which is why she took matters into her own hands. In the grand scheme of things, when it comes to race-based conspiratorial thinking, such merely interpersonal matters are almost never weighty enough to hang governmental plots upon, even as they often ground everyday fears about minor racial offenses (an empty cab passing you by, a flight attendant forgetting your drink, a police officer not recognizing your face as you shuttle by him in your own office building).

The justifications for larger-scale racial "conspiracies" (as opposed to less codified and more personal racial paranoias) are usually more specifically political. They are a function of the victim's antiestablishment views or powerful symbolic sway over a larger community, which serious conspiracy theorists can use to help explain just about every assassination in American history. The victims of conspiracies pose some kind of threat to the status quo, and so the deadly preemptive strike is meant to defuse a dangerous situation before it starts, not to pay back a woman for killing a neighbor's cat.

Even though Naylor adds some idiosyncratic bells and whistles to her version of racial paranoia, she is hardly the only prominent African American famous for linking paranoia and race. Malcolm X, when describing the hajj he took to Mecca in his autobiography, specifically mentions his belief that U.S. government agents were following him all along the journey. Paul Robeson, the well-known twentieth-century African American actor, singer, lawyer, and political activist, believed that government operatives were spying on him throughout the latter part of his life, both in the United States and abroad. His son still travels the country today carrying documentation about some of this surveillance, lobbying the government to declassify top-secret records on the matter, and claiming that his father's suicide attempts were the product of secret Central Intelligence Agency drug experiments and mind-altering techniques not all that different from the kinds Naylor describes in her book.

Of course, the old saying holds true in the cases of Malcolm X and Robeson: just because you're paranoid doesn't mean they're not after you. The two men had good reason to fear surveillance and plotting, even if they couldn't always have been right about when it was actually taking place. Unlike the relatively cloistered artist that Naylor admits to being in 1996, Robeson was quite political and public in his day. He fought lynching across the country, campaigned for Progressive Party candidates, and even supported the Soviet Union throughout the 1940s and 1950s, the latter position certainly not standing him in good stead during the McCarthy era's red scare. Malcolm X was slated to take the black American cause to the United Nations when he was killed. That would have been an international embarrassment with clear cold war gains for the Soviet Union. If the government was monitoring anyone, it would have been someone like Robeson or Malcolm X—and its spies would have had quite systematic ways of doing so.

University of Colorado professor Ward Churchill was once canonized within certain activist circles (long before his infamous statement that the 9/11 victims were "little

Eichmanns") for his research on Cointelpro.[15] This was the U.S. government's covert 1960s counterintelligence surveillance program that placed a great deal of emphasis on the potential threat to this country posed by militant black and Native American organizations. Government agents would even be sent undercover to infiltrate groups and to foment infighting and intragroup paranoia. The targeted organizations, which included the Black Panthers and the Nation of Islam, were considered dangerous and unpatriotic. They were also quite explicitly and undeniably political. They took to the streets. They marched. They protested. They used high-charged, antiestablishment rhetoric. In contrast, Naylor imagines herself chosen for surveillance over a seemingly inconsequential and apolitical squabble. She isn't a particularly partisan writer. She doesn't have a reputation for anything of the kind, which is part of why she calls on her passing support for the Million Man March as a sturdier political hook on which to hang her claims.

Of course, try as she might, Naylor has no smoking gun, no irrefutable anchor with which to ground her allegations. She can pile all the Internet-pilfered information she likes into her closing appendices, but her race-based assertions are still far from incontrovertible. In this sense, and maybe this sense alone, her idiosyncratic and eccentric form of racial paranoia is a fairly representative case.

The most prevalent rumors circulating within black communities today tend to have more in common with Cointelpro than with *1996,* concentrating on systematic political ideologies rather than personal attacks. The theories are based on racial paranoia and distrust, but they start with an unchallenged faith in racial identities as self-evidently real and discrete. For instance, there is the prevalent idea that Church's Chicken and other common fast-food restaurants are purposefully attempting to sterilize black men with their secret seasonings. Not only are racial groups discrete and real in this scenario, but races can be selectively targeted for physiological engineering and sterilization, for race-specific pharmacogenetic assault. There are claims that "Evian" water is spelled the way it is ("naive" backward) simply so that the company can thumb its nose at the very black community it is allegedly trying to poison with carcinogenic water. (The idea here is that black folks don't see this obvious play on words because they can't or won't read, which is the premise of an old joke about hiding $20 from a black person by putting it between the pages of a book.) Reebok had to take out newspaper ads to dismiss rumors about its supposed efforts to use the profits it made selling sneakers to support South African apartheid. And world-famous designer Tommy Hilfiger might still be fielding questions about statements he allegedly made over a decade ago that disparaged black consumers by explicitly denying any desire on his part to cater to the black clothing market.

Rumors about race, racism, and racial distrust are not just fringe beliefs held by a few hard-line crackpots, not even the kinds just mentioned. They define the surreal core of all racial stereotypes and race-based social policy. Race, as a concept, is only useful as a way to ground conspiratorial

claims—about research on inherent cognitive differences between social groups or about secret government surveillance
technologies. Race is one of the shortcuts we use to convince
ourselves that the social differences we see in the world
merely reflect more latent and inflexible differences in genes
or culture. And racial paranoia is the realization that we
are all far too afraid and polite to deal with any of these
assumptions head-on.

CHAPTER 4

Racial Paranoia's
Canonical Texts

While Gloria Naylor claimed to be describing factual recollections under the guise of fiction, John A. Williams, another African American novelist, marketed fiction as fact. When Williams set out to promote his 1967 novel, *The Man Who Cried I Am,* a slightly veiled commentary on the conflicted lives of writers Richard Wright, Chester Himes, and James Baldwin, among other 1960s icons, he did something pretty ingenious.[1] Williams plastered New York City subway trains with explicit details about the "King Alfred Plan," a harrowing government conspiracy "to detain and ultimately rid America of its Negroes." The specifics of the plot listed all the major federal, state, and local agencies as coconspirators. Even the president of the United States had a hand in it, as did the Central Intelligence Agency and the Federal Bureau of Investigation (working together and sharing vital information well before the creation of the Department of Homeland Security to integrate such multiagency efforts). The Departments of Justice, Defense, and the Interior were all involved, but the foot solders responsible for carrying out the plan on the ground

111

would include a combination of national guardsmen, state troopers, and local law-enforcement officers. The unsuspecting New York City transit riders who read the photocopied specifics of this conspiracy discovered a government plot to mount the most extensive, nationally coordinated military and policing operation ever to take place on American soil.

Everything would be sparked by the ratcheting up of "Negro violence" in the 1970s. At the onset of major Black Power–inspired race riots and urban rebellions, African American leaders (the Jesse Jacksons and Al Sharptons of the world, as well as organizational heads of groups such as the National Association for the Advancement of Colored People, the Congress of Racial Equality, and the Urban League) would be detained indefinitely, that is, the few who hadn't already been blackmailed or tapped for special overseas missions to get them out of the country when things finally went down.

The plan slices America up into ten distinctive geographical jurisdictions, and black soldiers are assigned to violent urban hotspots in each one almost immediately—in hopes of killing as many "combat-trained Minority servicemen as possible" during their clashes with black rioters. That way, according to the plan's unapologetic rationalizations, a more potentially dangerous threat than relatively unarmed black civilians would be contained, its numbers thinned.

The details those subway passengers read that day called for systematic racial disenfranchisement, boasting that black "members of congress [would] be unseated at once" as the opening move toward race-based martial law. The

frightening totality of this idea, which spread like wildfire
throughout many urban communities, captured the imagi-
nations of more than a few African Americans who were
already suspicious of a national government only one hundred years removed from officially condoning slavery, a
government just beginning to think seriously and systematically about reconciling its lofty principles with its legal
practices. Gil Scott-Heron, a critically acclaimed poet and
musician whose troubled personal life mirrors the highs
and lows of African American political struggles, even
wrote a song using the title from the Williams plot device,
a song where he ominously declares that "white paranoia
is here to say," so "places [concentration camps] are being
prepared [for blacks] night and day, night and day."

When subway riders picked up those mysteriously anonymous flyers, many of them must have been terrified by the
dreadful imagery painted. The fact that it was merely a publicity stunt, an excerpt from a fiery new novel, wasn't self-
evident or obvious, especially not to a rushing commuter
quickly removing stray pieces of paper from a subway seat.
And that ambiguity was purposeful. Williams played it
straight, not making it readily apparent at first glance that
the King Alfred Plan was part of a letter written by a fictional character in his new novel, a pivotal revelation at the
end of the story.

As longtime Harlem journalist Herb Boyd points out,
when most commuters came across this bit of promotional
material for the Williams book, some took it for fact, not
fiction—a racial version of Orson Welles's infamous 1939

broadcast, his radio adaptation of H. G. Wells's fictitious *The War of the Worlds,* during which Welles fooled at least some listeners into believing that Martians had actually begun attacking earth by way of New Jersey. There were disclaimers at the beginning and end of the program, but people were still overwhelmed by the spectacular bigness of the story itself and by Welles's use of a realist, documentarylike narrative style to relay the tale with breaking news reports between songs.

In pretending to cover an intergalactic event, Welles ended up creating his own "media event," angering many listeners with his "irresponsible" broadcast.[2] Of course, Mars attacking earth isn't the same thing as the King Alfred Plan's purported concentration camps and attempted racial genocide, phenomena that had already proved all too real in Nazi Germany before Williams began his publicity for *The Man Who Cried I Am.* But both minihoaxes fed into social fears already circulating throughout American society. After all, the novel's plan did seem strikingly close to racial-doomsday scenarios feared by many African Americans, particularly interpretations (in the 1950s and early 1960s) of President Richard Nixon's cosponsored McCarran Act, a McCarthy-era "anti-Communist law in which political subversives were to be rounded up and placed in concentration camps during a national emergency."[3]

Thanks in part to this ingenious marketing strategy, *The Man Who Cried I Am* is an honorary member of an unofficial canon of books most commonly used to ground racial-conspiracy theories within the African American community. The most popular texts and thinkers in this genre bolster claims about hidden racial plots and schemes against blacks, the kinds of arguments that provide a wider cultural context for the needling racial fears lodged far in the back of Dave Chappelle's mind when he decides, say, to leave for Africa out of the blue. These are the same fears that predetermine Cynthia McKinney's angry response to her building's security officer, not to mention the more extraordinary accusations of mind control and systematic surveillance offered up by Gloria Naylor in *1996*. Chappelle, McKinney, and Naylor may not have read any of the books, but their choices are certainly informed by the climate of racial cautiousness and distrust that this canon helps to generate.

The King Alfred Plan's origin story and recapitulation of long-standing worries about malicious and hidden threats to African Americans' life chances link personal forms of racial paranoia (about potentially racist television crew members, Capitol Hill security personnel, or National Security Agency–connected neighbors, people who would never admit to being racist in public) to larger racial conspiracies (about state-sanctioned genocide, something also publicly and adamantly denied by government officials). These latter theories institutionalize interpersonal fears that people have about the distance between what they see and what they get when it comes to racism in contemporary America. The canon of racial conspiracy, the books and themes that define its central arguments, constitute the pessimistic scaffolding that frames *de cardio* racism's everyday and fleeting forms of racial distrust.

If I were emphasizing whites' racial paranoia and the literature that promotes it, this chapter would look much different. I would have gone to a different section of the library entirely. That is a distinctive canon with a different set of theories and suspicions about blacks. Here, I just want to talk about the kinds of books and arguments that serve as common building blocks for race-based suspicions and paranoia within the black community, laying out some of the key claims informing African Americans' mild and extreme forms of racial distrust.

Many of the authors and titles I mention in this chapter are well known in Harlem, where I've conducted most of my anthropological research, or in other predominantly African American communities, even if these books haven't made their way onto the syllabi of many academics specializing in race and racism. The majority of these offerings—or the theories behind them—are central to blacks' feelings of cynicism and paranoia vis-à-vis white America. Journalist Samuel Yette's 1971 book, *The Choice,* is a scathing attack on "the Internal Security Act of 1950 (the McCarran Act) which, in effect, attempted to legitimize, *ex post facto,* the use of concentration camps during World War II . . . and to legitimize future concentration camps" for rebellious African Americans.[4] Yette cites the 1966 findings of fellow journalist Charles Allen Jr., findings about "camps . . . being 'quietly' erected at Wickenburg and Florence, Arizona, and El Reno, Oklahoma, the latter places having served as prisoner-of-war camps [for Japanese Americans] during World War II."[5] (Allen had been asked by an organization called the Citizens Committee for Constitutional Liberties to study the concentration camp accusations.[6]) These camps may have been built after America's military actions in Korea and Vietnam (as a holding facility for antiwar activists), but Yette believed that they would surely do double duty as an answer to Black Power and the urban rioting it spawned, especially since he maintained that the American government was purposefully inciting blacks to revolt as a justification and pretext for their draconian responses to that violence. John Williams might have scooped Yette by a few years, but they were both using the McCarran Act to indict America for secretly plotting future atrocities against its black citizens.

Novelists and journalists weren't the only ones interested in the McCarran Act and its racial implications. Shirley Chisholm, the first black congresswoman in the United States, spoke eloquently for the repeal of the McCarran Act during her tenure, arguing that only racism could explain why Japanese Americans were thrown into concentration camps during the 1940s while German Americans were not and why the government seemed to think that the Black Panthers embodied a kind of sedition that merited such treatment when "the KKK [Ku Klux Klan] and minutemen have armed themselves to the teeth" without any sustained and serious governmental attempt to stop them.[7]

Even without any specific discussion about the McCarran Act or the King Alfred Plan, when I was growing up in Brooklyn, New York, during the 1970s and 1980s, it was pretty common to overhear bitter accusations that housing-project complexes were being purposefully designed to achieve the concentration camp effect that so concerned

Williams, Yette, Allen, and Chisholm. Something like the spirit of their accusations animated everyday political conversations in the neighborhood and catalyzed community fears.[8] People wondered why African Americans were being herded into enclosed, high-rise project complexes in major American cities. To make surveillance easier? To better police and contain them? To segregate inhabitants from the rest of the city? Invariably, the argument went, highways were purposefully built around these self-contained mini-metropolises to cut off avenues of escape (when the time came) with massive roadways and the intractable thickness of cement barricades.

New York City planner Robert Moses was sometimes mentioned by name and considered one of the major conspirators. People claimed that he avoided wealthier middle-class neighborhoods and only bulldozed poorer minority communities whenever he wanted to make way for a new highway or any other urban renewal project. It seemed self-evident to most of my neighbors that major city roadways tended to snake themselves around New York City housing projects, including the one where we lived, like some kind of cement and vehicular corset squeezing itself too tightly around those unlucky enough to be stuck inside.[9] According to Yette, the point of such measures is soberingly simple: racial genocide, starting with "black guerilla fighters" and other activists cited in one House Un-American Activities Committee (HUAC) report from 1968, racial troublemakers that the HUAC document claimed could be "isolated and destroyed in a short period of time."[10]

The Choice and *The Man Who Cried I Am* epitomize the cultural significance of racial distrust, of African American misgivings about the nation's commitment to social equality and inclusiveness, and clearly other books foment the same kinds of skepticism and paranoia, books that further reinforce such African American perspectives on America.

This canon comprises "counterdiscourses" that exist separately from, and often in opposition to, more mainstream publications, writers, and researchers. The writers of such counterdiscourses position their work as correctives to the racial biases that predetermine, say, which titles make the *New York Times* Best Sellers List and which others get shut out. The authors of these offerings have sold hundreds of thousands of books, and they form a large interdisciplinary field of expanding scholarship, citing one another, adding new twists to older arguments, and building on colleagues' prior research and analyses. This growing body of literature directly or indirectly informs the beliefs of and debates among avid and casual readers alike. Whether people agree or disagree with their premises, these titles try to explain race's analytical and historical importance as a motivation for animus against African Americans, as an explanation for the existence of King Alfred–sized secret plots. They describe race as something that is still salient, even if purposefully less visible, in a post–civil rights era.

One crucial title in this library of race-based distrust is grounded in theories that have been around since at least the 1970s, when its author, psychologist Frances Cress-Welsing, first published her pamphlet-sized "psychogenetic" take titled "Color-Confrontation," the foundation for her 1991 book, *The Isis Papers: The Keys to the Colors*. Cress-Welsing's arguments rest on one foundational premise: white people are the ultimate paranoiacs because they fear "genetic annihilation." This fear, she argues, gets reworked into a viciously defensive posture, a "white supremacy power system/culture" intent on killing before being killed. Cress-Welsing links her claims to the hardwiring of biology: "whiteness is indeed a genetic inadequacy or a relative genetic deficiency state, based on the inability to produce the skin pigments of melanin."[11] This lack of melanin, what she calls "color absence," is "abnormal" (since most of the world isn't "afflicted" with it), and "this state of color absence acts always as a genetic recessive to the dominant genetic factor of color-production."[12]

At a subconscious level, Cress-Welsing divulges, whites actually recognize that "color always 'annihilates' (phenotypically and genetically speaking) the noncolor, white."[13] And she sets up a hierarchy of "color potential" with blacks at the top, whites at the bottom, and everyone else in between. As a response to these subconscious fears, whites fight to keep their race alive by stopping blacks from running roughshod through their gene pool. According to Cress-Welsing, whites feel genetically inferior and repress that sense with fantasies of racial superiority, ploys to repress their fears of inadequacy, even King Alfred–like plots to eliminate that racial threat altogether.

Few readers I've ever met have simply accepted all of Cress-Welsing's claims uncritically, but they have usually wanted to see for themselves why her book was considered

so controversial.[14] With the new human-genome work being conducted now, other researchers have attempted to
corner the market on how the tandem of race and genes
gets understood, and in ways that usually highlight the odd
overlaps (not definitive differences) between seemingly distinct populations.[15]

When literary scholar Henry Louis Gates used African
Ancestry (a company that houses the largest "African line-
age database" in the world) as part of his Public Broadcasting Service (PBS) documentary *African-American Lives*, he
wanted to help black celebrities find out a little genetic information about themselves. Viewers learned that portions
of black people's DNA might sometimes point to places
other than Africa. The pristine differences between ideal-
ized racial groups tend to get challenged more than reinforced with the use of sophisticated genetic technology. For
instance, it also turns out that we're all African, with mito-
chondrial Eve as our singular, if distant, foremother. What
the human genomic projects haven't found, experts will tell
you, is a supposed "black gene" for whites to fear, which
isn't to say that some well-respected geneticists aren't still
looking, even if they want to prove the exact opposite of
Cress-Welsing's theory by finding a genetic explanation for
differences in intelligence and other abilities that put blacks
at the bottom of the evolutionary ladder.

For Cress-Welsing, once she had fine-tuned her version
of a "unified field theory" explaining "white supremacy,"
everything she saw day in and day out began to make a
new kind of sense to her, including the symbolism of popular sports. Cress-Welsing maintains that all of the most

highly watched sporting events in America point directly to
white fears of genetic extinction at the hands of black
men.[16] In most major American sports, she points out,
black or dark balls are much larger than white ones. She's
thinking of "big brown balls" like footballs, basketballs,
and bowling balls and comparing them to the white
balls found in, say, baseball and golf. Those large black
balls are usually tossed through white nets (symbols, she
says, for white female genitalia), or they are used to knock
down white pins (emblematic of the vulnerable white male
phallus), but what happens to those smaller white balls?
They are constantly getting whacked around with long,
dark sticks. And I probably don't have to tell you what she
says that represents.

According to Cress-Welsing's "color-confrontation" hypothesis, the world is just a staging area for all of our repressed racial fears, for self-defense mechanisms aimed at
genetic survival. This is mostly subconscious, she says. It is
somatic memory, genetic memory. *De cardio* racism, racism of the heart, is reimagined as a kind of genetic racism,
racism of the genes. The "selfish gene" is decidedly racial
too.[17] This is where *de cardio* racism gets connected to the
ideas about genetic racism Cress-Welsing champions. If
even our recreational games are secretly coded to buttress
racist thinking, how much can we trust the seemingly innocent actions of the white people playing them? Not everybody who fears that racists may hide their racism believe
that we are all genetically programmed to be racist, but *de
cardio* racism can be made to mesh quite comfortably with
such presumptions.

If you entertain even the tiniest sliver of Cress-Welsing's theorizing, then the idea of AIDS as a government-created disease designed to kill black people all around the globe sounds like just another means to the same old end, another version of Williams's King Alfred Plan. Similarly, fried-chicken batter, malt liquor, certain beverages, and generally any products that seemed to be marketed exclusively to black communities have long served as culprits in conspiracy theories circulating around urban black America. Niche marketing can sometimes make black-only products suspect.[18] If it isn't good enough for middle-class white communities, why should blacks use it? Just because it's cheaper? If evil people wanted to target the black community for something terrible, they'd have some ready-made vehicles for doing so. Of course, if anybody was planning a massive racial attack, the target was assumed, first and foremost, to be young black *men*.

Haki Madhubuti, the poet who in 1967 cofounded Third World Press (the independent publisher of both Cress-Welsing's color-confrontation theory and Naylor's "fictionalized memoir," as well as Tavis Smiley's bestselling *The Covenant* and Chancellor Williams's *The Destruction of Black Civilization*) is famous for writing several canonical race-conspiracy books, many of which add a twist to the racial-genocide arguments found in Yette and Cress-Welsing. His *Black Men: Obsolete, Single, Dangerous? The Afrikan American Family in Transition* had become a classic in the genre by the early 1990s. Everybody seemed to be reading it. As an undergraduate at Howard University, I certainly did.

Black Men asks provocative and taboo questions. It explicitly wonders aloud about whether AIDS was manufactured to speed along a "purposeful destruction of the black world," inquiring into why "its origin is falsely and maliciously placed in the Afrikan community."[19] Madhubuti uses popular anthropologist Edward T. Hall's *Beyond Culture* to argue for a renewed approach to culture as a "shared understanding" that, for black people, must be geared toward group survival, not individualistic gain. African American men are doing themselves in, he claims, by buying into the versions of black manhood being sold back to them through the mass media, a manhood defined as violent, irresponsible, drug addicted, and politically disinterested.

For Jawanza Kunjufu, another canonized figure, this discussion of black men must start much earlier in the life cycle with an emphasis on black boys.[20] Citing both Cress-Welsing and his mentor Neely Fuller (Cress-Welsing's mentor as well), Kunjufu argues (quoting the likes of Thomas Jefferson, Abraham Lincoln, and Cecil Rhodes) that white "historians, politicians, academicians and writers" have long offered works that merely serve as "justification for White supremacy." He sees the conspiracy quite clearly and maintains that America has no desire for black boys to become truly competitive. They are scared of such competition, and in many different arenas, including the genetic playing field that Cress-Welsing emphasizes. Kunjufu distinguishes between active and passive conspirators, the latter including African American youths "consciously or unconsciously participating in their own genocide" by not working toward educational goals, failing to take proper care of their families, and refusing to focus on spirituality over materiality. Kunjufu, Cress-Welsing, and Madhubuti are three major thinkers in a much larger literary edifice that makes clear and explicit claims about the effects of racism on the lives and life chances of African Americans and that asks blacks to be quite skeptical, even paranoid, about white America.

Marimba Ani's *Yurugu: An African-Centered Critique of European Cultural Thought and Behavior* is a massive tome that links history, religion, psychology, anthropology, and linguistics into a grand theory about whites and their collective self-assessments.[21] She believes that once she can explain Europeans' sense of themselves, she'll be able to explain how they relate to other social groups. Ani contends that European culture is based on little more than a phony "rhetorical ethic" that it professes but hardly believes. She claims that when Europeans approach other cultures, they use "concepts of traditional European anthropology" that cannot adequately or accurately make sense of others without angling for a way to control and destroy them. Attacking the very epistemology of European scholarship, she challenges its emphasis on scientific detachment, an emphasis that she traces back to German philosophy, particularly Georg Hegel's and his privileging of reason over spirit.

African worldviews are categorically different from those found in the West, she avers, in a gesture not too different from the "clash of civilizations" hypothesis popularized by political scientist Samuel Huntington, only with the positive and negative poles reversed.[22] The "rhetorical ethic" she describes buttresses European attempts at "world domination" and has been negatively internalized by African Americans via what she calls "mind control," techniques used to teach other groups to believe lies about their own inferiority. This is clearly part of Kunjufu's conspiracy and akin to what psychologist Na'im Akbar, another member of the canon, labels the "chains and images of psychological slavery," those aspects of confinement and pathology that emerged with the terrors of slavery and have continued long afterward—even getting worse.[23] Akbar argues that "distorted" attitudes and thought processes still harm blacks more than a century after emancipation. With the "loss of self-knowledge [fostered by chattel] slavery," African Americans have had to be very purposeful about reconstructing a "community of self" to exorcise that history. Akbar practices an "African-centered" psychology similar to the versions of anthropology and "psychogenetics" offered up in *The Isis Papers* and *Yurugu*.

There are probably still many black undergraduates who stay up late at night reading Senegalese anthropologist Cheikh Anta Diop's *Civilization or Barbarism: An Authentic Anthropology*, along with the aforementioned Chancellor Williams book, *The Destruction of Black Civilization*, both classics in the racial-conspiracy canon.[24] Those books provide versions of the past that are far different from what those students usually learn in history classes listed in their universities' course catalogs. Williams's book is an ambitious six-thousand-year saga of racial struggles and skirmishes from ancient Egypt to contemporary Ghana. His point is to make a case for the historical depth of "white supremacy" and its single-minded attempt at black annihilation. Diop dramatizes some of that same history, specifically highlighting the scholastic cover-ups that keep such facts hidden.[25]

George G. M. James's *Stolen Legacy* is still the classic among classics in this genre, arguing that those thoughtful ancient Greeks weren't so thoughtful at all, that they actually stole their philosophy from even older Egyptian "mysteries."[26] James considers this particularly important because of an equally controversial contention: those Egyptians he's talking about were Africans, blacks, which is his answer to why European scholars wanted to conceal that part of the story. According to James, Aristotle studied under Africans. Then, he simply pretended to write the massive volumes found in Alexandria, volumes only there, James contends, thanks to Alexander the Great's plundering of Egypt.

Martin Bernal, a specialist in Chinese political history, wrote a much more academically cited version of this argument in an ambitious multipart study on the Afroasiatic roots of Western civilization.[27] Bernal maintains that the "ancient model" for understanding the relationship between Egypt and Greece recognized the latter's debts to the former (just as James contends), but that that position was carefully replaced by an "Aryan model" more aligned with racist assumptions in the West. Classicists dismissed him as an amateur, an "armchair archeologist," but many students still scarf down Bernal's fascinating critique—and not just the "extremists" on the campus.

Ancient Egypt has become a kind of fetish in these debates, but when people want to talk about the present (without any of the "Afrocentrism" that defines the aforementioned texts), they usually turn to *The COINTELPRO Papers*.[28] The now infamous Ward Churchill and his coauthor, Vander Wall, reproduce declassified government documents that help to chronicle the Federal Bureau of Investigation's campaigns against major American figures, both before the start of COINTELPRO and after it was "officially" dismantled. The logic of racial paranoia assumes just these kinds of conspiratorial government antics. If you aren't something of a racial skeptic before reading the photocopied documents, you probably will be afterward, and their revision of national history is a key contribution to the racial wariness that gives many blacks, even those who are equally committed Americans, reason to second-guess government rhetoric about race and equality. All of these rereadings of history are grounded in an ethic and rhetoric of racial paranoia, and all of these aforementioned authors reference at least two final themes in their books, education and economics, themes that they argue will determine whether blacks ever gain control of their own collective destiny.

If you were to check out *Essence* magazine's most recent survey of the top nonfiction paperbacks among their participating black booksellers, Carter G. Woodson's *The Miseducation of the Negro* would probably be somewhere on it.[29] This is the flagship text on education and the black community by one of the most important black historians of the early twentieth century. The book's title concretizes its take on current educational curricula imposed on black children. When Kunjufu, Cress-Welsing, and Madhubuti make their arguments, they also explicitly talk about education as a key part of black America's problems, devoting entire chapters to it. For Kunjufu, it is the crux of that conspiracy against black boys, America's opening salvo, and part of the reason why young black males do even worse than their female counterparts in school. Cress-Welsing condemns education in American for teaching blacks little more than "interiorization," and Madhubuti argues that poor education is a purposefully concocted part of the reason why black men disproportionately end up in such dire straits; it is alienating by design. The authors would all agree that the truths in their respective books are the last things children are being assigned to read because the revolutionary ideas might instill a confidence and swagger in black readers that would only make them more of a threat to everybody else.

Kunjufu has written a book, *Hip-hop v. MAAT,* in which he dismisses hip-hop culture as part of the educational problem in black America. Even though it helps unleash powerful "energy and creativity," hip-hop and "New Jack" culture privilege individualism over community and promote "at-risk behavior [that] could take a variety of forms including substance abuse, promiscuity, academic failure, and other characteristics."[30] MAAT, on the other hand, "is expressed in the seven cardinal virtues of righteousness, truth, justice, harmony, balance, reciprocity, and order."

He wants young people to give up hip-hop for MAAT, which he says dates back to "the old Egyptian kingdom (2750 though 2180 B.C.E.)," linking MAAT to Nguzo Saba, the African philosophy developed as part of Kwanzaa by Afrocentrist Maulana Karenga. If hip-hoppers think of themselves as streetcorner educators, then they are doing a terrible job of getting across the information that Kunjufu thinks is most important for the future of black America.

According to these same authors, the other vital thing young black people aren't being taught is economics—how money, resources, financing, and entrepreneurialism impact families and communities. If black televangelists offer a "prosperity gospel" that promises financial security for individual believers and their families, there is a cottage industry in racial paranoia's literary canon that emphasizes "collective economics," prosperity for the race as a whole (one of the seven principles of Kwanzaa). Kunjufu's *Black Economics: Solutions for Economic and Community Empowerment* was one of the most popular versions of this theme when my classmates and I were reading *The Isis Papers* and *The Destruction of Black Civilization* as undergraduates, but Claude Anderson's 2002 *PowerNomics: The National Plan to Empower Black America* takes Kunjufu's economic self-help ethos to another level, offering techniques like "ethno-aggregation" as economic principles to create group wealth, racial wealth.[31] Anderson also makes education central to his thesis, arguing that teaching economics demands teaching black people a new way to see themselves, a way that isn't predicated on racist American stereotypes.

Taken together, these books offer a kind of full-tilt and full-time paranoia, a version of racial distrust that oozes from every corner of every page. But most versions of racial paranoia aren't nearly as all encompassing or extreme. They operate much less ideologically, much less single-mindedly, and usually with only intermittent sparks of explicit public expression.

A more accurate exemplar of the way that racial paranoia may operate in someone's political life can be found in Kwame Ture's autobiography, *Ready for Revolution,* when the subject of Ture's own racial paranoia comes up. Born Stokely Carmichael on the island of Trinidad, Ture moved to the United States with his family as a child and, after graduating from Howard University, became one of the infamous 1960s embodiments of "black power" rhetoric and politics. Ture headed both the Student Nonviolent Coordinating Committee (SNCC) and the Black Panthers for a time, participated in the freedom rides and countless other voter registration drives, and was an outspoken critic of the Vietnam War. He left the United States in the late 1960s to live and work in Guinea, dying of prostate cancer there in 1998.

The book is mostly framed as the story of an activist who genuinely believes that black people have to deal with the racism endemic to institutions by challenging it, rolling up their sleeves and working to change the practices adversely impacting them. He believed in opting into the system, rhetorical guns blazing, as the best way to change it. Almost as an aside near the end of the book, Ture launches into conjecture about whether or not the American government might have given him cancer "to 'neutralize' me or set me up for assassination."[32] He had no definitive proof and didn't know for sure, but he thought it was plausible enough to mention and take seriously as an explanation for his illness, even offering it as a possibility to journalists and other people he met during his final few years. Is it just chance, he muses, that his old SNCC peers have extremely high rates of cancer?

Ture is quick to point out that people's objections to his theory about the government giving him cancer are "*always* operational, never moral." He finds this fact very telling.

> It was never an "Oh, no, our government would not do something that evil." It was rather "The government couldn't do that: they haven't the technical capability to give someone cancer." Perhaps. One certainly hopes so. But who among us knows what all lies buried under the blank of top-secret, national-security concealment under which certain agencies go about their clandestine business? In any case, what the skeptics' response reveals about citizen confidence in the morality of government is, I would say, cause for serious concern. Not that they wouldn't, but that they couldn't.[33]

In a move similar to the mind-control information found in Naylor's appendix to *1996*, Ture even provides some documentation to support the believability of his assertion, including "materials on secret, government-sponsored radiation experiments on unsuspecting American citizens" and published allegations that Israel's Mossad might have given several Palestinian terrorists leukemia. He doesn't have definitive proof that such technology exists, but he has no doubt that the American government would use it on its enemies if it did. To those most predisposed to agreeing with the principles espoused in Ture's book, this final tangent is a distraction from real politics, a cop-out, a detour away from genuine ideological struggle and into the wonderland of evil geniuses and government conspiracies.[34]

But racial paranoia works exactly the way Ture's autobiography represents it, and his rendering is even more accurate than that found in many of the works penned by the canonized authors highlighted above. It functions like the flip side of "black rage," an eruption of anger and resentment that flares up in a flash, seemingly out of proportion to the situation and the evidence, and then just as quickly subsides, seeping back into the crevices of its everyday hiding places, lying in wait for the next explosion.[35]

Even after decades of being on the fringe of culture, of filling bookshelves in a relatively small number of homes without being stocked by corporate megabookstores, racial paranoia's canon has made several occasional forays into the wider popular culture. It has been to the movies. One instance is yet another Eddie Murphy reference, his 1992 romantic comedy *Boomerang*. Murphy plays the ever-dashing Marcus Graham, a womanizing advertising executive who gets a taste of this own medicine when his new boss, Jacqueline Broyer, played by Robin Givens, treats him the same way he is used to treating the women he dates, using him for sex with little regard for his feelings (and absolutely no interest in being tied down in a monogamous relationship). Viewing the film with an eye for what it reveals about racial politics sidelines the romantic story and foregrounds the relationship between Marcus and his two best friends, Tyler and Gerard, played by comedians Martin Lawrence and David Alan Grier.

Gerard is a soft-spoken buppie (black urban professional), who is far too shy and indecisive to get the girl, Angela Lewis (played by Halle Berry). After a few uninspired dates with Gerard, Angela eventually ends up with Marcus. Tyler, on the other hand, isn't connected to any of the love triangles and quadrangles that propel the film along. And he's the only major character who is not. He's there, it seems, to serve another purpose: constant purveyor of racial paranoia.

Tyler sees everything that happens as racial. For instance, early in the film, when a white waitress explains to him that "asparagus spears" are served with the dish he wants to order, he tells Marcus and Gerard that she would have called them "asparagus tips" if the three of them weren't black. "She might as well have called us jungle bunnies" he exclaims. The guys assure him that he's making too much out of nothing at all, and the viewer is supposed to laugh at his paranoid extrapolations.

But some of the time Tyler is clearly right about things being "racial," like when a white salesperson dismissively eyes the three black men in a fancy New York fashion outlet, clearly equating blackness with poverty or criminality and thinking them up to no good. The salesman's racism is not very subtle at all. It is caricatured and self-evident—to them and to the film audience.[36]

In another of *Boomerang's* classic scenes, a moment that owes much of its power to *The Isis Papers,* the three guys are playing pool as Tyler tries to explain the racist symbolism behind that game. It isn't just a coincidence, he declares, that the game is premised on a white ball (white masculinity) chasing a black ball (black masculinity) and attempting to knock it off the table, while knocking off all the other colored balls (other racial groups) along the way. It is "racial," he claims, and not in a particularly subtle way.

Marcus and Gerard are usually dismissive when Tyler starts talking like this, but Marcus admits that his friend might be on to something with his billiards analysis, even completing the symbolic logic of Tyler's point by saying that the pool table is green to signify the earth and that once people "thought it was flat." Marcus gets it, which makes Tyler's day because he isn't like Tyler. He doesn't always see race, spotting it almost everywhere, behind every corner, saturating every exchange and social interaction.

In many ways, Tyler is heir to Frederick Douglass—or, at least, to Douglass's Master Covey, who would surreptitiously hide behind anything (trees, barn doors, roadside ditches) in hopes of surprising his slaves when they least expected it. He wanted them to work as hard when he wasn't around as they did when he was, and Covey figured that they would slow down if they didn't think they were always being watched. So, he wanted them to internalize a sense of being constantly surveilled, to believe their white overseer was always there, always watching, always ready to pounce.[37]

Tyler's racial paranoia is a caricatured rendition of just such internalization. For him, white racism and antiblack contempt are always lurking behind the scenes, hiding racist machinations in the most innocuous things. Tyler sees Master Covey everywhere, which means that the King Alfred Plan would have seemed like so much more common sense to him.

I've met very few African Americans with Tyler's level of heightened racial sensitivity. To be even more specific, I have met only three or four people with the kind of hyper-racialism Lawrence's rendition of Tyler lampoons. Many people have described moments when they went ballistic with someone over something racist that nobody else saw the same way or that nobody else agreed was racial at all, but few people maintain their "racial" lenses as rigidly as Tyler does. He represents a hyperform of racial sensitivity, a commitment to making everything an example of *de cardio* racism, a monochromatic way of seeing racism everywhere when it is being hidden anywhere, maybe even when a waitress describes asparagus as having "spears" instead of "tips" and says it all with a smile.

But even this take on Tyler's paranoia isn't completely fair. In fact, Ture's model is probably closer to Tyler's version too. Tyler's not completely single-minded. He'll be the first person to label something "racial," to call someone a racist, even over next to nothing at all, but he still has time to hang out at the gym, discuss dating options with his best friends, and offer up witty one-liners at their expense. Tyler can see racism around every corner. He can imagine racial discrimination's defining and constraining every life possibility, but he still leaves psychic and social space open for other things—for fun and free time, for sex and silliness. He may spot Douglass's Master Covey everywhere, watching him at every turn, but there are many more moments when that terrifying understanding of racism's ubiquity is muted, downplayed, temporarily forgotten. That's an important characteristic of racial paranoia. It can fluctuate from all encompassing to compartmentalized in an instant, and that dynamism is often lost in its more concentrated and ideological forms, in many of the arguments found in books framed by a singular focus on the potential white threat, relentless in their obsession with racial discrimination's inescapability. Racial paranoia is lived quite differently, however more subtly, with antennae up only intermittently, even in the everyday lives of many ideological hard-liners.

Peter Piper Picked Peppers, but Humpty Dumpty Got Pushed

The Productively Paranoid Stylings of Hip-hop's Spirituality

When I was growing up in Brooklyn, New York, in the 1970s and 1980s, most of the young people who lived in the Bayview Houses (the housing project complex I called home for the bulk of my childhood) spent their weekends watching Saturday-afternoon kung fu movies on television, flicking clay- or wax-filled bottle caps across concrete sidewalks in "skelly" games, and listening to Mr. Magic or DJ Red Alert late at night on the radio. We were hip-hop's first youth generation, enthusiastic local guinea pigs for its unanticipated global influences.[1]

Before music came to television and hip-hop went mainstream, Mr. Magic and Red Alert were two of the most important official ambassadors for hip-hop music, spinning records by MC Lyte and Heavy D, Big Daddy Kane and Audio Two, UTFO and The Treacherous Three, records that you couldn't hear many other places on the radio dial. As passionate listeners, we memorized the artists' lyrics and recited their rhymes for one another—that is, when we weren't writing and performing our own original couplets in school cafeterias or during afternoon treks home. Everybody wanted to be an MC or a DJ, and that was long before most people fully realized just how financially lucrative hip-hop would turn out to be.

The hip-hop songs we memorized in the 1980s and 1990s were full of talk about "Gods and Earths" (i.e., black men and black women), references to the esoteric philosophies that MCs called "mathematics," tales of "grafted devils" (the theory that whites were genetically engineered by a black scientist long ago), and much more along those same lines.[2] This terminology and rhetoric grew out of another movement sprouting from the same fertile concrete that nurtured hip-hop.

Quite a few of the young black guys in Bayview Houses, these same hip-hop fans, were also Five Percenters. Members of the Five Percent Nation believe that the black man in America is god, a saintly energy and entity, and all their other philosophies spring from that premise. Five Percenters change their names (to things like "Wisdom Knowledge," "Righteous Born" and "Sincere Divine"), explicitly call one another gods, and memorize their daily "mathematics" right alongside their hip-hop lyrics. "Mathematics" represent the spiritual teachings that Five Percenters have to learn and recite on cue, the philosophical truths that provide them with "knowledge of self" about the black man's godly status.

Even though I was never a member of the Five Percent Nation, I did have enough Bayview friends in the group that I was able to get some of my questions answered about their worldview. For instance, I learned about their conviction that certain powerful and elite social circles (which included high-level government officials and rich corporate tycoons) actually knew the truth about black people's celestial pedigree but purposefully hid the facts from wider public view. Most people don't realize this and won't accept it, Five Percenters will tell you, because there's an ongoing conspiracy organized by an evil 10 percent of the world's population to keep the masses (85 percent) in complete darkness. The job of the 5 percent left over is to dutifully pull the wool from over people's eyes and show them the black man's true divinity.

From the very beginning, hip-hop music was tailor-made for disseminating Five Percenters' beliefs. For one thing, hip-hop and the Five Percent Nation were born at about the same time. Clarence 13X split from the Nation of Islam's Mosque Number 7 in Harlem (once Malcolm X's mosque) in 1968, at about the same time that blacks a few miles away (in the South Bronx) were first starting to combine urban Americana with anglophone Caribbean and black British influences to form the earliest renditions of hip-hop style.[3] Some hip-hop artists explicitly considered themselves Five Percenters and attempted to use the new art form to help the masses find "truth."

Hip-hop with any apparent connection to Five Percenters' faith usually gets designated "conscious rap," a subgenre made up of songs specifically designed to endorse pro-black ideas (in the distinctive traditions of Afrocentrism, Pan-Africanism, and Black Nationalism).[4] The first conscious rap offerings of hip-hop acts such as Stetsasonic and Afrika Bambaataa existed on an ideological continuum with hip-hop groups made up of actual members from the Nation of Islam and the Five Percenters (including Brand Nubian and Poor Righteous Teachers). But conscious rappers didn't necessarily have to believe in the Five Percenters' theories of global religious conspiracies to sympathize with their educational bent or to invoke the organization's idiomatic expressions as a sign of authenticity and street credibility. A fan could have been listening to any number of hip-hop acts in the mid-1990s (not just "Nation" groups), and if they were listening closely enough, they would have learned more than a few of the basic beliefs central to Five Percenter and Nation of Islam theologies.

Even if all hip-hop artists didn't identify themselves as part of that enlightened 5 percent of "poor righteous teachers" tapped to save the world, many did position themselves explicitly as street professors espousing truths that went against the grain of conventional America's educational curricula, a similar critique to those provided by authors discussed in the last chapter, such as Jawanza Kunjufu, Frances Cress-Welsing, and Haki Madhubuti, to justify their own theoretical interventions on behalf of black America. For conscious rap groups such as X-Clan, the Jungle Brothers, and A Tribe Called Quest (as well as more mainstream acts, such as the Furious Five and Kool Moe Dee, who schooled listeners about life on the street), hip-hop was committed to reeducation in the wake of past miseducations of black people at the hands of public schools and elite colleges.

A critic might bookend this move to equate hip-hop MCs with teachers by citing KRS-One's late-1980s demand that his fans heed his ideas ("you must learn!") about ancient Egypt and black history, on the one hand, and a group like Dead Prez's early twenty-first-century dismissal of "They Schools" as little more than "brainwash camps," on the other. Neither of these last two acts has been affiliated with Islam as a foundational aspect of its reputation, but both represent the broader pedagogical metaphors that frame hip-hop artists' justifications for their work. Hip-hop is supposed to bring class into session, a new kind of class. The better the MC, the more irreproachable his or her teacherly credentials, with the listeners' homework being to study the lyrics and learn the lessons of these street philosophers. And one of the major themes in many of these lesson plans has always been a critical distrust of larger American society and its commitments to the urban communities that gave birth to hip-hop culture.

In contrast to a strictly romantic and utopian version of race relations in a post–civil rights context, one of the major themes of hip-hop music emphasizes the utility of a certain cynical paranoia vis-à-vis American society. Most of the earliest hip-hop songs played on the radio emphasized fun and good times, using easy-to-follow lyrics and a relatively slow verbal delivery to narrate tales about the horrors of dating and boasts about individual prowess. But as the genre got more technically sophisticated, its rhetoric and its very style became conducive to more suspicious readings of contemporary American life. As the rest of America sought to hide racism beneath a veneer of politically correct speech, hip-hop became increasingly paranoid about race, and not a small part of that diametrical difference is linked to the intrinsic racial skepticisms of groups such as the Five Percenters and the Nation of Islam, two of the earliest influences on hip-hop discourse.

If paranoia is usually dismissed by committed scholar-activists, critics like political scientist Adolph Reed, as merely a distraction from real politics, something that dissipates the galvanizing energies required for true social transformation, hip-hop artists call on racial paranoia as a kind of lightning rod for politicizing otherwise disaffected black youth, asking them to wake up, recognize the global conspiracies afoot, and get their urban lives in order. The founding assumptions behind hip-hop's take on black America are often strikingly similar to Five Percenter philosophies and to race-based conspiracy theories more generally. For example, there is little mere coincidence in hip-hop rhetoric, especially when that rhetoric focuses on the plight of poor blacks. Nothing happens to African Americans simply by chance or due to the disinterested contingencies of history. Everything is chalked up to purposeful trickery and conniving, social insensitivity and self-serving disinterest.[5] For instance, when Grand Master Flash and the Furious Five released their megahit "The Message" in 1982, the song's talk of poverty and hopelessness emphasized uncaring teachers who provide little more than a "bum education" and highlighted all the conspicuous features of ghetto life that conspire to precipitate the early death of many young black children. Their message seemed to be that staying alive from day to day in America's ghettoes was a bona fide miracle.

"The Message" helped open hip-hop's political floodgates, and many more rappers would provide snapshots of urban poverty in black America after Grand Master Flash's early salvo. Of course, most of these later accusations were "dropped" over heavy drumbeats and with recourse to intricate (sometimes very subtle) wordplay. Hip-hop lyricism is specifically about toying with the fact that words can have many different meanings, with the slightest change in tone and inflection redefining common terms, sometimes radically. Hip-hop revels in its own peculiar brand of linguistic sophistication, in the fact that words can imply any number of things, even the opposite of what uninitiated listeners might think.

Run DMC offered a well-known vocabulary lesson in one of their early songs, explaining to outsiders that when they said the word "bad" it was "not 'bad' meaning 'bad' but 'bad' meaning 'good.'" From the nineteenth and early twentieth centuries, linguists such as Ferdinand de Saussure and Charles Sanders Peirce provided detailed explanations for the many reasons why "bad" can be made to mean "good," and those reasons all pivot on the basic arbitrariness of language. The sounds we make with our mouths only stand for the ideas they represent because of convention, because we all say they do. Societies (speech communities) agree on specific relationships between certain combinations of sounds and the concepts they symbolize, but such links aren't natural or "motivated" by logical connections fastening particular sounds to the ideas they sound out.[6]

Hip-hop uses that semantic slippage to popularize new sets of agreements (for those in the know) about the relationship between given words and what they "represent." "Bad meaning good" is particularly powerful, of course, because it turns a negative into a positive, like the hip-hop community's obsessive reclamation of "nigger/nigga" as a term of endearment, applying it in opposition to its venomous historical uses. Hip-hop embraces the "power to define" itself, and Run DMC's one line alone speaks volumes about the group's desire to cross over, about their sense of themselves as teachers (responsible for teaching new fans how to listen accurately), and about hip-hop's emphasis on potential linguistic impenetrability as part of its cultural power.[7]

For fans to really make heads or tails of what hip-hop artists are saying, especially when the artists aren't explicitly defining their terms the way Run DMC did above (and particularly after hip-hop MCs started to ratchet up the speed and lyrical complexity of their rhyming styles in the 1990s), they had to take their time deciphering what was mostly unintelligible to casual listeners or even to many serious fans. And that is a key part of hip-hop's story: its general "incomprehensibility."[8] Hip-hop is such a potential conduit for conspiracy talk and racial paranoia in part because of its in-your-face secrecies, its ability to hide political views in plain sight. And this isn't just about euphemizing. The "Parental Advisory" stickers on their CDs prove that hip-hop artists can be clear and explicit when they want to be. However, fast rhyming, playing with the phonetics of language, and continually redefining words all conspire to make hip-hop almost as indecipherable as a foreign language for anyone not raised on its idiomatic expressions or committed to learning them. Fully comprehending hip-hop demands decoding its intricate use of language to the point where one is able to recognize relatively obscure and cloaked references to veiled philosophies found in African American versions of Islam or explicit invocations of alternative discourses on racism popularized by books such as *The Isis Papers*.

Hip-hop's useful incomprehensibility is also tied to the fact that it is hardly "easy listening." There is an obvious premium placed on lyrical flow and speed. But on top of that, the layering of hip-hop music with scratching, cutting, sampling, and other sound effects makes it that much more difficult to excavate all the hidden lyrical meanings beneath its complexly textured acoustic landscape.[9] Hip-hop plays with the very substance and texture of sound, reworking Jazz's "scat" tradition into "hip hop, a hippit, a hippit to the hip hip hop and you don't stop" nonsensicality, or transforming an MC's voice into a drum machine (in the form of a "human beat box"). Everything about hip-hop's aesthetic asks us to listen to the very materialities of meanings, which means hearing things in newfangled ways.

This all helps make hip-hop's form, its very structure and sensibility, conducive to a kind of conspiring in broad daylight. Incomprehensibility and the layering of beats, scratches, cuts, and the like, collude to make hip-hop a masterful secret keeper. At the same time, there is also a specific hip-hop mindset predicated on the dominant belief that you can't really trust what you see. If the genre has one mantra, it is that the eyes deceive—or prove downright ineffective: "You can't see me." "You're blind, baby." "Can't trust it." Hip-hoppers from Public Enemy to Jay-Z are adamant about the inadequacy of vision, which is part of the reason why matters of authenticity and credibility are endlessly debated.[10] You don't just spy a self-professed hip-hop "gangsta," say, and naively accept that he isn't, in fact, a "perpetrator," a "studio gangsta," someone who plays the role of criminal to raise record sales. In hip-hop, what you see is never what you get. Listeners have learned to be skeptical of spectacles, even as the spectacle is also a form of presentation that most hip-hop artists embrace. This is what makes things so complex. Hip-hop is invested in "appearances" even as it simultaneously denounces them for being misleading: distrust of the mere "image" is combined with fondness for making a fetish out of precisely those things (the artist's look, bling-bling fashions, etc.) that aren't supposed to be trusted. This is one of hip-hop's most productive and fascinating paradoxes.

So, if hip-hop doesn't trust eyewitnesses to supply it with evidence on authenticity and credibility, what does it use? In hip-hop, truth isn't seen; it is felt. It is a fact of the soul and spirit more than anything else. You are supposed to feel the "real" of that popular mandate to "keep it real." And if you don't feel it, there's nothing else you can do.

This hip-hop philosophy is succinctly captured in the question that hip-hop artists ask one another (and their listeners) almost neurotically: "You feel me?" Do you feel me? Can you feel me? That isn't just an idle inquiry. There is an important principle behind it. Hip-hop is offering up its own epistemology, its way of knowing the world. To "feel" means to test the world, but differently from what social scientists might label naive empiricism. "You feel me?" ensures that hip-hop doesn't rely too simplistically on what people can prove with mathematical formulas or scientific experiments. Something about the truth, about real life, is more powerfully felt than statistically proven, more intuited than seen, which is the precise sensibility that grounds racial paranoia. The racial slights are real (for Cynthia McKinney, for Dave Chappelle, for Gloria Naylor) at least partially because they feel real, and no visible displays to the contrary can completely refute that.

"Feeling" short-circuits more traditional corroboration techniques—and not just seeing. It is unreceptive to most forms of external verification. Hip-hop artist Jay-Z, for one, rhymes about this pointedly, crystallizing hip-hop's attitude to perfection: "I put my hand on my heart. That means I feel you. Real recognize real and you('re) looking familiar." To "feel" someone is to connect to them beyond words or otherwise superficial similarities. Familiarity is something you sense, not what your gullible eyes might try to validate. That isn't the same thing as saying that hip-hop advocates blindness. It imagines a way of knowing a person that can see inside them, can look past the surface and connect on some more fundamental ground.

This idea of seeing something that isn't observable to the naked eye is a classic motif for conspiracies and paranoia, which is why you can't just disabuse people of their seemingly misplaced paranoia by splashing them with the cool, crisp waters of reason. Racial paranoia exceeds rational debate. "You feel me" because you can feel me. That's it. You get a vibe, something as ephemeral and invisible as a hunch. It isn't about cognitive and intellectual vetting. You just sense, intuit, with something similar to the blinklike efficiency and immediacy Malcolm Gladwell described.[11] Hip-hop places a premium on such implicit feeling, treats it as obvious and self-evident, automatic and hardwired.

It is this feeling, this way of knowing by sensing, that also makes racial identity so real for people. Like anything else worthy of the designation "culture," racial identities work most efficiently when we can't even see them, when they become second nature and we can't even imagine ourselves otherwise. People don't believe in social identities just because they are logical or reasonable. "Believing" means using a very different heuristic entirely. And this privileging of belief is caught up in hip-hop's entrenched faith-based leanings more generally, in hip-hop's spiritual fundamentalisms.

Critics are far more interested in criticizing the music's obvious vulgarity than in talking about hip-hop's emphatic spirituality. They call hip-hop artists out for their shameless misogyny and homophobia. Detractors decry the violence and nihilism glamorized by hip-hop gangstas. Or they dismiss much of the music and culture for its embrace of commercialism and apolitical ostentation. Those are all important critiques, but they only begin to scratch the surface of more serious discussions about hip-hop's social relevance and spiritual ethic.[12]

When people do comment on the connection between hip-hop and religion, it is usually to puzzle over the dissonance of "Christian hip-hop" (as popularized by, say, Kirk Franklin and Compton Virtue), which proselytizes through Bible-inspired lyrics. Or they lampoon secular hip-hop artists who spend most of their albums cursing and depicting brutal forms of barbarity, only to turn around and solemnly thank God on nationally televised programs for helping them win prestigious music awards. Those award-show gestures are dismissed as insincere or hypocritical. But the thing to realize about hip-hop is that it is an unabashedly spiritual art form, even if it espouses a kind of spirituality very different from what a casual (or disinterested) listener might expect.

Hip-hop's spirituality is related to its emphasis on feeling over seeing, faith over sight, and that isn't just for converts to Islam and the Five Percent Nation. It is also about a profound kind of brutal Christianity, the kind that allows MCs to gun down "bitches" on one track and sincerely praise God on another, without this necessarily being a contradiction. Instead, hip-hop offers another kind of religiosity, hip-hop's "you feel me" spirituality. This emphasis on "feeling" provides the foundation for hip-hop's incessant spirituality, its ubiquitous invocations of God in songs penned by the likes of DMX, 50 Cent, and R. Kelly (to name just three of the people most criticized for religious hypocrisy). These artists would tell you that you can't judge them because you can't "see" them, can't "feel" them—not really, not what's inside. God knows my heart, they declare, which is why Tupac Shakur could believe that nobody else was in a position to judge him. God can see into hearts, definitively spying *de cardio* racisms (or any other secrets) with no problem at all. And so, it's what you feel (in your heart of hearts) in the place where you commune with God alone, not what someone else thinks he can see (or even prove), that serves as the basis for hip-hop's claims of social invulnerability and purposeful inaccessibility. Sometimes what's in that heart might be drastically different from what you see on the outside. What you see can be the exact opposite of what you get.

Hip-hop's serious commitment to spirituality reveals the ways in which this powerful cultural form helps to transmit contemporary racial paranoia across the globe. Through both the narratives that artists emphasize in their songs and the media's irrational responses to hip-hop's potential violence, we uncover an important story about how different forms of paranoia coalesce at the center of this vibrant cultural space. From a discussion of "grafted devils" to claims about corrupt police officers and the government-sanctioned introduction of drugs and diseases into black communities, hip-hop music has helped to popularize and disseminate some of the most dominant stories of racial paranoia making the rounds today.

Hip-hop is stocked with paranoid stylings, and it is also an art form about which many people, fans and nonfans alike, have become increasingly paranoid. Perhaps no person exemplifies the perceived dangers of hip-hop's corrosive influence more than John Walker Lindh, the twenty-one-year-old white suburbanite from Northern California captured in Afghanistan in 2001 while fighting for the Taliban. America was slowly beginning to recover from the wreckage of 9/11, and Lindh's soot-blackened and scraggly-bearded face represented the country's worst nightmare: one of its own lined up staunchly on the wrong side of the country's newly declared "war on terror." Not too long after Lindh was apprehended, once journalists started to piece together his story, it became a little clearer how he had ended up waging war against U.S. soldiers, how he had gotten seduced into high treason. Hip-hop made him do it.

Before he converted to Islam, before he took off for Yemen and Pakistan to study Arabic, Lindh was a serious hip-hop fan. He knew all the big MCs, studied and memorized their lyrics, and even entertained thoughts of becoming a hip-hop artist himself.[13] He was one of those teenage "wiggers" and "wannabes" that Bakari Kitwana analyzes in his examination of hip-hop culture's appeal to white youth, including and especially young activists.[14] But Lindh didn't just enjoy hip-hop; he was obsessed with it. Lindh appears to have been so enamored with black culture that he seemingly wanted to be black himself, to claim hip-hop as his racial birthright. At the very least, Lindh pretended to be black whenever he could get away with it, "passing" while posting his thoughts about hip-hop all over the Internet in the mid-1990s.[15] Under a string of pseudonyms, Lindh left revealing traces of his complicated beliefs about the music and its superstars.

From what he wrote as a young white teenager (again, claiming to be African American), Lindh was a bit of a rap purist, if not an outright hip-hop snob. He attacked artists for "spreading stereotypes" and selling out to corporate America, sacrificing black interests for a lucrative recording contract.[16] Lindh dismissed NWA for celebrating the self-destructiveness of marijuana and malt liquor. He labeled Bay Area pimp-hop artist Too $hort a "house nigga" (a self-conscious reference to Malcolm X's already-mentioned critique). Too $hort, Lindh claimed, was "wacker than Marin County Caucasians," worse than the white folk Lindh knew and grew up with. In fact, Lindh was, himself, one of those very same Marin County Caucasians. Such low self-regard and disdain for his own local community undoubtedly played a crucial role in fomenting much of his angst, but hip-hop clearly provided the soundtrack.

Lindh had a problem with the politics of West Coast MCs, but he didn't just stick close to home. Old-schooler Marley Marl (one of hip-hop's New York pioneers) got blasted for "being fake like plastic" and crafting simplistic lyrics "to make money for the grafted." Lindh's reference to "the grafted" is important because it begins to hint at hip-hop's role in introducing him to his earliest understanding of Islam, long before he ever took off for Afghanistan. One of Lindh's first bits of sustained exposure to the religion came from hip-hop's connection to the Nation of Islam's version, where a diabolical black scientist named Yakub creates ("grafts") a demonic white race in his laboratory.[17]

While still in his mid-teens, Lindh seemed to so identify with hip-hop and some of the Nation of Islam–inflected beliefs of its early stars that he even attempted to embrace its mythological depiction of whites as laboratory-concocted devils, using that rhetoric to ground his criticisms of hip-hop artists as sellouts. Lindh was committed to blackness so thoroughly, so completely, that he felt immune to the sting of such antiwhite rhetoric, something similar to what neo-Nazi Leo Felton was able to pull off in New England at close to the same time.[18]

Felton, born to a black father and white mother in the 1960s, so identified with whiteness, with white identity, that he spent much of the late 1990s as an "Italian" neo-Nazi skinhead, starting fights with blacks (just because they were black) and plotting to blow up Jewish monuments in Boston. Felton actively and adamantly distanced himself from black Americans and clung to a relentless brand of white racism.

Questioned about this arguable contradiction, ostensibly being black while championing antiblack beliefs, Felton sounded like a seriously high-minded social theorist when he offered his response. Ask a group of academics in the sciences, humanities, and social sciences about race, ask them to define it for you and explain its significance, and chances are you'll get a potted answer about race being nothing more than "a social construction."[19] It isn't a real genetic and scientific fact, just a set of cultural beliefs hidden behind the facade of science. And Felton couldn't agree more. He doesn't think that race is biology, not at all.[20] In fact, he'd tell you, that is precisely the wrong way to understand it; you can't reduce racial identity to myths about genes and blood. Instead, Felton explains race as something you "feel" deep inside. It isn't material; it's spiritual, emotional. It is in your gut, your soul, your heart. And inside Felton's soul, deep down, he felt white, not black, regardless of his absentee black father or America's dogma about one drop of "black blood" disqualifying you from the purities of whiteness. Like Felton, Lindh seemed to invest in a version of race (at least as a teenager) that also cut against the grain of most people's assumptions about racial identification and even allowed him to spout (seemingly sincerely) racist principles about whites being "grafted" devils. He espoused this while managing to envision himself, a young white kid from northern California, as somehow exempt from its condemnation—except, of course, for the fact that he had to pass for black to do it.

Lindh eventually distanced himself more and more from the Nation of Islam's translation of that religion and from hip-hop culture altogether. But it had still been hip-hop that served as his point of entry into more orthodox forms of Islam. Hip-hop's expressions of religious belief started him out on his idiosyncratic journey to the front lines of Afghanistan through the careful study of groups such as Public Enemy and dismissive criticisms of just about everyone else. Hip-hop brought him to the altar and taught him a certain sense of spiritual discipline and reverence. Hip-hop gave Lindh his first substantial taste of Islam, and an undeniably American brand at that. John Walker Lindh represents one of white America's biggest paranoias about hip-hop music: it will turn their children into crazed and violent troublemakers. With Lindh as an "enemy combatant" alternative, controversial hip-hop superstar Eminem might not seem all that bad to any suburban soccer moms terrified by their kids' obsessive interest in hip-hop music and culture. But soccer moms shouldn't be singled out. Hip-hop artists have always recognized what Public Enemy once described as white America's more general "fear of a black planet" (i.e., wide-ranging panic that hip-hop culture will contaminate all of white America, transforming the nation in fundamental ways), and many hip-hop artists challenge such (imagined or real) white xenophobia quite directly in their lyrics, helping to illustrate the music's tricky relationship to African American versions of racial paranoia. Public Enemy's lead MC, Chuck D, once called hip-hop black America's CNN. He was absolutely right—and not just because it disseminates news straight from "the streets." It also packages that news for us, providing a sensationalist and skeptical framework for its social interpretation.

There have been some very high-profile cases of songs explicitly dealing with racial issues that many people would consider newsworthy. For example, hip-hop has crafted

many tunes emphasizing the fact that police in urban neighborhoods can't be trusted, black or white. The most famous
version of this is NWA's 1991 anthem "Fuck tha Police."
NWA rails against the entire Los Angeles Police Department for racial profiling, excessive force, corruption, and
the attempted murder of innocent black men. And the police only seem to do this, the group argues, because they'd
rather see black men struggling and in jail than thriving and
successful.

While there are innumerable references to such institutionalized racist practices throughout hip-hop, "Fuck
tha Police" transcends the topic, providing an example of
the move from racism to racial paranoia. For Ice Cube
and the rest of NWA, the fact that there are any crooked
officers indicts the entire police department, which is why
Cube can talk about the "bloodbath of cops" that he fan-
tasizes about killing in Los Angeles—and without compunction. Any person with a badge is implicated in the
racism of the few, and such a massive conspiracy is
thought to necessitate an equally extensive response.

NWA was hardly a group of Five Percenter or conscious
rappers, but many of their violent "gangsta" lyrics spoke
directly to paranoia vis-à-vis the police department and
other government agencies. There are no exceptions, and
everybody from the district attorney to the judge and war-
den are in on it. Hip-hop's emphasis on race, to the point
of racial paranoia, highlights what a conservative critic
like John McWhorter would disparage as racial fetishiza-
tion. But race was a fetish long before hip-hop got to the
scene, and it'll probably stay that way well after the next

new great musical genre has exceeded hip-hop's current popularity.

Like the Five Percenters and the Nation of Islam, many hip-hop artists believe that a good portion of what's most important about the workings of race in America are hidden, secret, even if they are actually quite "public secrets" that most people are simply afraid to invoke. Some hip-hop artists might actively distance themselves from (or downplay) the more mythical versions of these claims (about genetically "grafted devils" or a conspiring 10 percent literally working to help the devil gain world domination), but they still realize that racism is most powerful when it can't be seen, when it's lodged beneath the surface of things.

Hip-hoppers also highlight the *de cardio* subtleties of "perceived racism," of something qualitatively different from racisms of old. In his song "Mr. Nigger," for example, hip-hop MC Mos Def takes on racial profiling and overt racism, but the title of the song stems from his realization that there are probably very few times when he'll ever come up against the most brutal and shameless versions of racism, the versions that would have found whites calling blacks "niggers" to their faces only a few generations ago. So, Mos Def raps about how a racist cop will never explicitly say that he stopped a young black man because of race, but they'll both still "know" the unsaid truth. Mos Def realizes that whites are no longer willing to call blacks "niggers" in mixed company, but he is sure that they must still be doing it when they are alone—the same fear that Eddie Murphy parodied when he put on whiteface and went undercover in that *Saturday Night Live* skit.

Contemporary hip-hop artist Mos Def also declares (and this is where "racial paranoia" shows its sharpest teeth) that even if whites never say the word "nigger," their everyday "actions reveal how their hearts really feel." Mos Def cites flight attendants putting less water in black passengers' water glasses and double-checking to make sure that they really belong in first class when he talks about the global dynamics of racism. His examples are mostly based on reading between the lines of social politeness, deciphering euphemisms and practiced civility. But Mos Def still characterizes these *de cardio* racialisms as though he were describing the explicitly de jure kind. Mos Def equates the aforementioned slights with white people explicitly calling him a "nigger." He pretends that such a connection is absolutely certain and self-evident, leaving no room for doubt—which, of course, it does (even if his assessments are right). For Mos Def, even when he claims to see the telltale racist heart revealed, the behavior he actually chronicles is much subtler than that which his parents and grandparents would have generally had to interpret, more contestable than his definitive conclusions admit. They aren't less significant than earlier versions of racism, only stubbornly resistant to older models of disclosure and proof.

Chicago-based rapper Kanye West provides a representative example of how hip-hop links de jure, de facto, and *de cardio* forms of racism while carefully concealing its racial accusations altogether. Although he famously proclaimed that President George W. Bush "doesn't care about black people," he isn't always so unambiguous about racial matters in his lyrics. In his song "Heard 'Em Say," he rhymes, "And I know that the government administer aids. So I guess we just pray like the ministers say." West uses the double meanings of "administer" and "aids" to talk the talk of racial paranoia long before Hurricane Katrina. On one level, West is expressing the obvious fact that a government is supposed to aid its people, to provide assistance to citizens. But he's simultaneously voicing a profound skepticism by inferring that all folks can do then is pray, ostensibly because the government is not doing its job. But the implications don't stop there.

West also implies something even more sinister: the government purposefully administered (spread) AIDS to people. Not "aids," as in assistance, but AIDS, as in the disease that attacks the immune system, disproportionately infecting black women and men. This belief in AIDS as a man-made (government-deployed) drug has a long history. In fact, the Nation of Islam spent most of the 1990s arguing not only that AIDS had a suspicious etiology but that the drug provided to help those suffering from the disease, AZT, might do more harm than good to black people, advocating interferon as a safer alternative. Kanye West isn't a Five Percenter or a member of the Nation of Islam, but he does offer a version of racial paranoia (and racial-conspiracy theorizing) that is strikingly similar to theirs, using hip-hop's aesthetic and acoustic characteristics to disguise his accusations with polyvalent terminology that demands a close listen for complete comprehension.[21]

Are hip-hoppers right or just paranoid? If it is paranoia, is it "paranoia within reason" (as some anthropologists have labeled contemporary forms), another argument for not dismissing it out of hand?[22] With respect to African Americans, is this a "healthy paranoia" birthed from a cautious remembrance of America's sordid history of racial discrimination?[23] West's brand of paranoia is endemic to hip-hop, from the fears of crooked cops to DJs covering labels on the albums they "sample" so that other DJs can't steal their tunes. It isn't just the stuff of "grafted devils" that has hip-hop hardwired to deep-seated skepticism. Media outlets have exposed this skepticism and mistrust, some of which seems quite warranted. For example, those dramatic murders of Biggie Smalls and Tupac Shakur are shrouded in conspiracies and complicities. The 1990s have resulted less in fanciful Shakur sightings than in continued discussions about the possible depth of police complicity in his and Smalls's murders. Based on the work of investigative journalists following the Biggie Smalls case, there are certainly some strange ties linking major suspects to the Los Angeles Police Department.[24] This same adversarial relationship with law enforcement made it incredibly difficult to book hip-hop shows in many of the major venues throughout the 1980s and 1990s. There was a kind of "hip-hop tax" that raised the prices of those tickets relative to pop and heavy metal gatherings, even without hard evidence that hip-hop concerts produced markedly more actual violence. Sensationalized portrayals of hip-hop violence in the media seem to make concert promoters and city governments all the more paranoid about what might happen at a hip-hop performance in their town. Hip-hop has come to stand in for all kinds of potential violence, which means that hip-hop concerts are often treated differently, policed more stringently—and not just concerts.

I remember going to see the 50 Cent movie *Get Rich or Die Tryin'* in a suburb outside of Chicago in 2004 and being shocked to find police officers stationed inside the actual movie theater—not just in the lobby, not just on the sidewalk out front, but inside the movie theater itself. Six police officers stood at the front of the auditorium and watched us watch the film.[25]

In some ways, it makes sense that hip-hop brings out the paranoia in people. After all, it is a musical genre that highlights the role of racial paranoia in its very style and storytelling. The aesthetics of hip-hop promote open secrecies, the kinds that conspiracy theories thrive on. The acoustic layerings, the purposeful redefining of terms, and the verbal dexterities of its rhetoricians all promote a rigorous insiderism that shields casual listeners from some of hip-hop's more paranoid claims and fools them into missing the spiritual emphasis of the music, an emphasis that starts with a fundamental faith in "feeling" over seeing.[26] The more you can feel, the less you need to see. Literally.

In the 1998 film *Belly*, hip-hop MC Nas plays a well-meaning gangster and thief named Sincere, a hoodlum with a heart of gold. Even though he robs clubs for extra cash, we can still tell that he's a good person, that he really means well. God knows his heart, but so do we, the movie-goers. Sincere's partner, Tommy, played by hip-hop star DMX, actually morphs, by the end of the film, from a cold-blooded assassin into a sincere believer in the Nation of Islam–like religious organization that he was supposed to infiltrate and bring down for the government.

Made by hip-hop music-video director Hype Williams, *Belly* is about the dark impossibility of knowing what's inside other people—in their minds, in their hearts, in their souls, even in their bellies.[27] That philosophy, just like the hip-hop aesthetic described above, is carried over into the way the film is shot. Williams purposefully shoots the scenes dark, some almost pitch black, to the point that they seem underexposed. This darkness even makes it hard to see the action during certain sequences. You squint, use-lessly, trying to figure out what is going on. This emphasis on darkness, this humbling of vision and the access to knowledge it provides, is at the heart of the impenetra-bilities that hip-hop culture demands. And *Belly* is a great example of how those sensibilities—dark, spiritual and suspicious—follow hip-hop wherever it goes, even to the big screen.

CHAPTER 6

When Everyday Life
Becomes a Media Event

Not more than a couple of months after the attacks, a thirty-something New Yorker from Harlem talked with me about how traumatizing 9/11 had been for him. That fateful day, he flinched when both towers fell; he agonized over the unconfirmed stories of other hijacked planes in the air that morning. Even with all the angst and terror haunting him during that tragedy, he did find some solace in the fact that, despite it all, CNN was still covering everything, providing him with around-the-clock updates. He admitted that such hypermediation made things seem slightly less catastrophic somehow. It would have all been much more terrifying, he claimed, unbearable, if the cable feed had gone out, if the networks had been knocked off the air, and there had been no way for him to hear others (safely ensconced in their studios or braving it out "on location") relay a blow-by-blow account of what was happening. It was a kind of balm, even for someone who lived only a few short miles uptown from the soot, rubble, and death at ground zero. There was something faintly comforting about disastrous "breaking news" that wasn't so calamitous that it couldn't be properly framed and covered by the network news anchors. Even when we were all watching the towers fall, it was from a media vantage point made to seem all the sturdier for not succumbing to an equally horrifying fate.

Similarly, the parka-donning journalists delivering their pieces from the heart of the latest storm or its flooded aftermath provide the same kind of small-scale succor. Tragedies are somewhat (even imperceptibly) less tragic once the news media has found a way to narrate them, to summarize and recap their highlights. At the same time, the media help to place those tragic events more decidedly in the past—and they can do so almost immediately. Things are still present, clearly, the events only a few minutes or hours or days old, but this is a version of the present that journalists have found a way to package, frame, and review—over and over and over again, the same still images and candid video footage looped and rebroadcast.

Dave Chappelle's decision to end his successful sketch-comedy show with a spontaneous trip to Africa, Cynthia McKinney's infamous altercation with that Capitol Hill security guard, Gloria Naylor's claims about the government pummeling her brain with mind-control beams, Louis Farrakhan's conspiratorial queries about those breached New Orleans levees: these are all high-profile cases that millions of people followed in the media and discussed with colleagues around watercoolers, people irrevocably plugged into a global network that incessantly provides these kinds of stories.

We've all heard celebratory or ominous claims about the earth-shrinking speed of globalization, of seemingly instantaneous interactions across traditional geographical boundaries. Think of Thomas Friedman's catchy and persuasive description of the world as "flat," a powerful recuperation of pre-Columbian misunderstandings.[1] But this new flatness isn't just faulty planetary geometry. It highlights the extent to which our technological advances change the way we experience the world's massive interconnectedness.

We can receive almost immediate glimpses of the remotest parts of our world. We live in an age of rapid communication, experiencing the transmission of images and stories and rumors with blinking speed, as though our technological sophistication were finally catching up to our hardwired biological capacities. These fast-moving images allow us to pretend that we can see through our television screens and into, say, the tsunami-ravaged Indonesian coast—or even just to the other side of our city, where the latest metropolitan murder was committed. We live through most of our days negotiating incessant and omnipresent mass mediation. Media theorist Thomas de Zengotita describes this as living an inescapably mediated life, each one of us a "mediated person" awash in a broadcast-saturated world.[2]

Paranoia has characterized conceptions of the media for a long time, highlighting the kinds of irrational skepticisms and distrust that seem to always shadow technological innovations. Communications scholar Carolyn Marvin talks about electricity's beginnings (through oddities like telectroscopes and electronic corsets) as a way to challenge "progress" myths about efficiency as the singular engine for invention and technological development.[3] Technology is as much about culture as science, as much about traditional superstitions as newly discovered truths. Cultural historian Jeffrey Sconce shows that technological achievements in mass media actually promote hyperirrationalities among users, the kinds of irrationalities that cast machinery as, say, forms of witchcraft. And these irrationalities don't just define earlier deployments of media technology.

Anthropologists John and Jean Comaroff argue that our contemporary lives are defined by what they label "millennial capitalism," an irrational exuberance at the very core of an otherwise seemingly rational economic and social order. Even though we privilege reason as a guiding philosophical principle, we still sneak irrational commitments in through the back door of our everyday practices and desires. Sociologist Aneesh Aneesh contends that cutting-edge computer technology is only the latest and most powerful version of a long-standing attempt at "algocratic power," a form of rule by "the code" where alternative social options and irrationalities are already programmed out of possibility by the way machines predetermine our responses to them. Each of these scholars offers a different analysis of media technology, but they all hint at some of what makes it a key site of paranoid musings.[4]

During the early to mid-twentieth century, scholars began to canonize a version of media analysis that pivoted unapologetically on paranoia. Most famously, by the end of World War II, the so-called Frankfurt School theorists had created an influential body of literature reducing the mass media to mere ruse, a cover for (and ideological weapon of) fascism. They imagined it as only the newest example of what Karl Marx had already dismissively branded religion: an opiate of the masses, a tool for controlling people's political potential. To Frankfurt School thinkers, mass media meant "mass deception."[5] Not only did media producers exclusively control the meanings of their ideological offerings (with little wiggle room left over for audiences to redefine them), but they also found a way to impose that ideology onto just about every aspect of people's lives. There was no escape.

Critics argued that media makers pretended to provide what they could not. They even manufactured desires where there really were none. Nineteenth-century advertising agencies often called on the manipulative skills of hucksters from the "patent-medicine field"—fast-talkers with a gift for persuasion and sometimes a history of blatant misrepresentation—to market their wares.[6] According to the Frankfurt scholars, elites connivingly used the mass media to create "one-dimensional" human beings, distracted couch potatoes oblivious to the political maneuvers of the powerful.

Early critics called television's effects "narcotizing."[7] Media scholar Richard Butsch illustrates this skepticism of television by setting up a three-part story of mass media's history: our turn-of-the-century discovery of film was imagined to incite a kind of moblike mentality in viewers, catering to a chaotic crowd of savages, children, women, and

poor people. Although there were some positive developments in the 1920s and 1930s, which supposedly found
radio promoting democratic civic participation among
imaginative and active citizens, the invention of television a
couple of decades later caused America to backslide, producing pathetically atomized individuals ensconced in their
own private suburbias, "bowling alone" as Robert Putnam
famously put it, and unable or unwilling to enact full-
fledged civic engagement.[8] Where the Frankfurt School
might seem to lump all of the media together (Nazi propa-
ganda films, jazz-spewing radios, and newspapers' astrolog-
ical sections all being equally responsible for the destruction
of our critical faculties), Butsch sees a hierarchy in which
critics deem television much worse for us than radio and
film have ever been.

In other moments, people became even more paranoid
and suspicious of the television and radio, including some
scholars who penned pieces arguing that the electronic
media were being used to send the masses subliminal messages via hidden mind-control techniques, a broadcast version of the stuff Naylor describes in 1996. Journalists like
Wilson Bryan Key made a living in the 1970s and 1980s
arguing that there were hidden commands carefully placed
in mass-media broadcasts.[9] For Key, everything was really,
if subliminally, about sex. The media was loaded with secret invitations to sexual pleasure and fulfillment. Not only
was there little space for viewers to reject the media's
messages, but those messages were actually being carefully
engineered so that they could bypass our conscious brains
and head directly for our subconscious. What can the

viewer even hope to do against purposeful technological brainwashing?

The flames of paranoia are only further stoked by stories about the media's complicity in major cover-ups and scandals. In her analysis of one of the most widely discussed news stories in American history, President John F. Kennedy's assassination, Barbie Zelizer shows how easily journalists moved from simply investigating "the facts" to promoting themselves as authorities on them.[10] Gaps in knowledge, for instance, could be papered over for the sake of validating claims of journalistic expertise, a similar critique to the one leveled at anthropologists. And a lot more is being written about the impact of journalists (as real people) on our understanding of the news. Where Zelizer talks about journalistic coverage of a president's dead body, psychologist Anthony Feinstein wants to study the actual bodies of journalists themselves. Talking specifically about war journalists, he argues that we can't understand what's going on in places such as Afghanistan or Iraq without thinking about the emotional and psychological toll these regions have on the men and women charged with keeping us abreast of the situation there, a toll that must be informing the kinds of stories they write.[11]

In an analysis of why so many Americans seem to think that our government might have been involved in 9/11 (by making it happen, the hard version, or just knowing ahead of time and letting it happen anyway, the softer conspiracy theory), social critic Christopher Hayes also looks at journalists and how pathetically they sometimes cover the news.[12] Retooling and extending Zelizer's point, he argues that journalists aren't just interested in shoring up their own authority as presenters of truth; they also seem prone to taking what politicians say at face value. He argues that their lack of explicit skepticism or hostility (maybe to make sure that they can continue having access to important public figures) almost demands an oversuspicious pessimism from readers and viewers as a kind of stabilizing counterbalance.

According to many critics, journalists are already too comfortably in bed with the powerful, going to fancy cocktail parties, dancing with the stars, and becoming bona fide media celebrities in their own right. When cultural critic David Callahan claims that "Tipper Gore was right" for attacking mass-media excesses, he puzzles over why other Democrats seem so chummy with corporate capital's glossy bullhorn, Hollywood, and its branded movie icons.[13] Callahan thinks that Democrats mistake the left-leaning proclivities of many celebrity actors and producers for the right-wing structure of an entertainment industry that promotes sex and sensation for profit.

Meanwhile, Joseph Cappella and Kathleen Hall Jamieson maintain that media emphasis on style over substance in the coverage of politicians and their campaigns (partially a function of media makers' own cynicisms about American politics) is what actually fuels suspicion and distrust among American voters.[14] Whether they characterize the media's relationship to the power structure as overly cozy or cold, scholars blame much of today's heightened skepticisms on propensities specific to the current state of the mass media. The media's structure and design help to foment not just skepticism but racial paranoia.

Racial paranoia's social and psychological force, the substantial part it plays in people's understandings of race relations, is greatly augmented by mass-mediated stories, by their ability to accentuate and disseminate race-based suspicions across the nation and even the world. The media's very structure and style help to foment and embolden racial paranoia. The way we garner our information, through sensationalized overkill and hypercoverage, the twenty-four-hour news cycling of everything racial (from the latest drug bust of a celebrity athlete to the disappearance of white teenagers during Caribbean vacations), helps to create a different sense of daily living, a heightened racial everydayness, a rendition of ordinary life that seems threatened by the potential eruption of the extraordinary at every turn. And that eruption need not be on our block—or even in our hemisphere. Media coverage of everything from South Africa's apartheid to Haiti's political upheavals allows people to see race as a globally self-evident reality, something written on the strikingly similar bodies of human beings all across the world. The speed of global communication helps to grease the wheels of racial thinking by allowing us to confidently imagine that we can see the same few racial groups no matter where on earth our news crews point their cameras, making it easier for us to impose our culturally specific racial categories on groups halfway around the world (all because they look like the family who just moved in next door).

The fast-moving pace of our current news cycle combines with an insatiable market in sensationalism to dissuade many academics from entering that fray and going too public with their work. Faculty at leading universities feel that their colleagues will consider them less serious and rigorous if they get too "popular," too accessible. Anthropologists share these professional concerns, but they are also scared of going public for other reasons, especially because that often means they lose control of how their ideas about culture are appropriated. That's part of what happened in the 1960s and 1970s with the "culture of poverty" notion that anthropologist Oscar Lewis fashioned from his ethnographic research with poor Mexican families. Lewis was talking about the structural causes of negative cultural adaptations, but by the time his idea made it to Capitol Hill, it was mostly shorn of any discussion of structural forces at all, emphasizing culture as its own original and sustaining cause for poverty among certain groups.[15] That was an object lesson for many subsequent anthropologists, who shrank back from public debates for fear of future misappropriations.

The American Anthropological Association, a central organizational guild for anthropologists practicing in the United States, spends quite a bit of its time trying to get that spark back, to make sure that anthropology (a discipline based on face-to-face methods) stays relevant in an age of more mass-mediated social interactions. One of the biggest projects coming out of anthropology is the American Anthropological Association–sponsored multimillion-dollar RACE Project, a traveling "public education" museum that debuted in 2007. The point of the five-thousand-square-foot traveling exhibit is to "promote public understanding of myths and misunderstanding regarding ideas of race, racism, and human variation." It argues, in a nutshell, that race isn't real; racism is. The exhibit is set to travel around the country from 2007 to 2011, trying to disabuse people of their commonsense misconceptions about race.[16]

But if an emphasis on race brings anthropologists, and perhaps learned colleagues from other fields, back into the public sphere, the workings of the mass media can sometimes counter their momentum. Part of the reason why anthropologists continue to lose more and more of their public power is simple. It has to do with this "mediated" everyday world that scholars describe. Anthropology has never been a discipline based on conducting research with media and technology. That's exactly what anthropologists of the past were researching against. The discipline was formed to understand remote and "primitive" communities, those tribes and villages untainted by the vagaries of modern culture—those vagaries meaning, more than anything, the Industrial Revolution and its accompanying social transformations. The point was to treat these groups scientifically, using research on the lifestyle of hunter-gatherer societies to explain something about the preindustrial past of modern, mechanized Westerners.

The fact that the mass media can change the practices of a fairly obscure social science discipline is less important than the realization that those media also revolutionize the way we all experience everyday life, not just the ways it is studied. To understand 9/11 or Katrina is to understand how watching such events on television potentially changes the events themselves, as well as the people watching them. This is not like the fanciful notion that we are all living in our own private version of *The Truman Show,* our personal lives just television programs carefully produced all around us and without our knowledge. Instead, we are talking more about the kinds of lives lived by those television fans religiously watching Truman's life as it develops from infancy to adulthood all those many years. Do they do so at the expense of their own stories? Does it increase or decrease their ability to empathize with these mediated figures? Does it have to mean living life vicariously, in a kind of self-alienated way?[17]

We are always seeing ourselves through the images technology helps us to craft, forgetting that images produce mythological reflections of our own culturally skewed self-concepts. This odd discrepancy between mediatization and immediacy, the inescapable way our "media worlds" confound our everyday social worlds and the microsocial facts of face-to-face interactions, first hit home with me when I was still an undergraduate at Howard University in Washington, D.C.[18] My first year there coincided with the first years of a few other famous African Americans who decided to attend, including the infamous Tawana Brawley. As someone who grew up in New York City during the 1980s, I couldn't help but follow what was one of the biggest racial stories of the decade. Brawley was the black teenager who claimed that she was raped by six white men, including police officers and other state officials, in Wappinger Falls, New York. She was found smeared with excrement and with the word "nigger" scrawled all over her body.

The Reverend Al Sharpton was one of the activists who championed Brawley's case, demanding justice and using the media to make claims about a governmental cover-up, a conspiracy that he said extended all the way up to a New York State prosecutor, Steve Pagones, accused of being one of Brawley's rapists. When the grand jury finally met at the end of 1988, they didn't hand out a single indictment, which was read as either an indication of our racist judicial system or damning proof that Brawley's accusations were false, depending on who was doing the interpreting. What became very clear early on in the case, especially after Sharpton came on board, was that both sides would use the media as an important avenue to further sensationalize things in the court of public opinion. The sides were clearly drawn, and they still are, even if the mainstream media are quick to recap the Brawley saga, whenever they do, such as during the alleged-rape scandal involving the Duke University lacrosse team in 2006, as nothing more than an example of false racial allegations, end of story.

When we arrived at Howard in August of 1989, it only took a few weeks for word to spread around campus that Brawley had enrolled. And when I first met her, a very sweet and shy young woman with a magnetic smile, all of that media hysteria seemed very far away, like maybe it hadn't really happened at all. Although I never kept in touch with her after we left Howard, I do remember (especially as bright-eyed freshmen) the fabulous meals she prepared for a few of us, every once in a while, in her tiny campus apartment (most of us just had dorm rooms without kitchens). In fact, the first day my friends and I met her, she cooked us food and talked about school life as though none of what we all knew about her had ever taken place. But it had, and knowing how sweet and friendly she was to us, we all wanted to protect her from its aftermath, something we obviously couldn't do. At the time, Brawley was still a fairly big story in D.C. She was also in the midst of becoming Muslim, and we tried to support her with that as well. We even attempted, when we could, to intercept nasty hate mail left at the dorm's front desk for her, notes calling her every horrible thing in the book, notes left by black and white people alike.

We kept wondering, never bold enough to just come out and ask, what had really happened up in Wappinger Falls. How much of her story was true, and why didn't any of the facts stick? It wasn't that we didn't believe her. We mostly did. We had a somewhat contradictory response to the entire thing: one part dismissal of her accusations as a function of the grand jury's decision; one part unshakeable sense that anything we got from mainstream media sources about such a controversial subject would probably be suspect. We had grown up with a certain deep-rooted skepticism about the honesty of governmental officials and the fairness of the criminal justice system, and especially about the mass media. An alternative black press (black radio, black newspapers, black cable-access shows) based its founding premise on the discriminatory biases of the mainstream media. There wouldn't have

been a black press, at least not one organized as opposi-
tionally as ours historically has been, were it not for the
far-reaching fear that African Americans have always had
of mainstream media outlets and their investments in the
racial status quo.

With the fuller integration of black media professionals
into mainstream media venues after the protests of the
1960s, America still didn't end up with a black population
that fully trusted these mainstream media organs—or some
of the new black journalists who worked there. Or rather,
you had full trust and distrust at the exact same time—
pride, say, in the fact that Bryant Gumbel or Oprah Winfrey or Ed Bradley had achieved so much, but continued
misgivings about just how inclusive the media actually
were or about what backroom deals, what manner of "selling out," might have greased the wheel for particular
blacks' integration into the establishment. (That's why a
figure like Tavis Smiley is so fascinating: national appeal, a
pretty significant black following, or at least name recognition in diverse parts of the black community, and a media
profile that is decidedly countercultural, which helps to reinforce his credibility in certain skeptical black circles—all
that and his unapologetic Southern accent, usually masked
by mainstream media professionals who imagine that national legitimacy is compromised by any hint of a regional
dialect.)

I haven't spoken to Tawana Brawley since my early days
at Howard, but I still remember all those conversations we
had back then, when she wasn't around, about whether or

not she had lied, always coming to the same contradictory conclusion, the same impasse. She might have lied about something, but the media's ability to misrepresent and discredit demanded that we give her as much benefit of the doubt as we could muster.

Brawley's case created a national hysteria, but it was only an opening act for the race mongering that would characterize the O. J. Simpson case. Both of these scandals became racialized "media events" of the highest order. Danial Dayan and Elihu Katz write about "media events," describing them as ceremonial moments when television represents the social collective to itself, dramatically and ritualistically.[19] Dayan and Katz focus on special occasions such as royal weddings or presidential funerals, moments when the mass media frame the viewing of major events in ways that help to redefine the national (and even the international) community. Everyone is watching and appreciating that other people are doing the same—those people they know and the millions more they don't. Benedict Anderson has famously called this the making of "imagined communities," senses of togetherness and identification fostered by the media itself and subsequently crafted into politically charged social divisions.[20]

It doesn't just have to be preplanned media spectacles that serve as galvanizing and collectivizing media events, not just the live broadcasts of "contests, coronations, and conquests."[21] Some media events aren't planned. British scholar Paddy Scannell describes the latter events as "happenings," which simply befall us. He makes the distinction between "happenings" and "occasions" ("things we make to happen"), expanding the definition of media events from ceremonial occurrences to scandals and international disasters, which Dayan and Katz would readily concede.[22] This includes not just Lady Diana's wedding but also her tragic death in a Parisian tunnel, something that wasn't planned ahead of time (unless you believe another string of conspiracy theories, as some do, about government complicity in the accident). The attacks on the World Trade Center and the Pentagon in 2001 would be another obvious media event, as were the tsunami in 2005 and Hurricane Katrina. Dayan and Katz might object, but one could also add the disappearance of Natalee Holloway, the scandals around Mel Gibson's and Michael Richards's respective tirades, Cynthia McKinney's altercation, Chappelle's resignation, Paris Hilton's incarcerations, and so many other national news stories that seem to define the insatiable sensationalizing tactics of media news today. These are events we all watch, however distractedly. And we seem to be given very little choice in the matter.

Journalists and their camera operators are currently in Iraq all day, every day. And incessant reports come back to the United States about the number of car bombs, the rising death toll, plans for more troops, American reactions, the timetable for a pullout. The bloodshed and combat in Iraq are real, and human beings are dying there. But the Iraq war also constitutes a major and ongoing media event. Our experience of it here in the United States is undeniably mass mediated. It has almost become an event exclusive to its media coverage. This isn't exactly the same thing as French sociologist Jean Baudrillard declaring that the first Iraq war never took place, but he was trying to make a similar point about what happens when our experiences are so thoroughly covered by CNN and FOX News that they seem to lose a certain kind of experiential realness.[23]

Of course, many American families are directly impacted by the loss of loved ones in Iraq, but even that undeniable tragedy is often mediated: Cindy Sheehan's media-covered attempts to meet with President George W. Bush are just one example of that. Breaking coverage of 9/11 families debating the merits of a Hollywood rendition of their experiences is another; it's real and really mediated simultaneously. Even on the Iraqi side, where the war is right on top of the people living there and not just a faraway "news update," images of suicide bombers' last notes and terrorists' training videos inundate the airwaves. Saddam Hussein is hanged and a smuggled-in cell phone captures it for posterity.

Even when it isn't just about sensationalism, the media still can't help but act as a hothouse for cannibalistic journalism, feeding-frenzy reporting. If an editor at the *Washington Post* wants to avoid a sensational story that he think has no real merit, a kind of media-based gravitational force demands his paper take up the baton anyway—or else. To opt out is to risk accusations of irrelevance or even to create yet another "media event" as a consequence of that attempt. If NBC doesn't cover something the way other outlets are covering it (because they don't think it is a "real" story, as some people dismissed John Kerry's flubbed joke about the soldiers during the 2004 elections), the noncoverage itself will get coverage as but another ideological move from the left-wing media. Resistance, then, is really futile.

With incessant daily presentations of images and commentary on television, there is barely a notion of everyday life existing outside of these visualized media events that we all follow and debate. Racial paranoia is powered by the fact that everyday life has become a kind of televised media event, a series of tales that successively push one another out of the public's consciousness almost as quickly as they arrive. News media–propagated political scandals are examples (rewording Scannell even further) of things that we just make happen to us by further fetishizing them, obsessing over the next fifteen minutes of someone's celebrity or infamy before their eventual slide back into anonymity.

And this is part of the reason why Butsch might be right to place television in a separate category from film and maybe even radio (which almost operates as a kind of poor stepchild to the bells and whistles of TV). The point of the television is its ability to hail us directly and immediately. My wife and I recently hosted a party at our house and got so caught up with the fanfare inside that we hadn't the foggiest idea that police had arrived to cordon off the entire block at some point during the evening. I only found out about it when I walked a guest out the front door and was met by flashing lights and several police vehicles lined up at both corners. The first thing we did, of course, was turn on the television to see if one of the news channels had a "breaking" story about what was going on up the street. When that didn't materialize, we decided to check the 11 P.M. news for some kind of summary (long after the officers had left) of what the "bomb scare" (as one of my neighbors claimed it had been) was all about.

At no point did anyone think to step outside and speak with a police officer or to call the local precinct for specific facts about what had happened. We simply turned on the television and hoped to catch a report about this seemingly minor interruption to our otherwise festive evening. And if there wasn't a news story on the event during that evening's broadcast, it couldn't have been all that big a deal anyway.

It is the idea that "breaking news" can burst open the preplanned schedules of network affiliates that makes television so different from film. Even the Internet and radio, which have similar breaking-news dynamics, seem like little more than consolation prizes compared to the high-definition moving images of the television screen. Everyday life has become a kind of media event because of broadcast television's twenty-four-hour potential for such interruptions. This palpable potential for media interruptions, the breaking story, at any and every moment, cuts into the mundane everydayness of life; it's a feature that even determines whether we think "a police action" on our very block is worth ending a party early.

Newspapers add gravitas to this with their graphic headlines and verbiage. Radio stations provide a greater sense of ubiquity with their background soundtracks. Even motion pictures confirm the significances of past media events by immortalizing them in celluloid for the big screen, events that are now irrevocable parts of both history and popular culture (think of Oliver Stone's *JFK* and *World Trade Center* as two big-budget examples). Of course, since most of these concocted media events are not usually as intrinsically significant as the two events highlighted in the Stone movies just mentioned, to wait for Hollywood films about most of them is to risk a resounding "so-what" many years down the line. So the fast-tracking of these fictional stories, while the iron is still hot, leads to the much-maligned made-for-TV movie, the fate of tales about lower-form media events probably doomed to obscurity or irrelevance in the not-so-distant future. The only other option is that they will be resurrected much, much later by Hollywood, generations after the fact, but not as a hot topic of discourse, not as something ripped from the headlines, but more as a probing drama about some interesting, if forgotten, part of Americana. Imagine something like *Wappinger Falls* starring Meagan Goode. It could be a small "independent film" for which it would probably be all the better if people have already forgotten the original incident. Then ABC News could produce a substantive piece about the actual 1989 case during the film's opening weekend.

The civil rights and black power movements were media events even as they unfolded in the streets. And they have now morphed into a different kind of media event as we relive their canonized moments through popular footage of marches and protests, of water hoses and national guardsmen, of Angela Davis's Afro and George Wallace's gruffly barked defiance. "In its most radical stage," political scientist Adolph Reed writes, "black power lived and spread as a media event."[24] Maybe it does so even more now as powerful, grainy-filmed mementoes: those VHS copies of *Eyes on the Prize* collecting dust in university video libraries across the country.

When everything is a potential media event, there is a very real danger of flattening out important differences between more and less significant incidents. O. J. Simpson becomes the same as Robert Blake becomes the same as Michael Jackson becomes the same as Lindsey Lohan becomes the same as Winnie Mandela becomes the same as Malcolm X—ad infinitum. I'm part of that generation born without any direct experience of the civil rights movement. Thankfully, I've encountered the most blatant and dehumanizing forms of racism, at least in my adult life, as something that happens in movies or TV news footage, something rendered vividly in history books. Seeing all of this past racism (which was still unapologetic and unashamed in the years just before I was born) and being familiar with its long-standing and entrenched nature (in popular culture, in the elite halls of the academy, in American electoral politics) makes many blacks all the more surprised at how quickly it has been removed from public display, replaced with black-and-white news footage and motion pictures about life under Jim Crow.

Even if you haven't experience it in the present, if you didn't live through "the struggle," Public Broadcasting Service (PBS) documentaries and other mass-mediated narratives may be better anyway because they have an otherworldliness or "othertimeliness" to them, not to mention a positive ending: blacks win legal equality. I gave a talk on racial paranoia at a New England college, and a young black assistant professor, with tears in his eyes, described how his parents and grandparents had withstood the viciousness of Jim Crow and the angry white backlash against the civil rights movement. His point was that, for him, that era wasn't just a PBS documentary; it was also family history, which is true for many African Americans. He's right, but that doesn't mean that it hasn't also become a newfangled kind of media event, another way we watch footage of our collective past to reproduce ourselves as slightly reimagined communities.

Of course, none of this is to say that the media simply cause racial paranoia. Even if we can criticize particular instances of media coverage for clear racial biases, the mass media also serve as one of the few spaces left that consistently forces Americans to talk about race and racism—and not always politely. At the same time, in a world overrun by media events, few things play as well as the unveiling of paranoid fears. In fact, paranoia itself has been reduced to a mere media event. Ominous stories about attempted racial genocide (supposedly engineered by some fast-food chain or soda company) get labeled "real" simply because someone claims that they have a friend who saw a "special" about it on *Oprah* or PBS or somewhere.[25] Of course, the most distrustful racial paranoiacs harbor a

sneaking suspicion that any and all of these racially inflected media events are little more than distractions from
even harder-to-see racisms, the ones never caught on camera, never discussed on *Nightline*, the kinds that really,
truly should have us spooked.

Conclusion

The Vulnerabilities of
Multiracial Citizenship

In the early 1970s, psychologist Joseph White penned what is now one of the most classic formulations of black paranoia as a reasonable response to white racism. "Part of the objective condition of black people in this society is that of a paranoid condition," he writes. "There is, and has been, unwarranted, systematic persecution and exploitation of black people as a group. A black person who is not suspicious of the white culture is pathologically denying certain objective and basic realities of the black experience."[1] As sports writer Ralph Wiley once evocatively put it, these same racial suspicions are part of the reason "why black people tend to shout."[2]

More than three decades after White's initial formulation, racial paranoia still exists. It might be most comprehensible (to some people, maybe even obvious) at the abstract and macrosocial level that White highlights, but it is often far more difficult to judge and resolve during specific interpersonal exchanges, especially since America has powerfully and importantly shunned public displays of overt racism. Even if "black people as a group" might still be justified in displaying some general distrust of white America writ large (already a controversial contention), "the time-tested skepticism in black communities" must still provide space for distinctions between and among particular white citizens that blacks meet while going about their daily lives.[3] And most black people are crafting just such finer-toothed distinctions all the time. For comedian Dave Chappelle, it was only one white crewmember who seemed to be laughing at his blackfaced shtick in an ostensibly racist way, not every single white person on set. He was still paranoid, and he probably left for Africa because he knew a lot of people wouldn't be able to understand, or even believe, his racial suspicions.

The first step to take in combating *de cardio* racism and racial paranoia demands admitting that they exist and allowing people to express their racial fears out in the open, no matter how seemingly unwarranted or intuited. We can't pretend that *de cardio* racial fears aren't worthy of analysis simply because they don't resemble the de facto and de jure varieties. We live in a world where people still don't trust across racial lines, no matter how uncomfortable they feel about making that fact known in mixed company. Of course, part of the reason why *de cardio* racism's claims are dismissed out of hand usually stems from the fact that we want to be able to recognize racists in some clear and obvious way—even when we can't. As we pat ourselves on the back over past racial victories, we must realize that those same positive and necessary gains have only forced racist perspectives farther underground into intraracial "safe" spaces where people can vent about "others" under the cover of communal sameness. Only once we begin to move beyond self-satisfaction about the successes of the civil rights era can we start to solve the newest versions of race-based distrust that characterize contemporary American life.

Racism is still "an American dilemma," but it is a dilemma that has been transformed by the structural changes remapping our country's social hierarchies: the move from chattel slavery to sharecropping and agriculture to urbanization, the migrations from South to North, and the radical renunciations of blatantly racist social policies. We inhabit a new racial world, one where the racial masters and slaves have rewritten their positions on overt forms of race thinking. Where the white master could once talk about black slaves with little fear of state-sanctioned reprisals, now white America feels much more constrained in its racial discourse. Where black slaves once watched their every word (or lived with the threat of violent silencing), African Americans boast of telling it like it is and "keeping it real" no matter what. We need new methods and ideas to deal with our newest experiences of *de cardio* racism and racial paranoia. Someone doesn't have to scream "nigger" in a crowded grocery store for racism to be real, even if the subtleties of its current manifestations test our limits of social analysis and confound our traditional tools for recognizing racial animus.

Of course, as real as racial paranoia might be (especially among minorities in America), it usually doesn't constrain people's every move. Blacks aren't simply functional paranoiacs, a term that seems to imply flimsier incorporations of paranoid worldviews into people's everyday lives in ways that fall far short of producing a full and prosperous existence. Being racially paranoid means more than just existentially scraping by, barely able to cope with an otherwise debilitating phobia. And most African Americans don't let their fears about cloaked racial injustice and hatred totally incapacitate them. This resilience defines black versions of racial paranoia, versions that don't allow minor slights, *possible* racial slights, to completely wear them down. These are African Americans with tales of being conspicuously trailed in fancy boutiques and of not getting enough cream cheese spread on their orders at local delis (white patrons are supposedly served bagels overflowing with the stuff). They complain about social workers consistently giving them "funny" looks in government buildings and lament being subjected to wisecracks about "Congressional Black Caucus conventions" whenever they get together with one or two of their black colleagues in an office hallway. It is precisely these relatively minor issues that fuel racial paranoia: they are its bread and butter, the coin of its realm. The smaller the slight, the more telling its *de cardio* implications.

Once we give credence to such experiences and admit that racism persists and is now fundamentally different from any of its previous incarnations, we must next prepare ourselves as individuals and as a society for the task of actually dealing with the thorny issues of contemporary racial distrust and cynicism. We have to actually commit ourselves to doing something about it. This is the paramount issue. Do Americans want to deal with race? Are Americans willing to invest their time and their trust in one another? At the very least, are they willing to see the racial disparities that continue to define important social and economic differences between and among the citizenry?

Even with formal equality and public espousals of color blindness, America's racial gaps persist. Social scientists such as Troy Duster, Joe Feagin, Marjorie Shultz, Eduardo Bonilla-Silva, and David Wellman compellingly argue that race-based social differences are a result of structural racism, not black or Latino cultural pathologies or race-based genetic deficiencies. They also emphasize that contemporary racial discrimination isn't only about prejudice or conscious racial malice. Reducing racism to conventional forms of blatant white bigotry, they argue, completely misses the point.

Economist Glenn Loury argues that racial inequality's stubborn intractability is a decidedly American creation, not a result of inferior African proclivities stowed away with slaves during their transatlantic trip to the New World. He joins social psychologist Claude Steele in arguing that racial stereotypes and stigmas have real productive force, that they have the power to create specific social outcomes. According to Loury, "Racial stigma should be given pride of place over racial discrimination" if we ever want to figure out why racism and racial injustice persist and how they translate into social misery.[4] And with the increased economic vulnerability of all Americans, blacks and other minority groups boxed into the margins might be disproportionately afraid of sliding even further down the social ladder—or of secretly being pushed.

As political scientists Melissa Harris-Lacewell and Andrea Simpson have shown, black people's thoughts on white America are far too complex and multifaceted to be taken for granted.[5] Their positions can't be packaged as a singular perspective and tied up with a neat black bow. And the same should be said for racial paranoia. I've met many African Americans who claim complete obliviousness to any of the relatively inconsequential incidents that drive race-based social fears. They don't sweat the small stuff. They don't worry about racists, won't allow other people's narrow-mindedness to slow them down.

Invoking "paranoia" at all might be dismissed as just the kind of move rebuked by historian of social science Daryl Scott, who claims that blacks are too often cast as psychologically damaged goods. This rhetoric of racial damage is asked to do the work of making a case for why, say, segregation is harmful and should be outlawed. When psychologists Kenneth and Mamie Clark showed that black kids preferred white dolls over black ones, they enshrined a version of internalized black pathology that Scott imagines as a kind of Faustian racial pact. It concedes black inferiority and pathology for the sake of collective advancement up America's social ladder. It accepts a damaged premise as a way to catapult the race "from savage to Negro," in anthropologist Lee Baker's memorable phrasing of things. Scott argues that black humanity and dignity get lost along the way and that social scientists "should place the inner lives of people off limits."[6]

In fact, for many of the social scientists mentioned above, racial paranoia already takes the emphasis away from structural issues, placing it on the psyche of blacks themselves. The focus on racial paranoia might be interpreted as yet another way to de-emphasize the significance of race (all we have now is racial paranoia, not real racism) or to paint one more dysfunctional portrait of black folks as a means of letting white racism off the hook (see how political correctness has created a pathologically paranoid black psyche that sees racism everywhere; so just call blacks "niggers" again, and maybe we'll all be better off).

None of these positions does justice to the complicated nature of our present situation or to racial paranoia's social and political importance. I do want to argue that racial paranoia isn't racism, but racism is also still alive and well (even in its more explicit guises). I don't want to privilege individual psyches over larger structural forces. In fact, I want to argue that a structural transformation in the American racial order created current versions of race-based paranoia. All I suggest is that we not simply reduce accusations of racism to simplistic assessments of truth or falsehood. We shouldn't just try to vet them for provable accuracy and then go on to something else once we think we've shown a particular allegation to be unfounded. Instead, I want to remind us that we now live in a political atmosphere that promotes racial dissimulation and insincerity. The self-conscious parsing of racial speech brings a certain kind of distrust and bad faith into the center of every interracial conversation, even if through the back door and against some people's best intentions.

Political correctness nurtures contemporary forms of racial paranoia, forms that turn earlier American versions of racial indifference and cruelty on their heads. This upside-down world of racial suspicion and mistrust, a world that merges with our carefully manufactured culture of a political correctness, is one of the legacies of slavery and Jim Crow that can't be easily defeated with silent marches or courageous sit-ins. Racial paranoia is about the kinds of social impasses created when people can walk where they want, eat where they'd like, and still have the sneaking suspicion that the folks pouring them their coffee or passing them on the sidewalk might really not be all that happy to see them—and even more, disgusted that they can't make that unhappiness plain. It may be true that African Americans "are less concerned with what white people think about them than what they do to them."[7] But today's not-so-telltale heart can harbor secrets about potential racist actions (or purposeful inaction) in the not-so-distant future.

This is not just a racial story. Most of the current controversies in national and international headlines are specifically based on the slippage between what people say and what they might really mean, between politically acceptable discourses and the potentially ugly intentions hidden beneath them. I've been talking mostly about blacks and whites in the United States, but the same *de cardio* invisibilities that fan the flames of racial paranoia in a politically correct American culture are at the center of other debates. Take two of today's most controversial national issues: immigration and global terrorism. The immigration debate in the United States today is rhetorically distinct from traditionally more blatant forms of xenophobia. For one thing, there is little mention of race as a biological excuse for discrimination at our borders. Everything is about culture, not biology—cultures at war, cultures clashing, cultures under siege. Literary critic Walter Benn Michaels is just the loudest voice warning us against such weaponized versions of culture, versions that serve as little more than euphemisms for the entrenched racisms of old.[8]

Samuel Huntington's *Who We Are* is one of the most famous examples of such "culture" talk in the immigration debate.[9] He posits distinctively American cultural values threatened by Mexicanization. But this culture talk is careful to dissociate itself from old-time racisms. Likewise, CNN's Lou Dobbs doesn't phrase his tirades in exclusively racial terms but, instead, talks of safety, jobs, and terrorism. The attacks on Dobbs and Huntington still level charges of racism at them, but this isn't the unabashed racism of *Birth of a Nation,* D. W. Griffith's 1915 celebration of the Ku Klux Klan's valiant fight to reclaim the South from carpetbaggers and evil freedmen. Dobbs and Huntington aren't Klansmen and would never celebrate that part of America's history. But they still don't escape suspicion, fears about ulterior motives, about hidden animus and ill will. This is the stuff of *de cardio* racism. One side can't easily prove it; the other can't shake the accusations.

President George W. Bush argues that Iran's regime can't be trusted about its nuclear intentions because President Mahmoud Ahmadinejad can say one thing and do something totally different. Of course, Ahmadinejad also says things that are objectionable (reports of unabashed anti-Semitism that wouldn't be tolerated quite the same way in America's public sphere), but Bush is most skeptical about Iran's claim that it only wants nuclear energy for peaceful ends, nuclear energy that the Russians are helping to provide. Of course, even if Bush has Ahmadinejad pegged, we are talking about a geopolitical context in which the Iranian leader can't admit that he wants to use nuclear weapons against the West, which already helps to explain his difference from an Osama bin Laden. Anthropologist Roxanne Varzi channels this discrepancy (between what Iranians say and do) in a completely different direction, arguing that Iranian young people don the visual signs of acquiescence to Islamicist mandates even when they don't necessarily believe them, not in their heart of hearts, at least not the way an outsider might think. Varzi pins the hopes for Islamic democracy on the fact that Iranian youth can wear the clothing of religious orthodoxy without truly buying into the legitimacy of a hard-line version of infallible theocracy.[10] They can all wear the same religiously inflected clothing and believe very different things underneath it.

The idea that individuals could be hiding secrets is exactly why, for instance, "rendition" (sending "enemy combatants" to other countries for interrogation) has become such a hot story. We are told that it might take serious, possibly torturous, techniques to get to the deeper truths behind suspects' lies and deceptions. It is a higher-stakes version of the same issue that makes gossip magazines and TV shows so universally popular. It explains why we want to make functional magnetic resonance imaging the next holy grail of mind reading. We crave backstage access to people's thoughts because we know that there are some juicy secrets lodged somewhere back there.

Of course, in all of the *de cardio* scenarios we might imagine—illegal aliens working off the books, dangerous terrorists pretending to be hardworking American dreamers, black potential drug dealers driving their expensive cars—we don't always know who is who, not definitively, so racial profiling is an attempt to short-circuit uncertainty by stopping everyone who fits a general type. Then we'll see what they're up to, be it a black motorist in a fancy BMW on I–95 or the "Arab-looking" man in seat 3B. Racial profiling says, okay, fine, I'll just assume the worst and see if I'm right, so you better not be hiding a secret. You can't tell a modern racist by just looking. There are no indisputable physical features, no phrenological evidence in the shape of a skull about hidden traits or beliefs. To use a Rumsfeldian truism, "we don't [even] know what we don't know" about other people's racial feelings, but we try our best to find out.[11] And racial profiling is what happens when these unchecked desires and fears meet the destructiveness of "bad-faith" politicking, a dangerous combination.

When you wire skepticism and paranoia directly to questions of racial discrimination and inequality (and in a context where economic inequality is rising just as social safety nets are deteriorating precipitously), you then have a perfect storm for severe responses to severe times.[12] When you can't trust what you see, when what you see is probably not what you really get, you open the door for theories about Church's Chicken and Evian water and anything else that might be a hidden sign of what people are really feeling, really scheming.

Recent declines in blatant acts of racism might actually promote, ironically enough, more fear and distrust between racial groups, not less. Of course, it is still important to combat racism, but to fight racism in 2008 the way we fought racism in 1968 is to ignore important details of context and history. Moreover, political correctness alone, in some kind of larger policy vacuum, just makes a bad situation worse. Racial paranoia is a way of thinking about race and fearing racism that is immune to outward signs of racial acceptance and benevolence. Using the logic of racial paranoia, repressing discussions about race, or framing them in sanitized and acceptable ways could just be another strategy to avoid sanctions against hidden racist feelings. Public tolerance doesn't necessarily mean the absence of racism, and liberalism might just as likely be a cover for continued racial malice, racism with a poker face instead of a Klansman's mask.

That's exactly why the anti-Semitic ramblings of drunken Hollywood moviemakers and the angry racist outbursts of frustrated stand-up comics, outbursts laced with rage-filled name-calling and nostalgic remembrances of when whites could lynch blacks with impunity, are significant "racial events." It isn't just that they distract us from more serious questions of institutional racism and structural inequality. These aren't only major news stories because sensationalist mass media want to milk them for all they're worth. These moments also pull the rug out from under the politically correct niceties that some African Americans fear might be a cover for the same old racisms, just hidden in the rafters in stead of poised center stage.

According to the logic of racial paranoia, when push comes to shove, the racists will show their faces (maybe not tomorrow, but at some point), making a lie of America's claims of racial inclusion. This is why Michael Richards provided such an provocative story in 2005 and why many African Americans in the northern half of the country sometimes claim to yearn for the psychological upsides of Southern racists of old, people honest enough to at least let them know where they stand.

These fears about *de cardio* racism are prevalent among all Americans, not just African Americans, and they de-mand a different discussion about racism than we are trained (by civil rights activists and policy analysts) to have with one another. These nonfalsifiable suspicions about secretly racist hearts also further highlight the fact that race isn't just an intellectual idea that we can easily persuade people to disavow. As the stories in this book try to show, race is about emotion, affect, intuition. *De cardio* racism places a premium on what you sense, on something you feel, not on whether you can definitively prove those suspicions in any particular case.

How should society respond to these feelings, these un-verifiable instincts? The point isn't just to dismiss racial paranoia out of hand, to demand that people provide ir-refutable evidence for their accusations or shut the hell up already. Instead, we should think seriously about what these claims can teach us about race's stubborn obduracy, about its resistance to proofs and standard empirical confirmation.

Of course, researchers have already started trying to measure some of these subtler racial prejudices in experi-mental versions of what sociologist Orlando Patterson dis-missively labels "gotcha psychology," social-psychological research on what's been called "implicit prejudice," re-search claiming to show that Americans who think of them-selves as liberals still harbor ingrained racial biases against blacks. Asking test takers to quickly link black and white faces to positive and negative attributes, one famous Har-vard study stresses the fact that most respondents, liberals and conservatives, whites and even blacks, tend to have a hard time instinctively assessing black faces positively.

Some critics downplay the significance of Americans' publicly concealing their racial biases in mixed company, even as some of these same naysayers admit that most blacks and whites don't have many substantial relationships with one another. In fact, political scientist Robert Putnam argues that Americans who live in diverse communities are more likely to disengage from civic life than those who live in homogenous racial and ethnic enclaves. This just further highlights fellow political scientist Diana Mutz's persuasive contention that "participatory democracy" (civic engagement, people rolling up their sleeves and taking part in political life) and "deliberative democracy" (substantive discussions about political life) operate at cross-purposes to one another.[13] If the lack of racial intimacy breeds distrust, the increase of interracial contact only makes good-faith social dialogue and interaction a casualty of that social mistrust. Social distance can make the heart grow frightened, but it takes more than just passing a diverse array of strangers on the street to allay those fears.

On an interpersonal level, dealing honestly with racial paranoia means going out of your way to make friends across racial lines. It's trite, I know, but it is profoundly important. Most people don't inherit a multiracial social network. They are used to using that fact to justify their long-held fears about other social groups. Instead, combating racial paranoia means demanding that you don't reproduce racial segregation within your own social circles. When you're on the job, make sure you are having substantive relationships across racial lines. How many blacks have told me about whites who are kind and sweet at work but have never invited them home for dinner, never eaten with them at lunch? Or how many blacks might be kind to whites and still stop short of inviting them home to do the same? Even if it is uncomfortable the first time, it gets easier, especially if everyone is doing it.[14] In the years after many battles have been fought and won in America's

courtrooms, such personal initiatives can be decidedly political acts.

Fighting racial paranoia also means renting apartments
and buying homes with an eye toward ethnic and racial diversity in your neighborhood. You don't want to be a gen-
trifying urban pioneer, but moving out of a neighborhood
to get away from the ethnic minorities moving in (even if
one justifies it in strictly financial terms) is the wrong mentality to have. Figure out how to forge relationships. Even
if you think about it just in calculated and self-interested
terms, having a bigger house in a gated community in a dying country isn't victory. It's delaying (say, for your children to deal with) an inevitably ugly social endgame. Don't
be afraid to fight for your neighborhood by finding ways of
making newcomers feel welcome—and beating back your
own knee-jerk or family-taught biases.

If your kids only live in one America, the America of lav-
ish homes, relatively safe streets, and only a few token
minorities, they are being primed for reactionary racial
politics—whether they're black, white, or any other ethnicity. This isn't to say that you have to count the number of
blacks or Latinos in their daycare centers, but it should
worry you that they haven't had substantive relationships
with children of different racial backgrounds. Addressing
racial paranoia means actually teaching your kids to see
race, not to be oblivious of it. The issue isn't whether or
not we can see racial differences (for the immediate future,
we're stuck with that faulty biological notion). The issue is
how we see them. We should force ourselves to spy race all

the time. When we don't see such differences (at our parks, jobs, parties, and school functions), we should be afraid. *Look for race. Don't look away from it.*

You're not searching for scapegoats or stereotypes but to see who isn't there—and to think about why. That doesn't mean you're obsessing (even though race may not be a bad thing to obsess about productively anyway); it means you are aware that your kids only see racial difference when they spy the black nannies watching other people's babies in the parks or when greeting the workers who serve them lunch or clean their hallways at school. See race. And be mindful of when you don't see it. Not to see race in 2007 is to perpetuate a color blindness that might feel psychologically helpful (in the short term) but will only prove socially and politically catastrophic over the long haul. That doesn't mean you boycott your child's daycare center until it buses in more kids from the other side of the tracks, but it does mean making sure the absence is publicly noted, thematized, and discussed, not just taken for granted or relished (as a way to keep out the "problem children").[15]

It means listening to other people's positions, even if you just think of those perspectives as utterly self-serving. See how they justify those beliefs. What evidence do they use? How do they make pleas to universality and justice over simple self-interest and bias? Even the worst racists in the world imagine their positions to be just and moral. How do they do that? Where are the tensions within their own arguments? And ask the same questions of your own beliefs. Interrogate them. Challenge them. It's always much easier to see other people's racial biases, but make it your business to peel back the layers of your own taken-for-granted assumptions about race and difference. Be honest with yourself by first really listening and challenging yourself about race. The point isn't just to change your own mind or to punch holes in your own arguments, and there's always a limit to how self-conscious and self-reflexive we can even be. But the internal search for such honesty can make us less hubris filled in our racial pronouncements about the rest of the world. There is little we know about the larger racial landscape, little we take for granted about races and their differences, that we don't simply and naively accept based on socialized bias and cultural conventions. We are all race gamblers, and we bet the odds that we (very unscientifically) think we see. We have to unlearn those odds. Winning one small hand today might mean losing the house tomorrow.

As a voting bloc, are there policies people cognizant of racial paranoia's power should champion? Legislation they should push? There probably aren't particular pieces of legislation that will magically dissolve paranoid fears or *de cardio* racism, but we do have to make sure we commit ourselves to policies that place a premium on color consciousness, on all the ways that we might need to beat back the unhealthy and undemocratic irrationalities fueling our more short-sighted commitments to racial segregation. We promote racial paranoia when we combine discussions about color blindness with silent acceptance of continued structural differences in racial realities.

At the same time, race isn't a smoking gun. It doesn't explain, all by itself, every social issue in America —not even close. Katrina wasn't simply and exclusively about race, even if much of the media painted the situation in such a monochromatic way. It is always about race and racism seasoned with other forms of prejudice, indifference, and hate. So, we need social policies that don't just assume one well-placed shot will do. We also require ways of policing ourselves against our own worst tendencies, those that don't simply go away with the enactment of new laws. We must battle race as much in custom as in law, on the basketball courts as much as in the courtrooms. If people don't feel comfortable around other human beings because of supposed racial difference, they are sick. They have a problem. And the first thing to do on the road to recovery is to admit that. To the extent that political correctness doesn't provide space for folks to sincerely express their fears about others, it is a very real public victory that masks a different kind of social failure. The less that gets said in the public sphere, the more that must be getting vented backstage—in the many racially exclusive social settings Americans gladly perpetuate. Dealing with such unknown and hidden possibilities is an important part of what makes us human. We've had to negotiate the threat of potentially concealed bad intentions for almost as long as we've been on the planet, and that usually means finding other ways of plucking certainty from the firm grip of doubt, a truly magical feat, and in more ways than one.

British social anthropologist E. E. Evans-Pritchard was famous for studying "primitive" religions and arguing that even some of their most sensational aspects are fairly rational responses to pressing social problems and existential uncertainties. Take the Azande[16]: for them, there is no happenstance in the social order. Nothing just occurs by chance. An early death, a bad crop, a serious injury—all the outcome of one thing and one thing alone: witchcraft. Evans-Pritchard is quick to point out that the Azande understand that there are "natural" causes for events in the world. If lightning strikes a tree, and the tree falls, they know that the lightning caused it. But if the tree falls on a house while a family is eating dinner inside, the arbitrariness of nature just won't do. The Azande will remain suspicious about the specifics. Sure, the lightning fells a tree that destroys a home, but why that home, and why when those particular people were inside? The only explanation for such detail, according to the Azande, is witchcraft. They know what "caused" the tragedy, but they still have to make sense of "why" it happened. And witchcraft is always the best answer for questions of particularity when it comes to social tragedies.

Racial paranoia is a different version of a similar understanding. Sure, there are proximate causes for misfortunes, obvious chains of events that culminate in horrible misfortunes. But why these particular tragedies, and why do they seem to affect one group disproportionately? To make sense of the "why" demands more than just the laws of nature, more than talk about the physical causes of lightning. If the tree had fallen and there were no socially meaningful consequences to that event, the Azande would highlight "nature" as an open-and-shut explanation. Once the laws of nature translate into the senselessness of social calamity, however, a set of suspicions kick in, suspicions not too different from the racial paranoia we've been discussing here. It isn't that nature doesn't act erratically—it sure does—but that alone can't possibly do enough to fully explain why someone in particular is singled out for destruction, especially if that person is just minding his own business, eating a meal with his family when a tree squashes them to a pulp at the dinner table—not the house next door, not the house down the street, but their particular house, and right on their heads.

Racial paranoia imagines trees falling all over the village, but mostly on the houses of certain racialized community members. Trees upon trees upon trees fall—to the point where some villagers are afraid to even eat dinner anymore for fear of being crushed at their supper tables. These aren't just the fears "of a privileged class."[17] It isn't just the rich and famous, the black but privileged, who harbor such fear-filled tenseness. Many poorer African Americans are also haunted by forms of racial paranoia. Philosopher Cornel West flags the upshot of this fact in his continuing analyses of black youth and "nihilism." It isn't just that young black people don't care about the society, he says. They look around and see something that appears even more insidious: a society that doesn't seem to care about them. And just as the Azande would imagine it, these young people believe that the capriciousness of history alone doesn't fully explain why the people in their neighborhood are all living at the doorway to poverty when other communities, gated or not, are so rich and opulent. Lightning is only ever just lightning when it doesn't have social consequences.

Although racial paranoia might work a little like the Azande version of witchcraft (in its emphasis on secret, nefarious explanations for social tragedies), it makes no sense to dismiss accusations of racism as mere witch hunts or to pretend that racism can only ever be invoked when bold racists announce their hateful feelings with little regard for public approbation. We shouldn't long for a world without the sharp-toothed mandates of political correctness, a time when bigots belittled their racial "inferiors" out in the public square and lecherously unreconstructed sexists tormented female coworkers on the job. However, we do need to respond to social differences in other than quietist and defensive ways. That only has the slightest chance of happening if we can first force ourselves to be honest about our own investments in racial thinking—in what it does for us, what it does to us, and how it narrows all of our possibilities.

When political philosopher Danielle Allen talks about the need for "political friendships" and mutual sacrifice in contemporary American society, she is arguing for a kind of commitment to others that flies in the face of narrow, short-sighted versions of community.[18] She argues that such sacrifices, when shared freely and equally among all citizens, can allay the fears people have that others will take advantage of them. It can short-circuit a bit of what sociologist Herbert Blumer once called the "group position theory of prejudice," the zero-sum game racial groups concoct to imagine gains for others as translating into relative losses for them.[19] Allen thinks that we should all gain and lose, and we should be able to see others doing the same. When it looks like one group disproportionately bears the brunt of the losses (those heavy trees always crashing down on their group's dinner tables), it makes sense for them to get a little paranoid about how the game is being played.

These kinds of sacrifices demand that citizens embrace the role of "vulnerable observer," a suggestive phrasing that anthropologist Ruth Behar uses brilliantly to describe ways of seeing predicated on seers' accepting the limitations of their own sight and the ineluctable fact of being seen themselves at the same time. Seeing racism in the context of *de cardio* concerns requires all of us to accept our fates as vulnerable observers, realizing that our collective future depends on mutual trust and recognition. Being a vulnerable observer means not taking the easy way out. It means not letting yourself off the hook. It means trying to hear other people's less-than-generous readings of your hidden intentions, especially in the truncated context of politically corrected speech. This is why radio, of all the electronic media, might not be so quick to lose its social and cultural significance in the twenty-first century, even with the ubiquity of the Internet.[20]

For one thing, black radio is a hothouse for racial paranoia, and any serious listener to black radio can hear all the latest fears and conspiracies circulating within the black community in just the first fifteen minutes of any city's daily morning talk show. Sure, you get that material online too. But it is one thing to read a blog and quite another to listen to the voices of black people sincerely expressing their racial skepticisms live and in person. Black radio isn't the only thing interesting about contemporary radio as a cultural conduit for paranoia. The difference, say, between Don Imus and an even racier shock jock like Howard Stern pivots on how the latter talks almost obsessively about race. Even if you don't believe he's an equal-opportunity misanthrope, you could never listen to Stern's broadcast and think he's hiding (for better or worse) his ultimate feelings about race. He seems to put it all on the air. You might find his comments sexist and racist; he might make your blood boil; but you don't feel like he's hiding something. It is that fear of the hidden vis-à-vis race and racism that racial paranoia breeds upon, a fear that is related, but not reducible, to fears about racism per se. It is about not knowing, not being sure. We don't want everyone to try to be Howard Stern, but his comedy (at its best) promotes a kind of multiracial gesture toward honesty that hinges on his ability to say things that others are afraid to say. It unflinchingly demands a certain commitment to seeing race, even if it is a way of seeing race that is all the more frightening for its easy deployment of traditional racial stereotypes. Racial paranoia for African Americans is the fear that whites aren't saying what they really feel. Blacks, because of their social marginalization and the contingencies of transatlantic history, don't have to bite their tongues about race nearly as much as whites do. However, the whites who seem most comfortable talking about race are the ones who help to create interracial spaces that foster honest dialogue about racism shorn of the most obvious manifestations of insincerity and duplicity.

Ever the optimist, even as I argue for our entrenched and collective race-based paranoia, part of me still wants to hope that Howard Stern might just be a small step in the direction of exorcising our *de cardio* demons. And sometimes I'm even able to convince myself that some of this is a generational thing, that America's younger Facebook and MySpace crowd is learning to see multiracial friendships as much more natural than their parents do, as the rule more than the exception. That would be a positive gloss on, say, those white Floridian softballers who went to a campus party in blackface with the help of their black friends on the school's basketball team. Maybe these kinds of controversial and explicit racial gestures, ostensibly performed in a context of mutual trust and friendship, provide hope that nothing from our sordid racial past can haunt us the same way forever. This might not be exactly the kind of trust some political philosophers would call for (its sacrifices still so obviously lopsided), but it may be the only second chance that a country with our racial baggage can realistically expect.

Afterword
Racial Optimism Is Not the Opposite of Racial Paranoia

E ven though many of us have gotten used to the idea of
an African American family in the White House, we
should not forget how unthinkable such a scenario was
not too long ago, even just moments before it happened.
Once the 2008 presidential election was decided and the
seemingly impossible had actually occurred, Americans
began congratulating themselves for ushering in what they
thought would be a radically new racial order. But such an
abrupt cultural transformation is never that easy.

On November 5, 2008, the day after Barack Obama defeated John McCain to become the forty-fourth president
of the United States, I appeared as a guest on *The Agenda
with Steve Paikin*, a Toronto-based television program
that some of my friends described as Canada's answer to
Charlie Rose. Paikin, a thoughtful and precise interviewer,
wanted to know if Obama's election had changed "everything" in America. Had we awoken to a profoundly new
country that morning? Did Americans, especially African

Americans, feel better about their nation's ability to put its money where its mouth was with respect to racial equality?

I had made an appearance on Paikin's show a few months earlier to discuss *Racial Paranoia*. Then he had invited me back so that he could ask me a specific (and very fair) follow-up question: Did the election of its first black president signal the end of "racial paranoia" in America? That is, would an Obama presidency nullify my book's claims? Pre-Obama America might have been filled with race-based skepticisms and paranoia, but surely Obama's election signaled the beginning of a new racial moment. Consequently, as Paikin put it, did a little air come out of the tire of *Racial Paranoia*'s thesis?

Leading up to Obama's victory, the story of America's 2008 presidential election was very much one about racial politics, only with some unanticipated twists. For one, Obama was expected to be the racial candidate, America's first viable black presidential nominee. He was the one with a Kenyan father, and he had spent all of those years at an "Afrocentric" church run by a controversial reverend. Race was all over the election, and it seemed to be exclusively about Obama's historic run. However, Senator McCain lost, ironically enough, because he turned himself into the racial candidate. Let me explain.

Many social analysts have written about the so-called "browning of America," a relative decrease in the country's white population tied to continuing Latino immigration and higher birth rates among other ethnic groups. Obama ran his "post-racial" campaign with full consideration of just how such demographic shifts have changed the makeup of the electorate. He helped register more people of color than ever before, and he compellingly encouraged those voters to go out to the polls. He told them that this was their America, too.

In contrast, almost every decision McCain made seemed to reflect a profound under-appreciation of America's diverse body politic, even a denial of it, something bordering on nostalgia for myths about bygone years of American racial homogeneity. He chose a charismatic vice presidential running mate, Sarah Palin, who failed to demonstrate any explicit recognition of America's changing ethno-racial composition. She did a fantastic job energizing "the base" and continues to work magic with her party's rank-and-file. But for those who didn't already unequivocally consider themselves a part of that Republican core, she also gave the singular impression that her party's foundation was constituted by an only slightly euphemized commitment to white privilege.

The McCain campaign's late-game deployment of "Joe the Plumber" trafficked in the same indifference to America's changing demographic makeup. Joe the Plumber was supposed to stand in for average Americans, but he ended up further alienating many of the new black and brown voters who interpreted his support for McCain (and his public proclamations of Obama's supposed socialism and implied anti-Americanism) as an attempt to play a white version of "the race card" without explicitly invoking race at all. Obliviousness to the kinds of racial skepticisms that

I describe in this book allowed McCain to unknowingly antagonize and insult millions of newly registered American voters. This is part of what cost him the election.

The majority of just about every durable demographic and ethnic group in American society voted for Barack Obama in 2008. Almost every conceivable category of voters went for the Democrat except for two distinct groups: self-proclaimed conservatives and white Americans. If it had been up to white voters, McCain would have won the election handily, which is another way to potentially complicate any talk of Obama's victory signaling a completely new America. If the majority of white Americans still weren't willing to vote for a Democratic candidate in the context of a wildly unpopular war in Iraq and a massively hemorrhaging national economy (both chalked up, by most critics, to an incumbent Republican presidency), then what does that say about the contemporary legacies of white racism? Especially considering just about every other demographic group in the country was willing to "vote the bums out" of office. *Racial Paranoia* argues that such a question animates the center of African American political engagement. And given the history of America's racial investments, it probably couldn't be any other way.

But has Obama's actual presence in the White House begun to beat back African American cynicisms? When we began to take stock of Obama's presidency in 2009, early studies put some meat on the bones of Paikin's question regarding the racial implications of his historic victory.

Indeed, just four months after Obama's inauguration, a CBS/*New York Times* poll made national headlines by demonstrating record levels of African American optimism on issues of race. For the first time since CBS started such polling, most of the black respondents characterized race-relations positively. Just one summer earlier, only 29 percent of the blacks polled had described race-relations as "good," a figure that shot up to 59 percent in 2009 (not far below the 65 percent of whites with a similarly positive take on race that same year). Obama's victory effectively amplified the degree of racial optimism found in black America.[1] So there you have it. Racial paranoia's sound defeat, right? Not quite.

Political scientist Melissa Harris-Lacewell puts a fine point on some of the precariousness of black America's newfound racial optimism. "The best part of Jan. 20," she wrote in the *Philadelphia Inquirer*, discussing her take on the inauguration festivities, "was that Barack and Michelle got out of the bulletproof black Cadillac and walked the streets—and no one shot at them."[2] According to Harris-Lacewell, ostensible black optimism stems from the deep pit of racial skepticism and paranoia. Some blacks are hopeful, she claimed, because they are amazed that Obama made it through his first 100 days—without being assassinated.

There are Americans, and not just African Americans, who still admit that they briefly put on CNN every morning, just to make sure Obama has safely survived another night. It looks as if racial paranoia can co-exist with polls demonstrating racial optimism—an emergent sentiment that still imagines America's other racial shoe conceivably dropping. And at almost any time. The glass is half full, but have we plugged up all its holes? Even if we haven't, Obama thinks we can.

Back in March 2008, Obama gave his powerful "race speech" in Philadelphia's Constitution Center. I joked with my friends that it was as though he had stolen an early peek at *Racial Paranoia,* which published in hardcover the following month. In his address, Obama made several rhetorical moves that pivoted on claims I make in this book: he talked explicitly about American slavery and its legacy; he defended his connection to Reverend Jeremiah Wright by arguing the short-sightedness of calls for Americans to disown friends and relatives who voice racist rhetoric (a version of what some demanded of Obama vis-à-vis Wright); he made a case for racism's ubiquity, invoking his grandmother's fears of black male criminality; and he claimed that he could be committed to Wright's church and trust in his grandmother's love while stridently disagreeing with their racialist investments. In many ways, he argued for exactly what this book champions: honest discussions about race across ideological fault lines, instead of commitments to a public sphere scrubbed clean of racial language, a kind of post-racialism by repression and ostracism.

When Obama's attorney general, Eric Holder, another symbolic and substantive African American first, called America "a nation of cowards" with respect to open dialogue about race, he was also riffing on that same theme:

the need for direct and likely painful conversations, not pre-fabbed platitudes and politically corrected scripts. In many ways, Obama's speech and Holder's public reprimand have served as the beginning and end of Obama's explicit rhetorical engagement with race and racism. Even when Obama tried to comment on the intractability of racial profiling last July (when Harvard's Henry Louis Gates, Jr., was arrested in front of his own home for being indignant over accusations of breaking in), he had to retreat from his strident initial reactions, especially his characterization of the arrest as an example of stupidity. Obama might get away with giving a rousing speech at an NAACP dinner, complete with flourishes from the black homiletic tradition, but it appears far safer (politically speaking) for him to address the impact of racism by attacking more universal issues such as health care, employment, and educational access—issues that can get at racism's legacy without explicitly highlighting race at all. A rising tide helps all Americans. Blacks, too.

But might this just be a kinder, gentler version of racial paranoia? It pivots on a fear that the only way to deal with racism is by not directly dealing with it at all (i.e., by not alienating whites with calls for race-specific interventions). We might be able to get at certain aspects of racial discrimination from such a side door, but this maneuver is predicated on what is arguably one of the most cynical readings of all. What does it say about America's capacity for cross-racial empathy and community?

And this is hardly the only change that racial paranoia has undergone since the ascendancy of Obama. There are also fears that his presidency will give conservatives license to roll back some of America's formal commitments to racial justice. With an African American elected to the highest office in the land, how could racism explain lack of achievement for any other black people?

In such a context, Obama might be playing with fire by privileging race-neutral language as the most pragmatic mechanism for addressing racial realities, delegitimizing the explanatory power of racial arguments. His relative day-to-day silence on racial issues can be read as yet another reason to dismiss invocations of racism altogether. Journalist Tavis Smiley is the most vocal African American public figure who has consistently demanded that African Americans (and political progressives of all stripes) hold Obama "accountable" on questions of race.[3] The argument here is that Obama's victory and relatively "color-mute" public discourse actually bolster reactionary claims about the contemporary insignificance of race as a social, cultural, and political category.[4]

On the other end of the ideological spectrum, conservative critics such as Shelby Steele accuse Obama of explicitly invoking race *too much*. Steele went out on a limb before the 2008 election was decided with a book that envisioned Obama's ultimate defeat, folding that very prediction into its subtitle, *A Bound Man: Why We Are Excited About Obama and Why He Can't Win*.[5] In it, Steele argues that Obama is "bound" by America's myopic and misplaced

mathematics of race, a math of one-drop rules and simplistic invocations of racial impurity-by-addition ("black"
plus "white" equals the inauthentic "bi-racial"). Foremost,
Steele asserted, Obama's candidacy demanded that he play
the conciliatory role of "bargainer" in contradistinction to
America's more hard-lined racial "challenger" (represented
by people like Jesse Jackson), the latter described as using
"white guilt" to political advantage. According to Steele,
this meant that Obama had to come off as "post-racial"
during the election, and as decidedly not hostile or otherwise bitter toward whites. However, Steele argued, such
positive racial politics wouldn't necessarily stand Obama
in good stead with the more cynical and skeptical strands
of African American thinking on race—the strands I highlight in this book, central to African American opposi-
tional politics. As Steele saw things before the 2008
election, those very traits that made Obama palatable to
many liberal white voters potentially estranged him from
black ones, and vice versa. Obama's electoral coalition, as
depicted by Steele, was split right down the middle. (Of
course, this was all before we would be imagining a scenario wherein a newly inaugurated President Obama was
ostensibly turning bygone African American skeptics into
racial optimists.)

Steele also claims that Obama is equally "bound" by
his own misplaced efforts to actually embrace a more
open-minded form of "the same-old racial politics" as opposed to eschewing it altogether and declaring its utter
bankruptcy, which Steele would prefer. He even blasted

Obama's nomination of Judge Sonia Sotomayor to the Supreme Court last year for that very reason.

"The Sotomayor nomination commits the cardinal sin of identity politics," Steele wrote in the *Wall Street Journal*.[6] "It seeks to elevate people more for the political currency of their gender and ethnicity than for their individual merit. . . . Mr. Obama is promising one thing and practicing another, using his interracial background to suggest an America delivered from racial corruption even as he practices a crude form of racial patronage." Steele chided Obama for being "unoriginal and hackneyed" in his choice of a Latina judge.

Never mind that Sotomayor had an unassailable legal pedigree. Or that she had more years of judicial experience at the time of her nomination than just about all the other justices on the Court. Steele still dismissed the choice out of hand, painting President Obama as less a racial optimist than a racial opportunist, someone playing both racial sides against the middle for his own political aggrandizement. I think of these urgent invocations of "racial patronage" and "identity politics" as yet another form of contemporary racial paranoia. But whatever the case, racism and racial politics weren't voted into oblivion on November 4, 2008. They have just morphed into newly configured fronts of dispute and contestation.

* * *

As explicit forms of racist rhetoric are suppressed in public discourse (and potentially repressed by certain whites who don't want to be considered racists), our conversations across racial lines get less and less trustworthy. *De cardio* racism represents the idea that one of the ways in which African Americans, and others, try to square an egalitarian and explicitly inclusive public discussion about race with the perpetuation of racially inflected structural inequalities is by mining everyday inter-racial exchanges for subtle expressions of hidden bias, for race-stalking wolves trying to pass themselves off as color-blind sheep. This is exactly where the rubber of inter-racial contact meets the road of structural and historical realities.

While *Racial Paranoia* doesn't stop at such personal readings, it would be unproductive to simply dismiss these analyses (probing between the lines of everyday social life) as hypersensitive or ridiculously paranoid. This is how people responded to, say, comedian Dave Chappelle and former congresswoman Cynthia McKinney. It's also how some whites responded to the Gates arrest. But Gates, McKinney, and Chappelle aren't simply failing to strike up casual conversations across racial lines at their local coffeeshops. They are responding to structural transformations in America's racial landscape, transformations that potentially cloak racial inclinations and motivations behind the political firewall of race-neutral rhetoric. What detractors pooh-pooh as irrational racial paranoia might represent an appropriate, if incomplete, response to euphemized forms of racism today. Even a controversial figure such as Pat Buchanan, someone with no qualms about publicly privileging the hardships of working class whites over and against "affirmative action babies" couches his

position in the rhetoric of color-blind egalitarianism.[7] This
is a new racial order, indeed.

In many ways, the election of Obama just greases the
wheels for new versions of plausible deniability with respect to issues of race. That is a somewhat controversial
claim, and I don't think that a lot of people want to hear
it—on the political left or the political right. But these
"personal" readings, these "paranoid" readings, represent
a starting point for cultivating new language about race
that captures its unprecedented contemporary manifestations. For most of America's history, racists could be
unabashed with their racial venom. Championing segregation helped get you elected when only whites could safely
vote. By the turn of the twenty-first century, any whiff of
explicit racism could damage a politician's entire career.
That was a new America. And if those were unprecedented days (post-1960s and pre–President Obama), this
country has redefined "unprecedented" in terms of race
yet again with the 2008 election.[8]

And, in spite of all this, we do not live in a world where
racism and "reverse-racism" are one and the same. Racial
skepticism isn't just "a black thang." Whites can also be
racially skeptical, racially paranoid. But this does not
make the two forms of racial paranoia equivalent.

The Roberts Supreme Court, however, seems intent on
arguing that all forms of racial thinking are alike—and
equally unconstitutional when enlisted by governmental
agencies. But "race" is only intelligible as a social fact and
analytical tool when placed in the specific historical con-

text of its emergence and development. *Racial Paranoia* provides some of that context, at least in terms of the history of racism in the United States, with the purpose of showing that the racial landscape today must be examined with sensitivity to the sedimentary histories that form its many indigenous layers.

Racism in the twentieth century saw racial differences everywhere and shouted those findings from the rooftops. Racism in the twenty-first century, however, works by refusing to recognize it and chastising anyone for seeing racial ghosts that are supposedly not there. In many ways, there is a double-standard in America with respect to race, one that ironically promotes equality and equal-access by understanding racial differences as a function of historical differences—not biological or essential ones, and certainly not unchangeable ones.

Racial paranoia, as I've described and delineated here, is not about blaming black people's relative material poverty on their cynicism (a version, I think, of placing the cart before the horse and cursing the horse for not towing it). It is also not an attempt to pathologize black Americans—or to romanticize extreme and exotic forms of racial cynicism. Rather, any true path to "post-raciality" must start with a thorough revisiting of America's racial past, and an exorcizing of its racial demons.

We have a long way to go before new racial optimisms come close to representing anything more than repressed racial anxieties. But this does not seem to be President Obama's preoccupation. His optimism about America's racial possibilities appears durable and longstanding. However, there are many African Americans whose racial optimism is more tenuous. And polls indicating an emergent hopefulness should not be interpreted as a definitive end to the kinds of racial skepticism that I've emphasized in this book. If anything, we should recognize that these kinds of racial paranoia and skepticism have only ever been possible—in ways that don't degenerate into certifiable pathology or into existential angst that rips the skeptic asunder—because they have co-existed with slivers of optimism all the while. Obama has long been a kind of racial idealist, someone who wants to convince us all that trusting across racial lines is well worth the risk. This book shares some of that cautious hope.

We are, indeed, living in a new racial moment, uncharted racial territory, but it is built on the palpable remains of those racial pasts that still haunt us today—whether or not we admit to seeing them. And there is a palpable difference between moving toward the ever-receding horizon and getting stuck in the mud and muck of our own ideological intransigence by congratulating ourselves on completing a journey we've only just started. Obama's 2008 victory was an exhilarating place to temporarily pitch our tents, but we had better make sure to get up and keep moving in the morning.

Acknowledgments

The idea for this book began to take root while I was conducting anthropological research for another project, listening to a young black man in Washington, D.C., explain a few of the reasons why he felt that white people made his life so much more difficult than it needed to be. "They just don't give black people the benefit of the doubt," he said. "Simple as that. Everyone else gets the benefit of the doubt, but we don't, it seems like. No matter what." The more I thought about his comments, the more I found something compelling in this suggestion about the links between racism and assumed social certainties. Some of that thinking translated into my book on racial sincerity, but there was still more I wanted to write (and for a potentially larger audience) about the kinds of doubts that haunt our everyday experiences of racial difference in America. That desire became the launching pad for this book.

I actually started writing *Racial Paranoia* during my year as a Lilly Endowment Fellow at the National Humanities Center. I was supposed to be working on a book about global black Hebrewisms (at which I'm still plugging away), but I ended up only conducting archival and ethnographic research on that project as I embarked on writing this one. I am thankful to the National Humanities Center for providing that much-needed time away from the everyday demands of academic life and for similar support provided by a Woodrow Wilson Career Enhancement Award. *Racial Paranoia* would have been impossible without those generous gifts.

It also couldn't have been completed were it not for the enriching feedback I received from friends and colleagues. At Duke University, scholars read drafts of chapters or listened to versions of their arguments over meals and "coffee," especially Anne Allison, Lee Baker, Houston Baker, Grant Farred, Micah Gilmer, Andrew Janiak, Ralph Litzinger, Wahneema Lubiano, Mark Anthony Neal, Diane Nelson, Charlie Piot, Bianca Robinson, Ragini Srinivasan, Rebecca Stein, Netta Van Vliet, and Maurice Wallace. Once I arrived at the University of Pennsylvania, many of my new colleagues indulged me in just the same way, including Asif Agha, Herman Beavers, Camille Z. Charles, Jasmine Cobb, Michael X. Delli Carpini, Gautam Ghosh, David Grazian, Elihu Katz, Carolyn Marvin, Paul Messaris, Adriana Petryna, Guy Ramsey, Peggy Sanday, Barbara Savage, Katherine Sender, Kenneth Shropshire, Salamishah Tillet, Riley Snorton, Brian Spooner, Joe Turow, Todd Wolfson, Barbie Zelizer, and Tukufu Zuberi. I want to thank them all for their time and expertise.

I also gained a great deal from opportunities I had to present versions of this material at other academic institutions, including John Hopkins University's Center for Africana Studies, the University of California, Los Angeles's

Department of Anthropology, Boston College's Program in African and African Diaspora Studies, and the University of Delaware's Department of History. The scholars who attended these lectures, including Ben Vinson, Stanford Carpenter, Lester K. Spence, Katrina Bell McDonald, Cynthia Young, Sherry Ortner, Devon W. Carbado, Kyeyoung Park, H. Samy Alim, Jessica R. Cattelino, and David Suisman (along with many, many others), provided useful leads and persuasive suggestions. Susan McDonic supplied me with several chances to re-rehearse the book's core maneuvers in front of her classes at American University. She also offered critical feedback about the book's larger implications. Other people provided bits of wisdom that helped me more than they probably know, especially Prudence Carter, Gary Alan Fine, Richard Iton, E. Patrick Johnson, Manning Marable, Donald Moore, Leith Mullings, Katherine S. Newman, Sheri Parks, Mary Pattillo, Larry Shields, Martin Sumners, Dawn Crossland-Sumners, Roxanne Varzi, and Patricia Williams. Thank you all for your insight and inspiration.

Ellen Garrison provided brilliant editorial guidance at the start of my relationship with Basic Civitas, and Chris Greenberg offered his discerning feedback once he took over that role. Amanda Moon shepherded the project through its final stages, along with Kay Mariea and copyeditor Jen Kelland. Greg Houle did the early work to publicize *Racial Paranoia*, and Whitney Casser provided invaluable help on the paperback edition. I also want to thank Dan Kirklin for providing a list of corrections for the paperback edition. My agent, Andrew Stuart, worked closely with me on this project from the first few words on the first blank page, and my friend

Cora Daniels spent much of her spare time schooling me about the culture of trade publishing and its difference from the demands of an academic press, which spared me much angst and gnashing of teeth.

I want to thank my family for always showing me love and support, especially Ethlyn Roberts, Arlene Roberts, Jayon Stewart, Jason Roberts, Doris Thomas, Delroy Thomas, Voicelyn Manning, Jerry Martin, Marilyn Manning, and all the many cousins, aunts, uncles, and others that I don't get a chance to see nearly enough. My wife, Deborah A. Thomas, read every page with love and critical clarity. Thanks, sweetie. My little son, Oliver, was as much of a sport about the entire thing as an infant-cum-toddler could possibly be. And his heavenly smiles were fuel for my fatherly and writerly soul. Thanks, Big-O! Marleigh-moo, thanks to you, too.

Notes

PREFACE

1. For a critical treatment of the "race man" figure (in its most and least progressive incarnations), see Hazel Carby, *Race Men* (Cambridge, MA: Harvard University Press, 1998). Unlike the antiracist projects of Mooney and Gregory, Chappelle's comedy usually comes off as much less accusatory. Anthropologist Lanita Jacobs-Huey is currently researching the political sensibilities and aesthetic decisions of black comedians in Los Angeles post 9/11, comedians who successfully walk that treacherous tightrope between comedy and political soapboxing vis-à-vis issues of discrimination in contemporary America.

2. For a critique of Cosby's very public speeches about poor blacks' reproducing their own social problems, see Michael Eric Dyson, *Is Bill Cosby Right? Or Has the Black Middle Class Lost Its Mind?* (New York: Basic Civitas, 2005). For a vehement defense of Cosby's analysis, see Juan Williams, *Enough: The Phony Leaders, Dead-End Movement, and Culture of Failure That Are Undermining Black America—and What We Can Do about It* (New York: Crown Publishers, 2006). Cora Daniels also weighs in controversially on this debate (and its larger implications for all of American culture, not just black culture) in *Ghettonation: A Journey into the Land of Bling and the Home of the Shameless* (New York: Doubleday, 2007).

3. For an examination of blackface minstrelsy's role in helping to shape a particular kind of nationalist cultural identity
among diverse groups of American citizens, see Eric Lott, *Love
and Theft: Blackface Minstrelsy and the American Working Class*
(New York: Oxford University Press, 1993), and Michael Rogin,
*Blackface, White Noise: Jewish Immigrants in the Hollywood
Melting Pot* (Berkeley: University of California Press, 1996).

4. This quote is taken from Dave Chappelle's *Oprah Winfrey Show* interview, which first aired on February 3, 2006.

5. For a critical discussion of Bert Williams and his relationship to blackface, see Louis Chude-Sokei, *The Last "Darky":
Bert Williams, Black-on-Black Minstrelsy, and the African Diaspora* (Durham, NC: Duke University Press, 2005).

6. The subtlety and cultural nuance of this distinction are
reminiscent of a fairly famous differentiation that anthropologist
Clifford Geertz unpacks between a mere "twitch" and a more
purposefully significant "wink," a difference best teased out by
what he calls "thick description." Clifford Geertz, *The Interpretation of Cultures* (New York: Basic Books Classics, 2000).

INTRODUCTION

1. These accusations might seem more compelling to some
people if we consider the Katrina aftermath to be more of a
complicated cocktail combining racism with class marginalization. There are also a few critics who adamantly declare that
race had nothing to do with it, that Katrina was *only* about
class-based vulnerabilities. For the latter position, see Walter
Benn Michaels, *The Trouble with Diversity: How We Learned
to Love Identity and Ignore Inequality* (New York: Henry Holt,
2006). Of course, some post-Katrina studies have found that
more whites than blacks were killed in the storm (and its after-

math). Even still, the public perception was that blacks bore the brunt of the hurricane's deadly winds.

2. That racial skepticism existed even before people started hearing about the government-sanctioned "use of 78,000 pounds of dynamite on the levee" when Hurricane Betsy hit New Orleans in 1927. For details, see John M. Barry, *Rising Tide: The Great Mississippi Flood of 1927 and How It Changed America* (New York: Simon and Schuster, 1997), especially 238–58. Above quote is from p. 339. Particularly powerful offerings on Hurricane Katrina include Barry, *Rising Tide;* Douglas Brinkley, *The Great Deluge: Hurricane Katrina, New Orleans, and the Mississippi Gulf Coast* (New York: HarperCollins, 2006); Michael Eric Dyson, *Come Hell or High Water: Hurricane Katrina and the Color of Disaster* (New York: Basic Civitas, 2006); Jed Horne, *Breach of Faith: Hurricane Katrina and the Near Death of a Great American City* (New York: Random House, 2006). Each book makes some mention of African Americans entertaining the idea that the levees were purposefully dynamited. According to Brinkley, for instance, "Since 1927, African Americans in New Orleans had been distrustful of the levee boards, believing that if the white gentry did it once, they'd do it again" (*The Great Deluge,* 8). Dyson makes a similar claim: "It is little wonder that the desperate and destitute took easily to 'conspiracy theories' about the possible dynamiting of some of the levees in New Orleans to protect the whites and drown out the blacks. After all, such an event happened in the Great Flood of 1927. And since the forces that fueled such a heinous act still thrive, including white supremacy and a deep dislike for poor blacks, it stands to reason that many blacks might believe it could happen again. In this instance, conspiracy theories are secular, grassroots theodicies—most likely of the attributive mode—that seek to explain the evil that poor blacks endure at the hands of a culpable and callous society" (*Come Hell or High Water,* 196).

3. I have always been intrigued by the fact that Kanye West didn't even use the word "hate" to ground his explicit accusations against President Bush. He said "doesn't care about," which seems like an oddly understated way to make such a serious claim about presidential racism. There's something about that difference between "hate" and "doesn't care about" that elucidates how "racial paranoia" works today, slipping easily from grand claims to more humble inklings. I'll elaborate more on this in later chapters.

4. I want to call each one of these instances a form of "racial paranoia," distinguishing them from conventional understandings of racism.

5. For a definition of racism that privileges "material advantages" over scholars who reduce the phenomenon to prejudice, false consciousness, discursive formations, or ideology, see David Wellman, *Portraits of White Racism* (New York: Cambridge University Press, 1993).

6. Randall Robinson, *Quitting America: The Departure of a Black Man from His Native Land* (New York: Penguin, 2004).

7. This interview comes from "The Situation with Tucker Carlson," which aired on MSNBC, September 15, 2005.

8. Richard Hofstadter, *The Paranoid Style in American Politics and Other Essays* (Cambridge, MA: Harvard University Press, 1996).

9. Richard Hofstadter, "The Paranoid Style in American Politics," *Harper's Magazine*, November 1964, 77.

10. Wellman, *Portraits of White Racism,* 29.

11. Literary critic Salamishah Tillet describes this tension as African Americans' gaining "legal citizenship" amid continuing "civic estrangement." For a different examination of the racial exclusions that necessarily come with political inclusion, see Devon W. Carbado, "Racial Naturalization," *American Quarterly* 57, no 3 (September 2005): 633–58.

12. Leslie Houts Picca and Joe Feagin, *Two-Faced Racism: Whites in the Backstage and Frontstage* (New York: Routledge, 2007). These two sociologists show that white students have different racial postures for different social contexts: one for public consumption, the other (less-flattering) reserved for the safety of intimately intraracial company.

13. See Stephen L. Carter, *Reflections of an Affirmative Action Baby* (New York: Basic Books, 1991).

14. William Julius Wilson's *The Declining Significance of Race: Blacks and Changing American Institutions* (Chicago: University of Chicago Press, 1978) created quite a firestorm by seeming to make such a claim.

15. See John L. Jackson Jr., *Real Black: Adventures in Racial Sincerity* (Chicago: University of Chicago Press, 2005).

16. This example of a cabdriver passing up a black fare out of fear is relayed in Cornel West, *Race Matters* (New York: Vintage, 1994). A person doesn't need to be a card-carrying Klansman to foster (even inadvertently) various forms of racial discrimination. See Eduardo Bonilla-Silva, *Racism without Racists: Color-Blind Racism and the Persistence of Racial Inequality in the United States* (Lanham, MD: Rowman & Littlefield, 2003).

17. Malcolm Gladwell, *Blink: The Power of Thinking without Thinking* (New York: Little, Brown, 2005).

18. To talk about racial paranoia is not just to talk psychology. It isn't simply about psychologizing racial problems. Elisabeth Lasch-Quinn's 2001 book *Race Experts: How Racial Etiquette, Sensitivity Training, and New Age Therapy Hijacked the Civil Rights Revolution* (New York: W. W. Norton and Co., 2001) highlights the pitfalls of making race exclusively a story of group therapy and self-help. Racial therapy alone isn't the solution for racial paranoia, not if that means consciousness-raising exercises and sensitivity training. Besides, I'm an urban

Notes

anthropologist, not a psychologist. My methods of choice allow me to discuss social and cultural issues over psychological and intrapersonal ones. This means that my examination of racial paranoia is more about its social ramifications and historical derivations.

CHAPTER 1

1. This is an exchange reminiscent of the triumphantly modern(ist) moment epitomized by Indiana Jones, when Jones successfully shoots a whip-wielding "primitive" threatening to kill him. This is an important moment that film critic Manthia Diawara has previously discussed in lectures and in print.

2. Richard Majors and Janet Mancini Billson, *Cool Pose: The Dilemmas of Black Manhood in America* (New York: Lexington, 1992).

3. Ira Berlin, *Many Thousands Gone: The First Two Centuries of Slavery in North America* (Cambridge, MA: Belknap/Harvard University Press, 1998).

4. For a discussion of these regional differences, see Philip D. Morgan, *Slave Counterpoint: Black Culture in the Eighteenth-Century Chesapeake and Lowcountry* (Chapel Hill: University of North Carolina Press, 1989).

5. For more on these differences, see Susan Eva O'Donovan, *Becoming Free in the Cotton South* (Cambridge, MA: Harvard University Press, 2007).

6. For a discussion of this new evidence about Equiano's taking poetic license with his life story, see Vincent Carretta, *Equiano the African: Biography of a Self-made Man* (Atlanta: University of Georgia Press, 2005).

7. Jacqueline Jones, *Labor of Love, Labor of Sorrow: Black Women, Work, and the Family, from Slavery to the Present* (New York: Vintage, 1985).

8. For more of these stories, see *Anti-Slavery Tracts*, Series 2, Nos. 15–25 (Westport, CT: Negro University Presses, 1970).

9. Whites could sue other whites for property damage (if they injured or killed a slave), but that wasn't about the slave's intrinsic power vis-à-vis whites, even if they could potentially manipulate that space a bit.

10. Howard Zinn, *A People's History of the United States: 1492–Present* (New York: Perennial Classics, 2003), 193. Of course, there were also examples of slave masters who felt vindicated by their slaves' responses to the Civil War. Historian Winthrop Jordan quotes a letter from a Mississippi planter's gushing daughter to just that effect: "They often speak to me about the war and there was great rejoicing in the kitchen at the news of our recent victory in Virginia. What would those miserable abolitionists say to such manifestations of devotion and affection on the part of the poor maltreated slave, whose heart, according to them, is only the abode of hatred and revenge against their master—They know nothing of the bond that unites the master and servant." Quoted in David Brion Davis, *Inhuman Bondage: The Rise and Fall of Slavery in the New World* (New York: Oxford University Press, 2006), 226–27.

11. This medicalization of runaway slaves was originally espoused by Dr. Samuel A. Cartwright in a piece titled "Diseases and Peculiarities of the Negro Race," penned in 1851. John Guillory, "The Pro-Slavery Arguments of S. A. Cartwright," *Louisiana History* 9 (1968): 209–27.

12. Davis, *Inhuman Bondage*, 226. Paternalism could also compel slave masters to act more humanely.

13. See Betty Wood, *Slavery in Colonial America, 1619–1776* (Lanham, MD: Rowman & Littlefield, 2005), 65.

14. Recent scholarship by Michael Johnson provides a new twist to the theory that Vesey's supposed conspiracy was nothing more than talk (and even a partisan governmental hoax). According to Johnson, Mayor James Hamilton, Jr., created a false

conspiracy to use as a political issue against Governor Thomas Bennett, Jr., who owned some of the accused slaves. Michael P. Johnson, "Denmark Vesey and His Co-Conspirators," *William and Mary Quarterly* 58 (October 2001): 913–76. Robert Tinkler, *James Hamilton of South Carolina* (Baton Rouge: Louisiana State University Press, 2004), another biographer of Mayor Hamilton, believed that the mayor actually did think there was a slave plot involving some of the governor's slaves, whether or not he was just being hyperparanoid.

15. For more of this story of the black-on-black paranoia that tempered the celebration of fugitive slave Frederick Bailey's arrival north, see Fergus M. Bordewich, *Bound for Canaan: The Epic Story of the Underground Railroad, America's First Civil Rights Movement* (New York: Amistad, 2006), 178–81.

16. *Anti-Slavery Tracts*, Series 2, Nos. 15–25, 27.

17. James T. Campbell, *Middle Passages: African American Journeys to Africa, 1787–2005* (New York: Penguin Books 2006), 100–101.

18. For an examination of lynching photographs, see Hilton Als, Leon F. Litwack, and James Allen, *Without Sanctuary: Lynching Photography in America* (Santa Fe, NM: Twin Palm Publishers, 2000). Of course, blacks were not nearly the only ones lynched by such vigilante mobs, which is a point that shouldn't be lost. For a discussion of American lynching outside the Old South (specifically in California), which is not over-represented by black victims (Latinos carrying that burden instead), see Ken Gonzales-Day, *Lynching in the West, 1850–1935* (Durham, NC: Duke University Press, 2006). For a book-length treatment of "white guilt," see Shelby Steele, *White Guilt: How Blacks and Whites Together Destroyed the Promise of the Civil Rights Era* (New York: HarperCollins, 2006).

19. Of course, Brown's actions didn't foment more rebellions in the South. There were far fewer revolts in the United States than in other parts of the Americas, which historians such as

Stanley Elkins chalk up to the country's harsher, more debasing form of slavery.

20. See Kenneth Shropshire, *Being Sugar Ray: The Life of Sugar Ray Robinson, America's Greatest Boxer and the First Celebrity Athlete* (New York: Basic Civitas, 2006), for a discussion of the controversies that early-twentieth-century heavyweight champion Jack Johnson caused by exemplifying this black buck role, specifically in his scandalous public relationships with various white women. In fact, Joe Louis would have to be "handled" quite purposefully (when another black boxer was finally allowed to fight for the heavyweight championship decades later) so as to avoid similar rancor and rage from white boxing fans disgusted by such high-profile flaunting of black male–white female miscegenation.

21. Danielle S. Allen, *Talking to Strangers: Anxieties of Citizenship since Brown v. Board of Education* (Chicago: University of Chicago Press, 2004), 13.

22. This is a reference to the title of a famous poem about the benefits of interracial duplicity, a poem from a celebrated late-nineteenth-century black poet. Paul Laurence Dunbar, *The Collected Poetry of Paul Laurence Dunbar,* ed. Joanne M. Braxton (Charlottesville: University Press of Virginia, 1993).

23. For a discussion of post-*Brown* reactionary backlash, see Beverly Daniel Tatum, *Can We Talk About Race? and Other Conversations in an Era of School Resegregation* (Boston: Beacon Press, 2007).

24. Quoted in Glenn C. Loury, *The Anatomy of Racial Inequality* (Cambridge, MA: Harvard University Press, 2002), 6.

25. This isn't to say that racism isn't still very real in a formal judicial system. For an argument to just that effect, see Bruce Wright, *Black Robes, White Justice: Why Our Legal System Doesn't Work for Blacks* (New York: Kensington, 2002).

26. Of course, skeptics would say that the police are fulfilling this punitive function just as effectively today.

27. Historian Jacqueline Jones and others argue that house slaves didn't live the good life at all. Closer proximity to the master meant greater opportunities for horrific violence against one's person.

28. For a further examination of this point (and a critique of Malcolm X's house/field metaphor), see Adolph Reed Jr., *Stirring in the Jug: Black Politics in the Post-Segregation Era* (Minneapolis: University of Minnesota Press, 1999). The "members of the slave elite" is a term used by Michael Craton in *Testing the Chains: Resistance to Slavery in the British West Indies* (Ithaca, NY: Cornell University Press, 1983) to talk about slaves trained to do the kinds of jobs that these three men did: blacksmithing, carpentry, and reading and preaching the Bible.

29. Wood, *Slavery in Colonial America,* 37. And even if *all* these accusations against slaves weren't true, at least a few of them probably were.

30. Berlin, *Many Thousands Gone.*

31. "The full weight and meaning of the slaveholder's dominion" is a phrase from Saidiya V. Hartman, *Scenes of Subjection: Terror, Slavery and Self-Making in Nineteenth-Century America* (New York: Oxford University Press, 1997), 65. The second quote is from O'Donovan, *Becoming Free in the Cotton South,* 104. For a writing of the antebellum North back into the story of American slavery (as beneficiaries and not just emancipators), see Anne Farrow, Joel Lang, and Jenifer Frank, *Complicity: How the North Promoted, Prolonged, and Profited from Slavery* (New York: Ballantine Books, 2005).

32. Orlando Patterson captures the slave's many responses quite persuasively in *Slavery and Social Death: A Comparative Study* (Cambridge, MA: Harvard University Press, 1982): "Nor was the slave a wholly passive entity. He might, in relative terms, be powerless, but he always had some choice. He might react psychologically, play the slave, act dumb, exasperate. He might lie or steal. He might run away. He might injure or kill

others, including his slave master. Or he might engage in armed revolt. Barring all these, he might destroy his master's property by destroying himself. To be sure, only a small minority of slaves ever made such drastic choices. Most chose simply to behave with self-respect and do the best they could under the circumstances" (173).

33. Stanley Elkins, *Slavery* (Chicago: University of Chicago Press, 1977). There were debates between and among historians, sociologists and anthropologists about what slavery did to African culture. E. Franklin Frazier claimed that slavery exterminated African cultural practices and beliefs. Scholars like Melville Herskovits and Herbert Gutman (even if they sometimes overstated their revisionist claims) rightly disputed such broad-brushed dismissals.

34. See Orlando Patterson, *Rituals of Blood: Consequences of Slavery in Two American Centuries* (New York: Basic Civitas Books, 1998); Daniel P. Moynihan, *The Negro Family: The Case for National Action* (Westport, CT: Greenwood Press Reprint, 1981); E. Franklin Frazier, *The Negro Family in the United States* (Chicago: University of Chicago Press, 1939); Thomas Sowell, *Black Rednecks and White Liberals* (San Francisco: Encounter Books, 2005). In the latter, Sowell goes so far as to argue that "macho" black culture is little more than the reappropriation of cultural tendencies found among Southern antebellum white "rednecks and crackers," maladaptive and antisocial beliefs and behaviors that Southern colonists brought with them from "the Scottish highlands, Ireland, Wales, or the northern and western uplands of England." He also makes the point that slavery has always been a global phenomenon, not America's singular aberration.

35. Randall Robinson, *The Debt: What America Owes to Blacks* (New York: Plume, 2000).

36. In fact, blacks might actively disidentify with slavery. Nicholas Lemann relays Senator Harris Wofford's story of

E. Franklin Frazier's asking black students at Howard University in the 1950s to raise their hands if their families descended from slaves. Nary a hand would usually go up. Nicholas Lemann, *The Promised Land: The Great Black Migration and How It Changed America* (New York: Vintage Books, 1992). Lemann's telling of the story is cited in Debra J. Dickerson, *The End of Blackness: Returning the Souls of Black Folk to Their Rightful Owners* (New York: Pantheon Books, 2004), 8.

37. A glance at the index of recent hip-hop studies, even the most rigorous ones, will quickly show that their authors do not highlight slavery as a specifically important theme within the music. For instance, see Jeff Chang, *Can't Stop, Won't Stop: A History of the Hip-hop Generation* (New York: St. Martin's Press, 2005).

38. Elite/high-brown African American cultural offerings do seem to thematize slavery more consistently than more vernacular cultural products. I'm thinking of Toni Morrison's novel *Beloved,* which fictionalizes the actual story of a slave, Margaret Garner, who chose infanticide over allowing a child to face the brutal vulnerabilities of slavery. In 2007, Garner's story was even adapted into an opera. In 2007, Wynton Marsalis created *Blood on the Fields,* a jazz performance about two stolen slaves who fall in love despite the dangers all around them. Octavia Butler's sci-fi novel *Kindred* plays with the idea of a twentieth-century African American going back in time and facing the hazards of slavery, a much more serious treatment of the *Chappelle Show*'s skit. I want to thank Salamishah Tillet for reminding me of the Butler text. Of course, the narrative for Haile Gerima's film *Sankofa* pivots on the same premise.

39. For an anthropological discussion of *Roots* as a widely circulating cultural text, see Kamari Maxine Clarke, "Mapping Transnationality: Roots Tourism and the Institutionalization of Ethnic Heritage," in *Globalization and Race: Transformations in the Cultural Production of Blackness,* ed. Kamari Maxine

Clarke and Deborah A. Thomas, 133–53 (Durham, NC: Duke University Press, 2006).

40. Allen, *Talking to Strangers*, xvii.

CHAPTER 2

1. Frederick Douglass wasn't the only slave who claimed that purportedly Christian masters were usually much more brutal than anyone else.

2. See James T. Campbell, *Middle Passages: African American Journeys to Africa, 1787–2005* (New York: Penguin, 2007), 133–34.

3. See Forrest Woods, *The Arrogance of Faith: Christianity and Race in America from the Colonial Era to the Twentieth Century* (Boston, MA: Northeastern University Press, 1991).

4. Some argue that this talk of "exposing his father's nakedness" is actually code for son-mother incest, for the cuckolding of Noah, which seems more to merit a curse of this magnitude, especially if Canaan was the illegitimate love child. See Leviticus 20:11: "And the man that lieth with his father's wife hath uncovered his father's nakedness: both of them shall surely be put to death; their blood shall be upon them."

5. The New Testament's Ephesians 6:5–9 was also a popular text for showing God's nonjudgmental accounting for slavery— and His rules about how slaves and masters should interact: "Servants, be obedient to them that are your masters according to the flesh, with fear and trembling, in singleness of your heart, as unto Christ; Not with eyeservice, as menpleasers; but as the servants of Christ, doing the will of God from the heart; With good will doing service, as to the Lord, and not to men: Knowing that whatsoever good thing any man doeth, the same shall he receive of the Lord, whether he be bond or free. And, ye masters, do the same things unto them, forbearing threatening:

knowing that your Master also is in heaven; neither is there respect of persons with him."

6. For a discussion of America's founding "exclusionary inclusions," see Devon W. Carbado, "Racial Naturalization," *American Quarterly* 57 (2005): 633–58.

7. For an argument about science's relative unimportance (compared to religious belief) as a primary justification for American slavery, see Vincent Sarich and Frank Miele, *Race: The Reality of Human Differences* (Boulder, CO: Westview Press, 2004), especially 59–101.

8. For a discussion of religion and white vigilantism in the nineteenth century, see Orlando Patterson, *Rituals of Blood: Consequences of Slavery in Two American Centuries* (New York: Basic Civitas Books, 1989), and Edward J. Blum, *Reforging the White Republic: Race, Religion, and American Nationalism, 1865–1898* (Baton Rouge: Louisiana State University Press, 2007).

9. For a current retelling of this moment, see Nicholas Lemann, *Redemption: The Last Battle of the Civil War* (New York: Farrar, Straus and Giroux, 2006), in which he argues that you can't explain America's Civil War (or its aftermath) without taking that discussion all the way up to the mid-1870s and the racial violence that reversed the gains of Reconstruction. For an early critique of whitewashed renditions of the post–Civil War moment, see W. E. B. DuBois, *Black Reconstruction in America, 1860–1880* (New York: Atheneum, 1973).

10. See, for example, Manning Marable, *Race, Reform, and Rebellion: The Second Reconstruction and Beyond in Black America, 1945–2006* (Jackson, MS: University Press of Mississippi, 2007).

11. Ella Baker and others worked the political angle without an overcommitment to religion. See Barbara Ransby, *Ella Baker and the Black Freedom Movement: A Radical Democratic Vision* (Chapel Hill: University of North Carolina Press, 2003). For a particularly brief, but moving, tribute to Robert Carter,

see Manning Marable, *Living Black History: How Reimagining the African-American Past Can Remake America's Racial Future* (New York: Basic Civitas, 2006).

12. See Christian Smith, *The Emergence of Liberation Theology: Radical Religion and Social Movement Theory* (Chicago: University of Chicago Press, 1991).

13. Roger Lancaster, *Thanks to God and the Revolution: Popular Religion and Class Consciousness in the New Nicaragua* (New York: Columbia University Press, 1988).

14. Lancaster, *Thanks to God and the Revolution.*

15. For a popular rendition of America's founding commitments to religion, see Toby Mac and Michael Tait, *Under God* (Minneapolis: Bethany House, 2004). For a political scientist's take on black religion's substantive political import, see Frederick Harris, *Something Within: Religion in African-American Political Activism* (New York: Oxford University Press, 1999).

16. For a look at television during this transformative moment in mass mediation, see Karal Ann Marling, *As Seen on TV: The Visual Culture of Everyday Life in the 1950s* (Cambridge, MA: Harvard University Press, 1994).

17. Media scholar Heather Hendershot is completing a piece on cold war right-wing broadcasters, people she casts as the forefathers of everyone from Bill O'Reilly to Pat Robertson. Of course, the different interpretations of that Rodney King beating (as captured by an amateur videographer) point out video's inherent opacity. It is not just a self-evident recorder of fact in a way that wholly predetermines viewers' interpretations of what they see. We still have to imbue the images with meaning, which is subjective business.

18. For a discussion of how black Americans productively manipulated the geopolitical minefield of African decolonization, see Campbell, *Middle Passages,* especially 268–364.

19. Walt Harrington, "Well Wrought," *Washington Post Magazine,* July 29, 1988, 24.

20. Richard J. Herrnstein and Charles Murray, *The Bell Curve: Intelligence and Class Structure in American Life* (New York: Free Press, 2004).

21. TMZ's website attempts to explain their mission: "Named one of the year's 50 coolest websites by *Time* magazine, TMZ—a joint venture between Telepictures Productions and AOL—has enjoyed a meteoric rise to prominence by breaking the biggest stories in entertainment" (www.tmz.com/about).

22. For a theoretical treatment of technological reproducibility as the defining difference of modernity, see Walter Benjamin, "The Work of Art in the Age of Mechanical Reproduction," in *Illuminations*, 211–44 (New York: Random House, 1991).

23. If Orlando Patterson's *Slavery and Social Death: A Comparative Study* (Cambridge, MA: Harvard University Press, 1982) equates slavery with a form of social death, it might not be too much of a stretch to link emancipation (in a U.S. context) with the social death of a certain form of white invincibility.

24. William Julius Wilson, *The Declining Significance of Race: Blacks and Changing American Institutions* (Chicago: University of Chicago Press, 1979).

25. Wilson, *The Declining Significance of Race.*

26. Archie Bunker is an easy rhetorical target, and David Wellman, *Portraits of White Racism* (New York: Cambridge University Press, 1993), argues that part of the reason why this is the case stems from the fact that he is a caricature that lets more middle-class and elite white racists off the hook. *All in the Family* was an imagining of white racism that relegated it to the ignorant rants of working-class Americana, which Wellman judiciously debunks. Debra J. Dickerson, *The End of Blackness: Returning the Souls of Black Folk to Their Rightful Owners* (New York: Pantheon Books, 2004), also invokes Archie as a recognizable icon of blatant white racism, even highlighting the fact that racism is no longer as explicit as it once was. For her, the point of this move is to say that blacks should focus less attention on white America

and potential white racism and more on intraracial policing that she argues does more damage to black life chances and more harm to the civil rights movement's legacy.

27. Critics argue that political correctness implies censorship and endangers free speech by placing premature limitations on public discourse, especially in political forums and at American universities. For one of the most famous early critiques of PC-policing in schools during the current era of our culture wars, see Dinesh D'Souza, *Illiberal Education: The Politics of Race and Sex on Campus* (New York: The Free Press, 1991).

28. Gunnar Myrdal, *An American Dilemma: The Negro Problem in Modern Democracy* (New York: Pantheon Books, 1944), lxix.

29. Of course, the heel diggers are still around; they're just not invited to most of the high-profile public gatherings. For example, see Michael Levin, *Why Race Matters* (New York: New Century Books, 2005), in which the philosopher revisits all of the most controversial anthropological and psychological research on race and comes to the conclusions that "whites are on average better people than blacks. However shocking this statement may sound, I believe it is a truth that must be dealt with" (10).

30. For a cogent theory about how racial segregation (even "hypersegregation") gets reproduced without explicitly segregationist laws, see Douglas Massey and Nancy Denton, *American Apartheid: Segregation and the Making of the Underclass* (Cambridge, MA: Harvard University Press, 1998).

CHAPTER 3

1. Jennifer A. Richeson and Sophie Trawalter, "Why Do Interracial Interactions Impair Executive Function? A Resource Depletion Account," *Journal of Personality and Social Psychology* 88, no. 6 (2005): 934–47.

2. There is a long literature in the social sciences on continued racial segregation in America after the civil rights movement. One of the most cited examples is Douglas Massey and Nancy Denton, *American Apartheid: Segregation and the Making of the Underclass* (Cambridge, MA: Harvard University Press, 1998). For a more recent look at racial segregation (its causes and effects) in one West Coast city, see Camille Zubrinsky Charles, *Won't You Be My Neighbor? Race, Class and Residence in Los Angeles* (New York: Russell Sage Foundation, 2006).

3. Of course, this racial looking glass is replete with orthogonal questions such as, is it morally justifiable to have racial identities (group identities) at all? Should the state recognize them? Are their harder and softer versions that we should distinguish? For a philosophical discussion of these contentious issues, see Amy Gutmann, *Identity in America* (Princeton, NJ: Princeton University Press, 2003). There are also questions about the overall cultural health and developmental trajectory of African Americans. Is the plight of blacks getting better or worse? For a critique of the crisis discourse about contemporary black culture, see Algernon Austin, *Getting It Wrong: How Black Public Intellectuals Are Failing Black America* (New York: iUniverse, 2006). Then, there are all the claims about the links between race and intelligence, links used to explain away continued black-white achievement gaps with recourse to heredity.

4. For a deconstructionist critique of race that also challenges how one luminary of black studies and sociology (W. E. B. DuBois) essentialized the construct in his own work, see Kwame Anthony Appiah, *In My Father's House: Africa in the Philosophy of Culture* (Oxford: Oxford University Press, 1992).

5. Two recent examples include Jeffrey Cassisi, Dennis R. Combs, Chris Michael, and David L. Penn, "Perceived Racism as a Predictor of Paranoia among African Americans," *Journal*

of Black Psychology 32, no. 1 (2006): 87–104, and Gene H. Brody, Yi-Fu Chen, Velma McBride Murry, Xiaojia Ge, Ronald L. Simons, Frederick X. Gibbons, Meg Gerrard, and Carolyn E. Cutrona, "Perceived Discrimination and the Adjustment of African American Youths: A Five-Year Longitudinal Analysis with Contextual Moderation Effects," *Child Development* 77, no. 5 (2006): 1170–89. In the latter article, 714 preteens were studied to show that the links between "perceived discrimination" and subsequent depression or bad conduct are mitigated by nurturant treatment from family, friends, and guardians.

6. Two of the main versions of this study label the phenomenon "John Henryism" for black men and the "Sojourner Syndrome" for black women. See Sherman A. James, David S. Strogatz, Steven B. Wing, and Diane L. Ramsey, "Socioeconomic Status, John Henryism, and Hypertension in Blacks and Whites," *Johns Hopkins University School of Hygiene and Public Health* 26, no. 4 (1987): 664–73. For Sojourner Syndrome, see Leith Mullings and Alaka Wali, *Stress and Resilience: The Social Context of Reproduction in Central Harlem* (New York: Kluwer Academics/Plenum Publishers, 2001). And such everyday stresses aren't always about racial difference; class and status can work on your blood pressure and overall health just as well. See James Lynch, *The Broken Heart* (New York: Basic Books, 1979).

7. Daniel Gilbert, *Stumbling on Happiness* (New York: Knopf, 2006). Some people might think that ignorance or lack of education allowed these kids to use blackface without realizing how the administration would respond, but they were fairly high-achieving college students, and they had all taken history classes. *De cardio* racism can even be hidden from the very person who harbors it. They may not even admit racist feelings to themselves. If we were all self-aware and totally self-transparent, every psychotherapist in the country would be begging for bread.

8. Anthropologist Oscar Lewis popularized the "culture of poverty" argument in the 1950s and 1960s. Using ethnographic research in Mexico and other places, he argued that large structural forces beyond any individual's complete control establish cultural repertoires that can exacerbate poor people's marginalization. They can develop cultural traits that hinder their social and economic advancement. The same argument is retooled today to ground claims about the so-called "black underclass," claims that poor blacks have such a dysfunctional and poverty-reproducing culture that they aren't even able to take advantage of positive changes in their social environment, government aid, and other social programs. Their cultural practices reproduce their own penury, making them resistant to assistance. If someone's culture promotes laziness and the absence of a serious worth ethic (regardless of how the culture got that way), then creating jobs for its members or promoting job training will mostly be in vain. They have a culture, the theory goes, that doesn't even allow them to take advantage of such remedies. Of course, welfare is just supposed to make matters worse according to some conservative pundits, for instance, Charles Murray, *Losing Ground: American Social Policy, 1950–1980* (New York: Basic Books, 1994). I find that argument far less compelling than one about a "culture of racial paranoia" organizing contemporary American life, a paranoia that doesn't necessarily lead to pathology.

9. So many nineteenth-century whites supported the founding of Liberia and the potential emigration and colonization of free blacks partially because they feared that once emancipated, blacks would never be able to forgive their former tormentors and live peacefully among them. Past racial exploitation can make former masters just as racially paranoid as their erstwhile slaves.

10. Shelby Steele, *White Guilt: How Blacks and Whites Together Destroyed the Promise of the Civil Rights Era* (New

York: HarperCollins, 2006), 24. By equating white guilt with Black Power, Steele wants to argue that black political agency was only possible because whites felt badly about past racism and beat themselves up over it—and even allowed blacks to join in. Steele has a reference to George Wallace as "an honest bigot," which is relevant to my argument (17), and his discussion of racism lurking in "the hearts of men" presages the central metaphor I use here (32).

11. Gloria Naylor, *1996* (Chicago: Third World Press, 2005).

12. I think of this as something akin to a writer's low-tech equivalent of reading—and writing into—other people's minds, giving her tormenters a taste of their own invasive medicine.

13. In some ways, Naylor's situation was something like James Frey's in reverse. Where he had publishers asking him to change his novel into a memoir (because they could market it better), Naylor was forced to label her book "fiction" (seemingly against her wishes) because nobody would publish it as fact.

14. For more information on the Protocols of Zion, see Stephen Eric Bronner, *A Rumor about the Jews: Anti-Semitism, Conspiracy, and the Protocols of Zion* (Oxford: Oxford University Press, 2003).

15. Ward Churchill and Jim Vander Wall, *The COINTELPRO Papers: Documents from the FBI's Secret Wars against Dissent in the United States* (Boston: South End Press, 1990).

CHAPTER 4

1. John A. Williams, *The Man Who Cried I Am* (New York: Little, Brown, 1967).

2. For a discussion of "media events," see Daniel Dayan and Elihu Katz, *Media Events: The Live Broadcasting of History* (Cambridge, MA: Harvard University Press, 1992). I'll discuss this text more directly in chapter 6.

3. Nixon cosponsored the bill when he was a congressional representative from California. For a discussion of Nixon's role in the act (and the larger conspiratorial claims around it), see Samuel Yette, *The Choice: The Issue of Black Survival in America* (New York: Putnum, 1971).

4. Samuel F. Yette, *The Choice: The Issue of Black Survival in America* (New York: Putnam, 1971), 276.

5. Yette, *The Choice*, 277.

6. Allen published his findings in a 1969 pamphlet, "Concentration Camps USA."

7. Yette, *The Choice,* 288.

8. For a discussion of the ideological debates forged in black cultural spaces, see Melissa Victoria Harris-Lacewell, *Barbershops, Bibles and BET: Everyday Talk and Black Political Thought* (Princeton, NJ: Princeton University Press, 2004). For a view of Black intraracial debate as stifled by ideological litmus tests, see Debra J. Dickerson, *The End of Blackness: Returning the Souls of Black Folk to Their Rightful Owners* (New York: Pantheon, 2004). For a similar discussion of black cultural politics as the privileging of "ghetto culture," see Cora Daniels, *Ghettonation: A Journey into the Land of Bling and the Home of the Shameless* (New York: Doubleday, 2007).

9. There are, of course, many not-so-paranoid (but sometimes still quite critical) readings of Robert Moses and his urban revitalization projects. For a highly cited look at Moses's life and career, see Robert A. Cano, *The Power Broker: Robert Moses and the Fall of New York* (New York: Vintage, 1975).

10. Yette, *The Choice*, 34.

11. Frances Cress-Welsing, *The Isis Papers: The Keys to the Colors* (Chicago: Third World Press, 1991), 4

12. Cress-Welsing, *The Isis Papers*, 4.

13. Cress-Welsing, *The Isis Papers*, 4.

14. I won't go into all the critiques of Cress-Welsing's work, but there are clearly several reasons why many geneticists find

her arguments far too simplistic—and simply wrong. One of my senior colleagues in anthropology, a physical anthropologist who taught me at Howard University, spent a lot of time (while I was still an undergraduate) debunking Cress-Welsing's genetics during public forums.

15. Of course, all this new genomic work was completed after Cress-Welsing's book was published. For my own look at the African Ancestry process, see John L. Jackson, Jr., *Real Black: Adventures in Racial Sincerity* (Chicago: University of Chicago Press, 2005). Also, for a genetic and genealogical reading of Oprah Winfrey's past (and the methodological issues involved), see Henry Louis Gates, Jr., *Finding Oprah's Roots: Finding Your Own* (New York: Crown, 2007).

16. Cress-Welsing, *The Isis Papers*, lays this out schematically: "Ball games = war of the balls = war of the testicles = war of the genes = race war" (143).

17. For a discussion of our precultural mandate for self-preservation (even at the level of individual genes), see Richard Dawkins, *The Selfish Gene* (Oxford: Oxford University Press, 1976).

18. For a critical look at niche marketing and its broader social implications, see Joseph Turow, *Niche Envy: Marketing Discrimination in the Digital Age* (Cambridge, MA: MIT Press, 2006).

19. Haki R. Madhubuti, *Black Men: Obsolete, Single, Dangerous? The Afrikan American Family in Transition* (Chicago: Third World Press, 1991), 4.

20. Jawanza Kunjufu, *Countering the Conspiracy to Destroy Black Boys*, Vol. 3 (Chicago: African American Images, 2004).

21. Mirimba Ani, *Yurugu: An African-Centered Critique of European Cultural Thought and Behavior* (Trenton, NJ: Africa World Press, 1994).

22. Samuel Huntington, *The Clash of Civilizations and the Remaking of World Order* (New York: Free Press, 2002).

23. Na'im Akbar, *Community of Self* (Tallahassee, FL: Mind Productions, 1985); Na'im Akbar, *Chains and Images of Psychological Slavery* (Jersey City, NJ: New Mind Productions, 1984).

24. In some ways, black nationalism and Afrocentrism are categorically predicated on race-base suspicions and cynicism vis-à-vis whiteness, which isn't to say that the model lacks pragmatic/theoretical usefulness or intellectual validity. For a critique of nonrigorous definitions of "Afrocentrism," see Michael Hanchard, *Party/Politics: Horizons in Black Political Thought* (New York: Oxford, 2006), especially 87–97.

25. Cheikh Anta Diop, *Civilization or Barbarism: An Authentic Anthropology* (Chicago: Lawrence Hill Books, 1991), and Chancellor Williams, *The Destruction of Black Civilization: Great Issues of Race from 4500 B.C. to 2000 A.D.* (Chicago: Third World Press, 1987).

26. George G. M. James, *Stolen Legacy* (New York: Philosophical Library, 1973).

27. Martin Bernal, *Black Athena: The Afroasiatic Roots of Classical Civilization,* Vol. 1, *The Fabrication of Ancient Greece 1785–1985* (New Brunswick, NJ: Rutgers University Press, 1987). For a popular critique of Bernal, Diop, James, and this entire revisionist camp in Egyptology, see Mary Lefkowitz, *Not Out of Africa: How Afrocentrism Became an Excuse to Teach Myth as History* (New York: Basic Books, 1996).

28. Ward Churchill and Jim Vander Wall, *The COINTELPRO Papers: Documents from the FBI's Secret Wars against Dissent in the United States* (Boston: South End Press, 1990).

29. Carter G. Woodson, *The Mis-Education of the Negro* (Trenton, NJ: Africa World Press, 1990). For another truly canonical attempt at reeducating black minds within the racial distrust-paranoia genre (one that includes discussions of everything from dietary concerns to freemasonry, Egyptology to economics), see Anthony T. Browder, *From the Browder File: 22*

Essays on the African American Experience (Washington DC: Institute of Karmic Guidance, 1989).

30. Jawanza Kunjufu, *Hip-Hop v. MAAT: A Psycho/Social Analysis of Values* (Chicago: African American Images, 1993), iii.

31. Jawanza Kunjufu, *Black Economics: Solutions for Economic and Community Empowerment* (Chicago: African American Images, 1991); Claude Anderson, *PowerNomics: The National Plan to Empower Black America* (Bethesda, MD: PowerNomics, 2001).

32. Stokely Carmichael with Ekwueme Michael Thelwell, *Ready for Revolution: The Life and Struggles of Stokely Carmichael* (New York: Scribner, 2003), 752.

33. Carmichael with Thelwell, *Ready for Revolution*, 753.

34. Why would a person like Ture put such an accusation, and only four or five pages of it, at the end of such a carefully crafted book, into this important and official recasting of his life? If anything, such a serious claim might better organize the entire book, right? If he believed it, which he ostensibly did at some level, it should be a significant enough allegation to frame the entire manuscript, no? "Let me spend the next few hundred pages telling you why the government might be trying to kill me with cancer." Instead, we get a short and intense burst of astonishing charges for a few pages near the end of the book, seemingly out of nowhere, not really foreshadowed by (or necessarily integrated into) the rest of the book, and then a ceding of the microphone just as quickly. The book continues racing on with the end of its telling without much more recourse to the government's possible plot. Of course, we might want to believe that Thelwell's editorial hand had a part to play in this, but probably much less than some would imagine.

35. William H. Grier and Price M. Cobbs, *Black Rage* (New York: Basic Books, 1968).

36. Movies aren't generally good at representing subtle racism. Things usually have to be blatant, so that, as in this instance, the audience can determine unequivocally that Marcus, Tyler, and

Gerard are absolutely correct in their assessments of the store clerk's racism. This is part of the reason why mass-media renditions of race so often help cement notions of paranoia. Racism on film or television has to be clear and obvious to signal "racism" to viewers, an exaggerated flick of the nose by a smug salesperson needs to read self-evidently. And with enough cinematic and televisual priming, we start to expect such unmasked explicitness in the real world too. When we don't get it, we either dismiss cries of racism as unjustified hypersensitivity or pretend the offending actions are self-evidently racist anyway, even when they aren't, when they are restrained and almost impossible to prove. Thankfully, boldly obvious versions of unmasked racism are more media cliché than anything else these days—not all the time, but usually. These clichés still suffice for romantic Hollywood tales of heroes and villains, but they are hardly up to the challenge of representing how complicated and messy racism sometimes looks in our politically correct, post–civil rights present.

37. For a discussion of eighteenth-century philosopher Jeremy Bentham's design for the Panopticon, a prison that was meant to exemplify this kind of all-encompassing surveillance, see Michel Foucault, *Discipline and Punish: The Birth of the Prison* (New York: Random House, 1977), especially 195–230.

Chapter 5

1. Skelly is a street game we played on the sidewalk with bottle caps where you have to successfully negotiate a board (usually drawn out on the concrete itself) while hitting other competitors' bottle caps with your own and avoiding their attempts to do the same thing to you.

2. Although not a general Islamic principle, this idea of the black scientist Yakub's concocting whites in a laboratory is central to the Nation of Islam's traditional racial cosmology. For a

look at African American versions of Islam that place that phenomenon into a larger global context, see Melani McAlister, *Epic Encounters: Culture, Media, and U.S. Interests in the Middle East, 1945–2000* (Berkeley: University of California Press, 2001), especially chapter 2, "The Middle East in African American Cultural Politics, 1955–1972," 84–124.

3. For a discussion of the Five Percenters and their relationship to New York City politics, see Barry Gottehrer, *The Mayor's Man* (Garden City, NY: Doubleday, 1975). Hip-hop's origin story is more complex and controversial than some believe, and "hip-hop experts" (in the academy and outside of it) have been debating its finer points for years.

4. There are many hip-hop artists who emphasize the belief that corporations are conspiring against "conscious rap," using their multinational power to promote the worst forms of self-degrading and depolitical rap. For some context to these accusations, see S. Craig Watkins, *Hip Hop Matters: Politics, Pop Culture, and the Struggle for the Soul of a Movement* (Boston: Beacon Press, 2005).

5. Everything is chalked up to what some hip-hop artists call "tricknology," a popular term birthed out of the tendency of groups like the Five Percenters, the Black Hebrews (in Israel), and the Rastafarians (in Jamaica) to coin new words as a way of challenging assumptions embedded in old ones (for instance, instead of "understanding" the world you are implored to "overstand" it). "Tricknology" marks technology's susceptibility to manipulation at the hands of secret groups hell-bent on engineering global (and racist) conspiracies.

6. We create meanings with words more than merely reflect them. Some advocates of political correctness argue that this is precisely why language matters—in the Sapir-Whorfian sense that they determine our world, rather that just passively reflecting it.

7. The African Hebrews of Jerusalem talk a lot about "the power to define," renaming many common terms that they believe

are misnamed: a "diet" becomes a "live-it," the "Dead Sea" is the "Sea of Life," and you "rise" (not "fall") into love. My next book project is an extended ethnographic study of this fascinating and thriving transnational African American community based in southern Israel.

8. For a discussion of hip-hop's "impenetrability" in the context of a larger analysis of its politics and aesthetics, see Imani Perry, *Prophets of the Hood: Politics and Poetics in Hip-Hop* (Durham, NC: Duke University Press, 2004), especially 50–51.

9. Hip-hop's seemingly hurly-burly aesthetic actively promotes indecipherability and exclusion, making it much easier for artists to offer up their racial conspiracies in songs that can be played over the radio without many listeners being the wiser.

10. For more on vision, its imagined seductions and shortcomings, see Martin Jay, *Downcast Eyes: The Denigration of Vision in Twentieth-Century French Thought* (Berkeley: University of California Press, 1993), and David Michael Levin, ed., *Modernity and the Hegemony of Vision* (Berkeley: University of California Press, 1993).

11. Malcolm Gladwell, *Blink: The Power of Thinking without Thinking* (New York: Little, Brown, 2005).

12. There are many powerful books on hip-hop. For one recent anthology of hip-hop, see Murray Forman and Mark Anthony Neal, *That's the Joint: The Hip-Hop Studies Reader* (New York: Routledge, 2004). One of the canonical takes on hip-hop is Tricia Rose, *Black Noise: Rap Music and Black Culture in Contemporary America* (Middletown, CT: Wesleyan University Press, 1994).

13. For an overview of John Walker Lindh's life (and an argument that links questions of sexuality to a theory about how he ended up in Afghanistan), read Sara Jess and Gabriel Beck, *John Walker Lindh: American Taliban* (California: University Press, 2002). For a look at Islam's emphasis on hip-hop, see Felicia M. Miyakama, *Five Percenter Rap: God Hops Music, Message, and*

Black Muslim Mission (Bloomington: Indiana University Press, 2005). For a general overview of hip-hop history, see Jeff Chang, *Can't Stop, Won't Stop: A History of the Hip-Hop Generation* (New York: St. Martin's Press, 2005).

14. Bakari Kitwana, *Why White Kids Love Hip-Hop: Wankstas, Wiggers, Wannabes, and the New Reality of Race in America* (New York: Basic Civitas, 2005).

15. James Best, "Black Like Me: John Walker Lindh's Hip-Hop Daze," *East Bay Express,* September 3, 2003. Also see Jess and Beck, *John Walker Lindh: American Taliban.*

16. Of course, even Dr. Dre sneaks conspiratorial references into his lyrics, and not just the kinds I discuss later in this chapter with respect to NWA, his former group. In "Been There, Done That," Dre rhymes, "If money is the root, I want the whole damn tree/Ain't trying to stick around for the Illuminati." Even his emphasis on making money doesn't stop him from referencing one of global conspiracy theories' biggest culprits.

17. For a contextualized discussion of this religious group, see Edward E. Curtis IV, *Black Muslim Religion in the Nation of Islam, 1960–1975* (Chapel Hill: University of North Carolina Press, 2006). There are many significant books on African American Muslims not affiliated with the Nation of Islam; one of my favorites is Carolyn Rouse, *Engaged Surrender: African American Women and Islam* (Berkeley: University of California Press, 2004). This Nation of Islam invocation of genes and race (Yakub's grafting of whiteness) dovetails quite easily with Cress-Welsing and the other genetic arguments for interracial antagonism (even if Cress-Welsing doesn't necessarily posit the black origins of "recessive" whiteness in a laboratory).

18. Paul Tough, "The Black White Supremacist," *The New York Times,* May 25, 2003.

19. The idea goes back as far as Emile Durkheim's notion of "social facts" (even to Georg Hegel and before), but one of the more recently canonized versions of the argument is found in

Peter L. Berger and Thomas Luckmann, *The Social Construction of Reality: A Treatise in the Sociology of Knowledge* (New York: Anchor Books, 1967).

20. Tough, "The Black White Supremacist."

21. In yet another song, when Kanye West raps about racism being alive and hidden in contemporary America, the evidence he uses to make his case is the fact that he is even forced to show his ID when he goes to shop at a place like Sam's Club. Of course, Sam's Club makes everyone show their Sam's Club ID, don't they? But who has to show another form of ID on top of that, just to make sure that the faded-out Sam's Club ID is theirs?

22. See George Marcus, *Paranoia within Reason: A Casebook on Conspiracy as Explanation* (Chicago: University of Chicago Press, 1999).

23. See William H. Grier and Price M. Cobbs, *Black Rage* (New York: Basic Books, 1968); Eugene B. Redmond, "Introduction: The Ancient and Recent Voices within Henry Dumas," *Black American Literature Forum* 22, no. 2 (summer 1988): 143–54.

24. Randall Sullivan, *Labyrinth: A Detective Investigates the Murders of Tupac Shakur and Notorious B.I.G., the Implication of Death Row Records' Suge Knight, and the Origins of the Los Angeles Police Scandal* (New York: Grove Press, 2002).

25. We can also ask Detroit's so-called hip-hop mayor, Kwame Kirkpatrick, about the negative associations that glom onto hip-hop and its ambassadors, associations that have helped fuel attacks on his administration since the first day he took office. For more discussion about him, see Natalie Hopkinson and Natalie Y. Moore, *Deconstructing Tyrone: A New Look at Black Masculinity in the Hip-Hop Generation* (San Francisco: Cleis Press, 2006).

26. I should just shout out to one twenty-eight-year-old hip-hop fan who told me that he's sure the FBI isn't fooled by hip-hop (or by its incomprehensibility): "They know," he said. "They hire folks to know."

27. Even the movie poster is all black, all blackness, with just the two main actors' heads and hands indicating that they are even there.

CHAPTER 6

1. Thomas L. Friedman, *The World Is Flat: A Brief History of the Twenty-first Century* (New York: Farrar, Straus and Giroux, 2005).

2. Thomas de Zengotita, *Mediated: How the Media Shapes Your World and the Way You Live in It* (New York: Bloomsbury, 2005).

3. Carolyn Marvin, *When Old Technologies Were New: Thinking about Electric Communication in the Late Nineteenth Century* (Oxford: Oxford University Press, 1988). Paul Starr, *The Creation of the Media: Political Origins of Modern Communication* (New York: Basic Books, 2004), argues that media technology progresses not out of pure scientific improvement, but as a function of political maneuverings and conflicts.

4. Jeffrey Sconce, *Haunted Media: Electronic Presence from Telegraphy to Television* (Durham, NC: Duke University Press, 2000). Jean Comaroff and John Comaroff, "Millennial Capitalism: First Thoughts on a Second Coming," *Public Culture* 12, no. 2 (2000): 291–343. Aneesh Aneesh, *Virtual Migration: The Programming of Globalization* (Durham, NC: Duke University Press, 2006).

5. Max Horkheimer and Theodor A. Adorno, *The Dialectic of Enlightenment* (New York: Continuum, 1976).

6. Joseph Turow, *Niche Envy: Marketing Discrimination in the Digital Age* (Cambridge, MA: MIT Press, 2006).

7. Add Paul Lazarsfeld and Robert K. Morton, "Mass Communication, Popular Taste, and Organized Social Action," in *The Communication of Ideas,* ed. Lynn Bryson, 95–118 (New York:

Harper and Brothers, 1948). Also, Herbert Marcuse, *One-Dimensional Man: Studies in the Ideology of Advanced Industrial Society* (Boston: Beacon Press, 1991).

8. This summary is based on my notes from a paper Richard Butsch presented, "Crowds, Publics and Individuals" at the University of Pennsylvania's Annenberg School for Communication as part of the Annenberg Scholars Program in Culture and Communication Symposium, "Back to the Future: Explorations in the Communication of History," Philadelphia, December 1, 2006. Robert D. Putnam, *Bowling Alone: The Collapse and Revival of American Community* (New York: Simon and Schuster, 2000).

9. Wilson Brian Key, *Media Sexploitation* (New York: Signet, 1976).

10. Barbie Zelizer, *Covering the Body: The Kennedy Assassination, the Media, and the Shaping of Collective Memory* (Chicago: University of Chicago Press, 1992).

11. Anthony Feinstein, *Journalists under Fire: The Psychological Hazards of Covering War* (Baltimore: Johns Hopkins University Press, 2006).

12. Christopher Hayes, "9/11: The Roots of Paranoia," *The Nation*, December 25, 2006, 11–14.

13. David Callahan, *The Moral Center: How We Can Reclaim Our Country from Die-Hard Extremists, Rogue Corporations, Hollywood Hacks, and Pretend Patriots* (New York: Harcourt Inc., 2006).

14. Joseph N. Cappella and Kathleen Hall Jamieson, *Spiral of Cynicism: The Press and the Public Good* (New York: Oxford University Press, 1997).

15. Oscar Lewis, *Children of Sanchez* (New York: Vintage, 1963).

16. Sociologists and political scientists have similar "manifestos."

17. For engagements with (and contested answers to) these kinds of questions, see Luc Boltanski and Graham D. Burchell, *Distant Suffering: Morality, Media, and Politics* (Cambridge:

Cambridge University Press, 1999), and John Ellis, *Seeing Things: Television in the Age of Uncertainty* (London: I. B. Tauris and Co., 2002).

18. For an important anthology of anthropological attempts to research "media worlds," see Faye D. Ginsburg, Lila Abu-Lughod, and Brian Larkin, eds., *Media Worlds: Anthropology on New Terrain* (Berkeley: University of California Press, 2002).

19. Daniel Dayan and Elihu Katz, *Media Events: The Live Broadcasting of History* (Cambridge, MA: Harvard University Press, 1992).

20. Benedict Anderson, *Imagined Communities: Reflections on the Origin and Spread of Nationalism* (New York: Verso, 1991).

21. This is based on my notes from a lecture, "Media Events and the Politics of the Present," presented by Paddy Scannell at the University of Pennsylvania's Annenberg School for Communication, Philadelphia, October 13, 2006.

22. See Elihu Katz and Tamar Liebes, "No More Peace: How Disaster, Terror and War Have Upstaged Media Events," *International Journal of Communication* 1, no. 1 (2007): 157–66. They were originally just trying to challenge Daniel J. Boorstin's suggestion in *The Image: A Guide to Pseudo-Events in America* (New York: Vintage, 1992) that such "media events" were by definition phony and inauthentic.

23. Jean Baudrillard, *The Gulf War Did Not Take Place* (Bloomington: Indiana University Press, 2004). Talking about the first Gulf War, he argues that the violence and death were real, but that the United States and Iraq were fighting such different kinds of battles (one virtual, the other conventional) that it was not really a war so much as a one-sided charade.

24. Adolph Reed Jr., *Stirrings in the Jug: Black Politics in the Post-Segregation Era* (Minneapolis: University of Minnesota Press, 1999), 72

25. For a scholarly look at such race-based conspiracy theories and their reliance on alleged media coverage for proof,

see Patricia A. Turner, *I Heard It Through the Grapevine: Rumor in African-American Culture* (Berkeley: University of California Press, 1994), and Gary Alan Fine and Patricia A. Turner, *Whispers on the Color Live: Rumor and Race in America* (Berkeley: University of California Press, 2004).

CONCLUSION

1. Joseph L. White, "Toward a Black Psychology," in *Black Psychology*, ed. Reginald L. Jones, 5–14 (Berkeley: Cobb and Henry Publishers, 1991), 12. Noliwe Rooks, *White Money/ Black Power: The Surprising History of African American Studies and Crisis of Race in Higher Education* (Boston: Beacon Press, 2006), quotes her colleague Cornel West as offering a similar analysis. "An oppressed people are a paranoid people," West says. "But that doesn't mean they're crazy" (6). Racial paranoia is both disturbing and compelling at the same time: disturbing because it can rely (especially after the formal gains of the 1960s) on seemingly minor social slights, racial mountains that look like glorified molehills; compelling because there is something to be said for "healthy" skepticism about American commitments to racial justice and equality. For another one of the most often-cited discussions of potentially "healthy paranoia" among African Americans, see William H. Grier and Price M. Cobbs, *Black Rage* (New York: Basic Books, 1968), especially 154–80. Danielle S. Allen, in *Talking to Strangers: Anxieties of Citizenship since Brown v. Board of Education* (Chicago: University of Chicago Press, 2004), argues that American citizenship is defined by such racial distrust, especially as inflected by racially monolithic constructions of citizenship and fettered access to the public sphere.

2. Ralph Wiley, *Why Black People Tend to Shout: Cold Facts and Wry Views from a Black Man's World* (New York: Penguin, 1992). For a look at how differently placed black men

think about the larger social world, see Alford A. Young, Jr., *The Minds of Marginalized Black Men: Making Sense of Mobility, Opportunity, and Future Life Chances* (Princeton, NJ: Princeton University Press, 2006).

3. Michael Dawson, *Black Visions: The Roots of Contemporary African-American Political Ideologies* (Chicago: University of Chicago Press, 2001), 86.

4. Glen C. Loury, *The Anatomy of Racial Inequality* (Cambridge, MA: Harvard University Press, 2002). For a look at how African American youths negotiate America's social landscape with an eye toward the discrepancies between differently valued forms of cultural capital, see Prudence L. Carter, *Keepin' It Real: School Success beyond Black and White* (New York: Oxford, 2005).

5. Melissa Harris-Lacewell, *Barbershops, Bibles, and BET: Everyday Talk and Black Political Thought* (Princeton, NJ: Princeton University Press, 2004), and Andrea Y. Simpson, *The Tie that Binds: Identity and Political Attitudes in the Post–Civil Rights Generation* (New York: New York University Press, 1998). For an even more damning look at how these political and ideological differences between and among black people promote forms of "secondary marginalization" that allow for intraracial negligence, exploitation, and oppression, see Cathy J. Cohen, *The Boundaries of Blackness: AIDS and the Breakdown of Black Politics* (Chicago: University of Chicago Press, 1999).

6. For more on how the social sciences, especially anthropology, were deployed during the civil rights struggle, see Lee D. Baker, *From Savage to Negro: Anthropology and the Construction of Race, 1896–1954* (Berkeley: University of California Press, 1998), and Daryl Michael Scott, *Contempt and Pity: Social Policy and the Image of the Damaged Black Psyche, 1880–1996* (Chapel Hill: University of North Carolina Press, 1997). The quote is from Scott, *Contempt and Pity*, xix.

7. Robert C. Smith, *Racism in the Post–Civil Rights Era: Now You See It, Now You Don't* (Albany: State University of

New York Press, 1995), 41. Of course, arguing for the importance of racial paranoia, or that political correctness might help to reinforce such paranoia among black Americans, can be dismissed as just another way of "blaming the victim," as a request for blacks to get over their "irrational" paranoia and move on already.

8. See Walter Benn Michaels, "Race into Culture: A Critical Genealogy of Cultural Identity," *Critical Inquiry* 18, no. 4 (summer 1992): 655–85.

9. Samuel Huntington, *Who Are We? The Challenges to America's National Identity* (New York: Simon and Schuster, 2004).

10. Roxanne Varzi, *Warring Souls: Youth, Media and Martyrdom in Post-Revolution Iran* (Durham, NC: Duke University Press, 2006). For a differently pitched argument about the possibilities of Islamic democracy (one of the issues at stake in *Warring Souls*), see Noah Feldman, *After Jihad: America and the Struggle for Islamic Democracy* (New York: Farrar, Straus, and Giroux, 2003).

11. Of course, you don't have to put all your eggs in a racial basket to be skeptical of governmental activities. The eclectic "truth movement" of folks who believe the U.S. government either had advance knowledge of 9/11 (or did the deed themselves) is a prominent current example of American paranoia. Even if they aren't actively out there publicizing this government's purported role in the mass murders of 9/11, as many as 30 percent of the American people seem to believe some version of American complicity in the tragedy.

12. For a detailed analysis of Americans' growing vulnerabilities, see Jacob Hacker, *The Great Risk Shift: The Assault on American Jobs, Families, Health Care, and Retirement and How You Can Fight Back* (Oxford: Oxford University Press, 2006). For a classic anthropological take on some of these same vulnerabilities, see Katherine S. Newman, *Falling from Grace:*

The Experience of Downward Mobility in the American Middle Class (New York: Free Press, 1988).

13. Diana Mutz, *Hearing the Other Side: Deliberative vs. Participatory Democracy* (Cambridge: Cambridge University Press, 2006).

14. And these interracial relationships don't have to mean relinquishing your commitments to racial community. There is also a clearly racialized component to our collective structural vulnerabilities. For a discussion of how race-based vulnerabilities inform differences between the black and white middle classes, see Mary Pattillo-McCoy, *Black Picket Fences: Privilege and Peril among the Black Middle Class* (Chicago: University of Chicago Press, 1999).

15. For a discussion of how racial silences reproduce racial hierarchies in school settings, see Mica Pollock, *Colormute: Race Talk Dilemmas in an American School* (Princeton, NJ: Princeton University Press, 2005).

16. E. E. Evans-Pritchard, *Witchcraft, Oracles and Magic among the Azande* (Oxford: Oxford University Press, 1976)

17. Ellis Cose, *The Rage of a Privileged Class: Why Do Prosperous Blacks Still Have the Blues?* (New York: Harper Perennial, 1995). Stokely Carmichael brings up Cose's book near the end of his autobiography, saying that he "lost patience with it rather quickly," characterizing it as "one extended, self-pitying whine from people who should have known better" (770).

18. Danielle S. Allen, *Talking to Strangers: Anxieties of Citizenship since Brown v. Board of Education* (Chicago: University of Chicago Press, 2004).

19. Lawrence D. Bobo, "Prejudice as Group Position: Microfoundations of a Sociological Approach to Racism and Race Relations," *Journal of Social Issues* 55, no. 3 (1999): 445–72.

20. See Ruth Behar, *The Vulnerable Observer: Anthropology That Breaks Your Heart* (Boston, MA: Beacon Press, 1997).

AFTERWORD

1. Other polls show less dramatic change in the degree of African American optimism on issues of race. In a CNN/Essence Magazine/Opinion Research Corp. poll released in July 2009, 55 percent of African Americans described racial discrimination as a serious problem, about the same percent they found in 2000. This survey received much less public attention.

2. Melissa Harris-Lacewell, "Why Blacks Are More Optimistic About Race," *Philadelphia Inquirer*, May 1, 2009.

3. Tavis Smiley (with Stephanie Robinson), *Making America as Good as Its Promise* (New York: Atria Books, 2009).

4. Mica Pollock, *Colormute: Race Talk Dilemmas in an American School* (Princeton: Princeton University Press, 2005).

5. Shelby Steele, *A Bound Man: Why We Are Excited About Obama and Why He Can't Win* (New York: Free Press, 2007).

6. Shelby Steele, "Sotomayor and the Politics of Race," *Wall Street Journal*, June 9, 2009.

7. Stephen L. Carter, *Reflections of an Affirmative Action Baby* (New York: Basic Books, 1991).

8. The structural roots of racism are precisely what set the stage for our current post–Civil Rights dilemma. Race is structured differently in a "browning America," in ways that are hardly reducible to the seemingly bi-chromatic make-up of the Old South. I will concede that I probably have under-played the theme of multiracialism a bit in this book, but I did so because I wanted to talk about a different structural configuration of race relations, a configuration that begins with the profoundly formative time of chattel slavery in the United States and reads subsequent developments (histories of Latino immigration and multiracialization) with that founding premise as a starting point. Racial paranoia isn't just about blacks and whites, but a schematic rendition of that dyadic dynamic provides a basic benchmark for other forms of race-based paranoia in an increasingly multi-ethnic America.

Index